Human No More

HUMAN NO MORE

Digital Subjectivities, Unhuman Subjects, and the End of Anthropology

EDITED BY NEIL L. WHITEHEAD
AND MICHAEL WESCH

University Press of Colorado
Boulder

Published by University Press of Colorado
5589 Arapahoe Avenue, Suite 206C
Boulder, Colorado 80303

AAUP 1937 2012

The University Press of Colorado is a proud member of
the Association of American University Presses.

The University Press of Colorado is a cooperative publishing enterprise supported, in part, by
Adams State University, Colorado State University, Fort Lewis College, Metropolitan State University of Denver, Regis University, University of Colorado, University of Northern Colorado,
Utah State University, and Western State Colorado University.

Library of Congress Cataloging-in-Publication Data

Human no more : digital subjectivities, unhuman subjects, and the end of anthropology /
edited by Neil L. Whitehead and Michael Wesch.
    p. cm.
  Includes bibliographical references and index.
  ISBN 978-1-60732-169-9 (cloth) — ISBN 978-1-60732-189-7 (pbk.) — ISBN
978-1-60732-170-5 (ebook)
  1. Anthropology—Philosophy. 2. Cybernetics—Philosophy. 3. Online social networks. 4.
Computers and civilization. 5. Virtual reality. I. Whitehead, Neil L. II. Wesch, Michael.
  GN33.H944 2012
  303.48'34—dc23
                                    2012025788

To Neil Whitehead
1956–2012

Cowards die many times before their deaths;
The valiant never taste of death but once.

Neil's soul substance burst from his tired body into the larger universe this morning. Those of you who know him well realize how significant it is that a packet of vital energy such as his has come forth with a fierceness. Please allow as much of his soul substance as you can stand to enter and live within you now, so that he will come to rest in dozens of bodies and continue to burst into the world through your mouth, through your eyes through your breath and through your tears.

—STEPHANIE ALEMÁN (on Neil Whitehead's Facebook wall, March 22, 2012)

Of course this news isn't believable. So in order to find out, I went to Facebook. And I'm sorry to discover confirmation that it is. Ah Facebook. Neil would have enjoyed this.

—JANET MARION CHERNELA (on Neil Whitehead's Facebook wall, March 23, 2012)

Contents

Human No More

Introduction

Human No More

Neil L. Whitehead and Michael Wesch

Over the last decade the growing possibilities of living in online worlds have continued to undermine and throw into question traditional anthropological conceptions of place-based ethnography. Such conceptions were already facing criticism for artificially bounding, limiting, and reifying "culture" in a world in which transnational cultural flows are commonplace. Online worlds add yet another dimension to this critique, providing examples of social forms that stretch and often break the definitions and boundaries of "communities" and "groups" and blurring our taken-for-granted distinctions between the human, bestial, and mechanical, thereby forcing us to rethink our notions of what might constitute the "subjects" that we study.

However, in this volume we also use the insight that the challenges of ethnography in online worlds presents to broaden our critique of ethnography. We do this by asking how the occluded worlds of digital culture, and also those of hidden and marginalized persons, can be better integrated into anthropological thinking and how the ethnography of both the "unhuman"

DOI: 10.5876/9781607321705.c00

1

and the "digital" leads to exciting possibilities for reconfiguring the notion of what is human. But why would an academic discipline that is founded on the notion of the "human" (*anthropos*) saw off the very branch of the "tree of knowledge" on which it rests? How can anthropology properly acknowledge the cultural and historical contingency of the category "human" unless this entails the end of anthropology itself?

Through the chapters that follow, we demonstrate that such questioning is not the end of anthropology but, to the contrary, a fruitful endeavor leading to the discovery of new ends and purposes for our enduring commitment to engage and interpret other lifeways. A critical examination of the "human" sheds light on how the anthropocentric presumptions of much anthropology ignore not just the "unhuman" but also the "animal" and the "not-quite-human" (transgendered, disabled, or psychologically impaired persons), inevitably leading to a challenge, and perhaps an outright rejection, of the whole category of the human, at least as a core concept for anthropological theory.

Anthropology is only one academic discipline currently engaged with the posthuman (Wolfe 2010), but arguably anthropology has the most to contribute to such debates through ethnographic engagement with cultural worlds in which Western Enlightenment definitions and exclusions (Latour 1993) are not so prominent. In this regard, the essays here demonstrate that new forms of ethnographic engagement with "unhuman" populations (as in the chapters by Heckenberger, Whitehead, and Wisniewski) can inform and be informed by studies of online phenomena that also challenge and subvert traditional notions of the human.

The chapters here illustrate emergent cultural contexts in which embodied, "rational" individuals are but one of the forms of agency present in virtual and socially occluded worlds. As Matt Bernius demonstrates, software programs create chatbots, spambots, searchbots, and even ballot-stuffing bots, some of which are fully equipped to interact with "real humans" socially, sexually, and financially. Such bots appear alongside and engage with simulacra of our offline selves.

Anthropologists such as Donna Haraway (1991) were pioneers in drawing out the possibilities and implications of the posthuman, but the challenges and questions that arise from such insights and observations are often ignored in mainstream anthropology, safely put aside while getting on with the "real" work of doing real ethnography "in the field." Perhaps it is only now, amid a mass engagement and subjective incorporation of the reality of the online into everyday life and imperial ambitions of pharmaceutical and bioengineering corporations to control Life itself, that such early critiques and insights become central to the prospects of anthropology in the twenty-first century. And as the Internet and other new media forms increasingly integrate with even the most mundane aspects of everyday life in even the most remote regions of the world, and the "virtual" blurs with and ultimately becomes the "real," issues raised by an anthropology of the virtual necessarily become the issues for anthropology at large.

HUMAN NO MORE?

The theme of these chapters—human no more?—resonates as a question throughout. Although Whitehead answers firmly in the affirmative and eagerly embraces the posthuman as a potential liberation from the late capitalist disciplines of the corporeal and the mental, others more cautiously question whether we are in fact posthuman at all and whether we should radically rethink anthropology. This is partly the reaction of Anne Allison (whose afterword was originally a response to the American Anthropological Association (AAA) panel at which these chapters were first presented), but her highly constructive and open-ended engagement with the question of "humanity" contrasts with other commentators (Boellstorff 2008) who find the prospect of the posthuman threatening, both subjectively and with regard to the preservation of the iconic founding figures of the discipline. Just as the idea of the "postmodern" provoked surprisingly conservative reactions among otherwise innovative thinkers such as Johannes Fabian, Marshall Sahlins, and Eric Wolf (Whitehead 2004), it is important to distinguish the critique of anthropology's intellectual frameworks, which the asking of questions about the "human" permits, from the assumption that "posthumanism" is a disguised political gambit aimed at taking over the profession.

Attempting to avoid such pitfalls, and in a similar vein to Allison, Tufekci notes that the first symbols ever created allowed for a form of "disembodiment" by separating the thought from the human, arguing that "the essence of humanity is that we have always been both symbolic and embodied." "We were always human," she suggests. "Or maybe, said alternatively, we were always posthuman." Tufekci and others in this volume discover that even in these virtual worlds that create always expanding possibilities for disembodied sociality, embodiment remains crucial. It is the body that "centers and unites us," even as we play with different social roles and personas. "Typing on a keyboard," Tufekci suggests, does not "create an ontological split within the body." But, as Tufekci rightly points out, this still begs the question of what we are to make of emerging technologies that now promise to immerse us in fully realistic simulated worlds—skin suits, goggles, and other devices that will bring digital inputs seamlessly into our increasingly augmented intelligence—or those futuristic Kurzwellian visions of nanobots swarming through our bodies, giving us access to all the information on the web from inside our own skin while repairing and rebuilding our cells and transporting us into virtual worlds whenever we desire (Kurzwell 2005). Moreover, this also begs questions about the role of symbolizing and embodiment for animals and those "not-quite-humans."

Nonetheless, the bodily disciplines imposed by subjective engagements through such technological devices do represent a historical and cultural rupture and disjuncture. Thus, it is not our potential forms of disembodiment that make us posthuman but rather the way in which this historical movement away from prior cultural forms of embodiment are understood. As a result, Tufekci necessarily oscillates between the formulation "we were always human" and the formulation "we were always posthuman," precisely because the notion of the "human" is always a contingent category and different regimes of "humanity" have been deployed throughout history to produce the exclusions and inclusions so necessary for the construction of power through difference. The whole realm of ecstatic experience through ritual and shamanism, for example, is a perfect example of the persistent presence of an instability in the human/non-human boundary and in ideas about embodiment. Consequently, the ethnographic literature on shamanism, particularly from Amazonia (see Whitehead, this volume), has been inspirational and reinvigorating for this kind of discussion, especially for some of our authors (see also Alemán, Hoesterey, Wisniewski). Bringing not just cross-cultural but historical sensibilities to our analyses thus allows us to see both the contingency of current posthuman forms and also how there have been perhaps many "posthumanisms."

In the final sentence of *Les Mots et les Choses* Michel Foucault suggested that "[a]s the archaeology of our thought easily shows—the Human is an invention of a recent date. And one perhaps nearing its end . . . If those arrangements were to disappear, as the ground of Classical thought did at the end of the 18th century, then one might predict that Human would be washed away, like a face drawn in the sand at the edge of the sea" (Foucault 1966, 386; translated by Whitehead). It is regarding this perception of the emergence of new (if not unique) cultural and ontological worlds that all the contributors are in agreement. Some may be uneasy with the term, its implications, its sometimes utopian rhetoric, and its lack of singularity in theoretical formulations, but we all agree that it is a term that, as Lévi-Strauss (1966) said of animals, is "good to think with." As Jennifer Cool notes, "engaging the figure of the posthuman proves valuable to understanding questions of virtuality, materiality, and embodiment that attend the reconfigured relations of space, time, and being in the cultural worlds of computer-mediated sociality."

EXPLORING POSTHUMAN LIMITS AND POSSIBILITIES

As a longtime researcher in virtual worlds, Cool leads these selections with a study of Cyborganic, a community of web geeks based in San Francisco that since the first days of the web in the early 1990s have been pioneers of the different possibilities for sociality online, creating the precursors to blogs, status updates, and other forms of digital communication that now seem commonplace. Most interestingly, the community has continuously interacted through both online and offline means, allowing Cool to examine the "complex symbiosis" of online and offline modes of sociality.

Matthew Bernius provides an example that is especially "good to think" in this regard by examining how the "human" is manufactured in the creation of artificial intelligence (AI). As he demonstrates, AI-bots are becoming increasingly common in chatrooms, creating a social space in which not all "subjects" (or apparent subjects) are human. In a second example, Bernius looks at the Virtual Peers project at Northwestern University, where animated AI characters on screen are paired with digital objects throughout the physical environment, so that "the virtual peer is a complex system that extends itself into much of the environment in which she and her human interlocutors interact." As tracking systems, two-dimensional barcodes, sensors, and other digital objects become increasingly part of our everyday lived spaces of sociality, such an example becomes especially important to examine.

Jenny Ryan moves us into the realm of the truly "posthuman," exploring how the dead live on through their digital traces and in virtual spaces where grievers gather to share and post their memories. Perhaps most interesting in this regard is the way in which most posters address their comments directly to the deceased. Here Ryan makes the point that "embodiment" may need to be reconfigured as the highly immersive nature of online interaction can create the sense that the deceased is really "there," even after death. Perhaps nothing could say this more forcefully than the protest movement against Facebook's policy of removing personal information from profiles after somebody dies, aptly named "Facebook Memoralization Is Misguided: Dead Friends are Still People."

For decades now scholars have speculated about and documented the possibilities of identity play online in virtual worlds (see, e.g., Rheingold 1993; Turkle 1995), a notion captured in the public imagination by the now classic *New Yorker* cartoon "On the Internet, nobody knows you are a dog." But more recent forms of online sociality, such as Facebook, allow for what Zeynep Tufekci calls "grassroots surveillance," in which ubiquitous peer surveillance of the most mundane activities monitored through status updates, photos, and videos make identity play much harder. In a play on the *New Yorker* title at a panel discussion Tufekci noted, "On the Internet, everybody knows you are a dog."

As Wesch notes in his contribution to this volume, each digital platform, virtual space, or tool creates its own structure for participation, which can in turn be played with and at times remade by the participants themselves. Facebook and other platforms require persistent and mostly verifiable identities, whereas others allow for more identity play, pseudonymity, or anonymity. Some connect people around the world; others emphasize local connections. Some are text-only, others audio-only; some use video and some mix all three. Some are synchronous whereas others are asynchronous. Some are open, others closed. Some are archived, providing a running history of social interactions; others are not. Every feature shapes the possibilities for sociality. In the end, the most pertinent and active structuring principle of online sociality is not a simple list of features and characteristics but instead an open-ended range of possibilities limited only by human imagination, allowing new forms of sociality to emerge.

Wesch examines one of these new forms in the phenomenon of Anonymous, an "ongoing collective happening" that challenges our traditional notion of identity and group as all interlocutors on the site remain anonymous, communicating through text, links, and imagery. Their peculiar form of sociality, along with the values they express, presents a scathing critique of our cultural obsession with individualism and identity and the cult of celebrity that emerges from this obsession. Moreover, following the furor around Wikileaks and the support Anonymous gave to the figure of Julian Assange, as well as ongoing AnonOps against various governments and their agencies, there is an important way in which Anonymous's challenges to individualism and identity represent a potentially new form of political engagement and resistance.

Traditional notions of human identity become increasingly irrelevant to life as it is lived even as they begin to seem the most pertinent to the procedures of power and governance. As Wesch forcefully illustrates, we must recognize the ways in which "identity" is used as a way of rendering people legible to those who exercise power; and this remains a powerful structural element in current academic practice, no less than in the panopticon of the security state. In this way, questions of identity emerge as less important for scientific fact than for the way in which such notions validate the truth of the cultural quest for ever-expanding discovery and knowledge of others.

RETHINKING FIELDWORK IN THE AGE OF THE POSTHUMAN

This discursive panorama—in which we may really have become human no more—raises important questions about the emergence of a "posthuman" anthropology—an anthropology in which the human subject, a historically contingent conception, is no longer the sole focus of attention. In such a context traditional Malinowskian formulas of "participant observation" need to be critically assessed because it is the manner of our participation in online and offline worlds, rather than the limits and qualities of our observations, that urgently needs to be thought through more carefully (Whitehead, in press).

Radhika Gajjala has been rethinking "participant observation" during her two decades of research on South Asian diasporas, developing an especially acute sense of how different media "mediate" the communities we study. In this volume, she teams up with her colleague Sue Ellen McComas to explore how Indian diasporas have been mediated across generations, from pre-digital mediated narratives to a study of how members of a diaspora interact as avatars among the scripted objects of Second Life. There she has the opportunity to re-encounter those recurring critical questions that she has raised in earlier work: How do ethnographic practices and the ethnographer evolve in the online context? How are they revolutionized? What constitutes the field?

For Gray Graffam, the "field" is the World of Warcraft, a virtual reality and massive social space that to date has more than 10 million players. In adapting ethnography to suit this field, Graffam found that interviews with players outside the game lacked the proper context that provides the performative cues for people to "be themselves" and answer his questions effectively. Fieldwork experiences like this remind us that observation of any kind (online and offline) is by definition utterly dependent on the forms of participation that the ethnographer may choose or have available.

Such issues affect ethnography even as it is most traditionally conceived, especially as there is a growing worldwide cultural investment in online life, even among the most remote and marginal populations. In this volume, Stephanie Alemán reports on her experiences in a remote Guyanese village where the Waiwai first encounter the Internet and start to present themselves online. In one telling example, a young Waiwai man presents himself on Facebook "in a Taekwondo uniform and pose, and another, in a gangsta pose with a knit hat, with dark glasses and headphones and making hand signs." Meanwhile, as the anthropologist, Alemán has collected images of him in more traditional "native activities": adorned in full black body paint, shooting a bow and arrow, and dancing in the communal house. Alemán begins to see a clear dilemma for many anthropologists today: how do we represent those who can and will represent themselves? How do we address "their multiple and complex entailments with the regional and global networks to which they not only now have access but actively seek to engage"?

Such anxieties are explored in James Hoesterey's encounter with a TV reality show about the Mek of Irian Jaya that shamelessly re-creates colonial subjectivities by feeding a prurient interest in the savage violence and sexuality of others, while simultaneously portraying the protagonists, Mark and Olly, as kind, enlightened, likable, and sensitive explorers. At the American Anthropological Meetings in 2009, when Hoesterey first presented the story of how the "first contact" with these "primitives" was elaborately constructed for television, the anthropologists in the audience responded with gales of laughter. Such laughter was perhaps related to the fact that although we anthropologists like to draw strong lines between what we do and what Mark and Olly do, the differences between us are not so great. As Hoesterey demonstrates, the anthropological critique of pop ethnography reveals deep disciplinary anxieties about our expertise and role in the representation of others.

In this context of increasing anthropological anxiety, there is a growing need for the ethnographer to explicitly theorize participation no less adequately than we have painstakingly theorized observation and representation. As Wisniewski notes in this volume about his study of the invisible caboclos of Brazil in which he teamed up with two hippie "vagabond ethnographers," "theorizing participation will give us a clearer understanding of how ethnographic knowledge is produced, revealing it as a shared product, an intersubjective product, not just of and about humans but of and about human interaction with all categories in a way that does not privilege or overvalue the role of the anthropologist in its production."

The need to theorize participation extends beyond the emerging contexts of online life to all spaces of virtuality where traditional notions of the human limit us or fail altogether. As Michael Heckenberger points out in this volume, not all "virtual realities" are digital or online, so the import of engaging digital subjectivities for wider theory lies precisely in how it may offer the possibility of eluding the Foucaldian/Marcusian nexus of knowledge-power-media. In São Paulo, public discourses about public health and security create the unhuman *nóias*, a drug addict who has taken center stage as the persona of the irrational and subnormal in public discourse. Also referred to as zombies, inhabiting a space between life and death, such unhumans invoke different forms and moments of marginalization and oppression than those of the South Asian digital online residents, but nonetheless they experience displacement and disorientation similar to that produced in social encounters within a geographical diaspora. Like the zombies of the cityscapes, the diasporic are also engaged in an attempt to reframe their cultural identities to stave off the threat of cultural—if not physical—genocide through the effects of a rampant globalization.

Thinking about how such potential marginalization of the already marginal plays out is important for ethnographers to keep in mind because, as with globalization, what we are witnessing may be a reordering of differences and inequalities rather than their dissolution. At the same time the potential for digital media to create new spaces and opportunities for empowerment and resistance are apparent from Asia to Amazonia to America.

BEYOND HUMAN NO MORE

Issues of constituting an ethnographic locus and representing the "humanity" of marginal groups, such as prostitutes, criminals, and even "insurgents" or "guerillas," present all ethnographic approaches with theoretical and ethical challenges. This is because the "human subject" is not a given in online or offline contexts. Anthropologists currently researching issues in disability studies and science and technology studies, as well as animal rights and biological anthropology, thus all have important contributions to make to this emergent discussion of the fact that we may have become "human no more." Culture, language, ritual, symbol, and their performative embodiment are thus no longer adequate criteria for defining a notional "human subject."

In fact, such categories have revealed a vast field of social and cultural continuities among the human, animal, and technological.

Current notions of biopower, the deployment of artificial intelligence and robotic systems in warfare and law enforcement, and the cultural logic of cinematic and televisual representations are all indications of the urgency with which anthropology should engage its new subjects.

Regardless of where one stands on the question of the posthuman, it is clear that a jailbreak from late modernity does not go unchallenged. Stalwart symbols and institutions, such as hungry profiteers and militarized governance, seek to delimit the "human terrain" in both online and offline contexts, creating yet one more piece of the complex contexts and new spaces of cultural and social significance that have proliferated in the last decade. Here the "native populations"—the freaks, geeks, weirdos, techies, and net-addicts—like the savages at the margins of an earlier colonial order, defy simple inclusion into the frameworks of the state and its ethnographies.

Living with the Mek, or the caboclos or the Waiwai, no less than the character-subjects of Anonymous or the online worlds of Second Life or My(Death)Space, must now take account of the endless interplay between offline and online subjectivity, while also expanding our notions and understandings of the vast potential of human diversity and social interaction.

The stakes are high. Quoting Judith Butler, Heckenberger nicely observes how our cultural frames for thinking the human set limits on certain lives that are not considered lives at all: "[V]iolence against those who are already not quite living, living in a state of suspension between life and death, leaves a mark that is no mark." These are the "killable bodies" discussed by Giorgio Agamben (1995) in his characterization of contemporary power and governance. As Wisniewski notes in this volume, it is time to expand and refine our approach so that we are equipped to grapple with the relationship between humans and technology, while also recognizing that humans are part of much larger systems that include relationships with animals, insects, microorganisms, spirits, and people who are not always considered human by others. And as humans become more digitally connected, we must also recognize that the sociality that emerges from such connections might not always be immediately analogous to traditional social formations and may involve unhuman actors and agencies (which may or may not be conceptualized or treated as human). This signals an end to anthropology of a certain kind and the necessity for inventing new ends and new methodologies for anthropological research that will better interpret such changing and emergent cultural worlds.

REFERENCES

Agamben, Giorgio. 1995. *Homo Sacer: Sovereign Power and Bare Life*. Trans. D. Heller-Roazen. Stanford, CA: Stanford University Press.

Boellstorff, Tom. 2008. *Coming of Age in Second Life: An Anthropologist Explores the Virtually Human*. Princeton, NJ: Princeton University Press.

Foucault, Michel. 1966. *Les Mots et Les Choses*. Paris: Flammarion et Cie.

Haraway, Donna Jeanne. 1991. *Simians, Cyborgs, and Women: The Reinvention of Nature*. New York: Routledge.

Kurzwell, Ray. 2005. *The Singularity Is Near*. New York: Penguin.

Latour, Bruno. 1993. *We Have Never Been Modern*. Cambridge, MA: Harvard University Press.

Lévi-Strauss, Claude. 1966. *The Savage Mind*. Chicago: University of Chicago Press.

Rheingold, Howard. 1993. *The Virtual Community*. Boston, MA: Addison Wesley. http://www.rheingold.com/vc/book/

Turkle, Sherry. 1995. *Life on the Screen: Identity in the Age of the Internet*. New York: Simon & Schuster.

Whitehead, Neil L. 2004. "Power, Culture, and History: The Legacies of Wolf, Sahlins, and Fabian; Envisioning Power—Ideologies of Dominance and Crisis, Eric Wolf (California, 1999, 300 pp.); Culture in Practice—Collected Essays, Marshall David Sahlins (Zone Books, 2000, 600 pp.); Anthropology with an Attitude—Critical Essays, Johannes Fabian (Stanford, 2001, 256 pp.)." *Ethnohistory* (Columbus, Ohio) 51 (1): 181–5. http://dx.doi.org/10.1215/00141801-51-1-181.

Whitehead, Neil L. In press. "Ethnography, Knowledge, Torture and Silence." In *Virtual War and Magical Death: Technologies and Imaginaries for Terror and Killing*, ed. Neil L. Whitehead and Sverker Finnstrom. Durham, NC: Duke University Press.

Wolfe, Cary. 2010. *What Is Posthumanism?* Minneapolis: University of Minnesota Press.

The Mutual Co-Construction of Online and Onground in Cyborganic

Making an Ethnography of Networked Social Media Speak to Challenges of the Posthuman

Jennifer Cool

For approximately ten years I was a participant-observer of Cyborganic, a group of San Francisco web geeks who combined online and face-to-face interaction in a conscious project to build community "on both sides of the screen." Cyborganic members brought *Wired* magazine online; launched *Hotwired*, the first ad-supported online magazine; set up web production for CNET.com; led the Apache open-source software project; and staffed and started dozens of Internet enterprises, such as Craig's List, during the first decade of the web's development as a popular platform (1993–2003). Cyborganic pioneered self-publishing and featured some of the earliest online diaries before these were called "blogs," most notably *Links from the Underground* by Justin Hall, a "founding father of personal blogging" (Rosen 2004), and *Brainstorms* by author Howard Rheingold. The new imaginaries and practices of networked, social media that Cyborganics integrated in their daily lives during this period are recognizable today in Facebook,[1] Twitter,[2] and a variety of other forms of many-to-many online media centered on self-publishing, user-generated content, and social networks.

DOI: 10.5876/9781607321705.c01

Although online life challenges traditional assumptions of place-based ethnography and the anthropological subject, my Cyborganic study shows how practices of networked social media can reconfigure experiences and imaginaries of place, identity, and embodiment without dematerializing these as sites of subjectivity or rendering them obsolete as sources of anthropological insight. Indeed, the interdependence or mutuality of Cyborganic's online and onground (face-to-face) aspects has been a key finding of my study. This mutuality can be seen large-scale in the importance of place to the economic and cultural history of networked media and small-scale in the new media practices of Cyborganics. Attention to the mutuality of online and onground suggests ways to think through challenges to inherited conceptions of the anthropological subject posed not only by the proliferation of online life but by earlier critiques of the discipline (postcolonialist, feminist, and postmodernist) that similarly challenged assumed relations of social and material worlds. That, in thumbnail, is the overarching argument this chapter presents in two parts. Part 1 focuses on the Cyborganic case, drawing on ethnographic description and analysis to illustrate the formative role of place in the cultural construction of networked social media and give tangible examples of the mutual co-construction of online and onground. In Part 2, I take a broader, theoretical scope, arguing that my analysis of online/onground mutuality in Cyborganic offers ways to think through challenges to inherited conceptions of the anthropological subject that I discuss as "challenges of the posthuman."

Throughout this work, I use the terms *online* and *onground* to talk about ways networked media were integrated in the whole of my Cyborganic informants' lives. *Online* is the conventional term for computer-mediated communication, and I came up with *onground* because I needed a convenient way to refer to aspects of Cyborganic that were not, or not only, online (e.g., working and living together, interacting face-to-face). Instead of *offline* I decided *onground* was more descriptive of these place-based aspects of Cyborganic. However, it is vital to make clear that the distinction between onground and online is not that the former is material and the latter immaterial. However tempting and common sense that assumption, online communications clearly have material bases in physical hardware (machines and wires) and material forces of production and consumption.

The work of geographer Edward Soja is particularly valuable to thinking about how computer-mediated sociality challenges the assumptions of place-based ethnography. Soja argues that, just as the physical world can be divided in to *space*, *time*, and *matter*, the abstract dimensions of *spatiality*, *temporality*, and *social being* "together comprise all facets of human existence" (Soja 1989, 25). He calls this triad the "ontological[3] nexus of space-time-being." These basic dimensions of human existence are not natural or given but rather social constructions that shape empirical reality and are simultaneously shaped by it (Soja 1989, 25). That is, the relation between the physical triad (space, time, matter) and existential triad (spatiality, temporality, and social being) is already mediated through language and socialization. Computer-mediated communication blurs and shifts relations of spatiality, temporality, and social being—Soja's basic facets of human existence—and thus calls into question traditional conceptions of the anthropological subject. Although the tremendous growth of real-time, global, information networks untethers social being from many of the spatial and temporal constraints to which it had been tied, it does not dematerialize these facets of human existence. Soja's theory helps conceptualize these relationships and informs the concept of colocation developed in my analysis of Cyborganic in Part 1. It also informs my approach to questions of virtuality, materiality, and embodiment that have long attended the study of life online (Turkle 1984, 1995; Stone 1991, 1995; Dibbell 1998) and figure centrally in competing visions of the posthuman presented in Part 2.

PART 1

Online/Onground Mutuality in Cyborganic

Started in an apartment in a two-story Victorian in San Francisco's Mission/SOMA (South of Market) district, Cyborganic was a neighborhood cooperative, social clique, artist organization, professional network, and Internet start-up business. The Cyborganic business concept can be traced back to 1990, and the community can be traced to the San Francisco rave scene of the early 1990s and the SFRaves mailing list started in 1992. Described by *Rolling Stone* magazine as "a community of webheads who live in and around an apartment on Ramona Street on the outskirts of . . . Multimedia Gulch" (Goodell 1995) and by *Wired News* as "an influential early Web community" (Boutin 2002), Cyborganic's central project was to create a "home on both sides of the screen" (Cyborganic Gardens website, 1995).

Onground as a local, face-to-face community, Cyborganic comprised three concentric, overlapping entities. First, there were several group households on a single block of Ramona Avenue, known as "The Ramona Empire," which had a peak of approximately twenty residents during the years 1995–1999. Second, there was the Ramona LAN (local area network), a physical network of computers, wires, and buildings whose maximum reach was across eleven separate rental apartments, providing approximately thirty-five people with full-time residential connections to the Internet for more than a decade. The third and largest of Cyborganic's face-to-face venues were weekly community potluck dinners, known as Thursday Night Dinner, or TND. With approximately 100 regular attendees from August 1995 through the end of

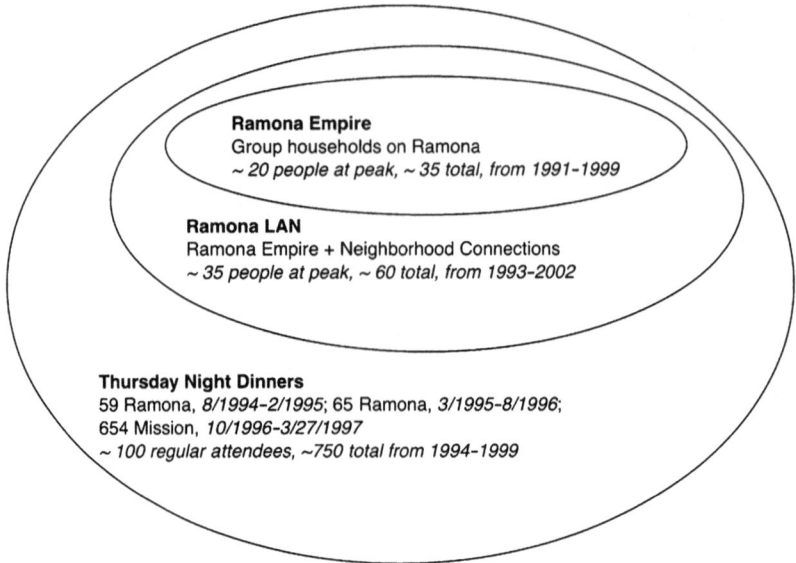

FIGURE 1.1.

Cyborganic as a place-based, face-to-face community. Peaks reflect the largest number of simultaneous members in each group. Totals are the number of members over the life of the group.

1996, TND was, as *Wired News* put it, "the place to be for San Francisco's up-and-coming Web workers" during the dot-com boom of the 1990s (Boutin 2002). These three place-based parts of Cyborganic—the Ramona Empire, local area network, and Thursday Night Dinners—are diagrammed above in Figure 1.1.

Online, Cyborganic included the following forums, illustrated in Figure 1.2. Cyborganic's web and mail servers hosted approximately 100 user accounts and more than 100 virtual domains between 1994 and 2002. The cc list, a community e-mail list, was the most central of Cyborganic's online forums. Launched in 1994 with 33 subscribers, it grew to 152 subscribers by mid-1996, had a peak of more than 200 in 1997, and remained active through 2002. Cyborganic also had a website, Cyborganic Gardens, which showcased the community and business and hosted member homepages and projects. Cyborganic had thirty-four member homepages when the website went online in April 1995 and eighty-six from January 1996 through the winter of 1997 when it went offline. Finally, Cyborganic's online venues included the space bar, a text-based synchronous conferencing system, or "chat," that was active from April 1995 until mid-2008.

Web & Mail Servers **1994–2002** Hosting, Publishing Tools, and Help Pages for: ~100 users ~100 domains	**Mailing List (cc list)** **1994–2002** 220+ subscribers at peak ~33 regular posters over life of the list
Website (Cyborganic Gardens) **1995–1997** ~86 homepages 200+ Cyborganic pages Publicly Viewable, Only Members Publish to Site	**Space bar** **1995–2008** ~30 space bar regulars 250+ logins at peak

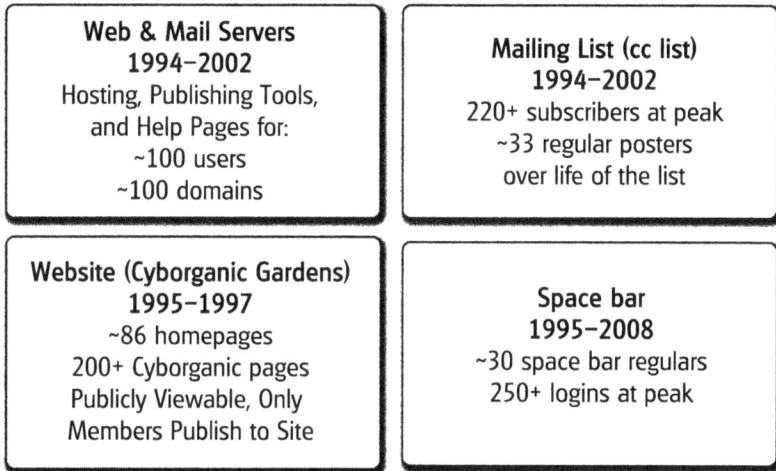

FIGURE 1.2.
Cyborganic online.

Cyborganic's Place-Based Legacies: Silicon Valley and Bay Area Countercultures

In the large-scale view, my ethnography situates Cyborganic genealogically in relation to two cultural histories: first, of Silicon Valley as a region of technological and economic innovation; and second, of Bay Area countercultures and the role these played in the social construction of networked personal computing. Both highlight the formative role of place—physical colocation in particular places and the embodied, face-to-face sociality that this affords—in the development of networked media.

From the "community of technical scholars" envisioned in 1927 by Fredrick Terman, the Stanford professor who played a key role in the creation of Silicon Valley, to the "faires," hobbyist clubs, and local businesses that ushered in personal computing in the 1970s (Freiberger and Swaine 2000), spatial proximity and face-to-face sociality have been central to the development of information technologies. Scholars of urban development (Saxenian 1993, 1994; Castells and Hall 1994) and economic history (Kenney 2000) identify Silicon Valley as an example of the "technopole" and emphasize the crucial role of place and culture in technical innovation and "dynamic economic growth" (Castells and Hall 1994, 8). More recent studies have demonstrated the extraordinary spatial concentration of the Internet industry and the continued importance of geography in the network age (Zook 2005; Saxenian 2006). During the 1990s the SOMA district in San Francisco, where Cyborganic formed, emerged as "a new Silicon Valley," about forty miles to the north, in a process of "short-distance decentralization" (Castells and Hall 1994, 235) in which technopoles spawn nearby satellites. My ethnography of Cyborganic demonstrates how spatial proximity and face-to-face sociality worked together in SOMA in the 1990s to "foster dynamically evolving networks of relationships" among emerging businesses and outposts of larger enterprises, in "a kind of fishnet organization" (IFTF 1997, 2).

The significance of place and embodiment can be seen, for example, in the fact that Cyborganic was an age cohort (a group of people of the same generation) that came together through a variety of kin, high school, college, and occupational networks. Figure 1.3 diagrams the network of firms, projects, and professional and recreational communities in which Cyborganic formed, tracing its connections to the new businesses and software projects through which web publishing developed in San Francisco in the 1990s. Although a few lines of connection in Figure 1.3 represent Internet connectivity as well, all lines represent flows of people, ideas, and collaborative action. In this diagram, the multiple, overlapping, graphic shapes (cloud, diamond, rectangle) illustrate the overlap and interconnection of social forms—businesses, voluntary projects, and communities of work and leisure—and, thus, of work and play, professional and personal. The concentration of Internet firms, projects, and communities in San Francisco's tiny SOMA district (less than one square mile) illustrates the interdependence of onground and online sociality. These were the small-scale social forms and boundaries my Cyborganic subjects negotiated as producers and consumers of new forms of networked media during the first phase of the web's development as a popular platform during the 1990s.

The other relevant regional legacy for Cyborganic is that of the Bay Area as a center of 1960s and 1970s American countercultures. The vital role of these countercultures in the emergence of networked personal computing and virtual community has been well documented in a variety of contexts (Roszak 1986a, 1986b; Brand 1995; Abbate 1999; Castells 2001; Roy 2001; Markhoff 2005; Turner 2005, 2007). Communications scholar Fred Turner (2005, 2007) traces the role of Bay Area countercultures in the emergence of online communities through the WELL (Figure 1.3, top left), an online community and business founded in 1985 by Stewart Brand and Larry Brilliant. WELL stands for Whole Earth 'Lectronic Link and is a reference to Brand's earlier enterprise, *The Whole Earth Catalog*, a handbook of the hippie generation. Profiled in Rheingold's *The Virtual Community* (1993), the WELL is one of the oldest online communities and also one of the most studied (Smith 1992; Figallo 1993; Hafner 1997; Wellman and Gulia 1999; Kollock 1999). The WELL, Turner argues, "not only modeled the interactive possibilities of computer-mediated communication but also translated a countercultural vision of the proper relationship between technology and sociability into a resource for imagining and managing life in the network economy" (Turner

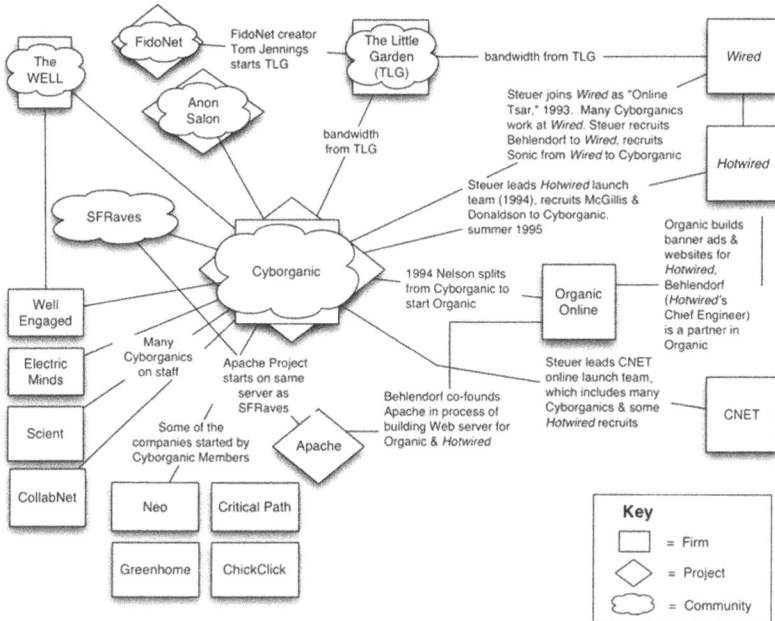

FIGURE 1.3.
Cyborganic network of firms, projects, and communities, San Francisco, 1993–1999.

2005, 491). Cyborganic inherited from the WELL a small but formative membership and, more significantly, the entrepreneurial and utopian vision to start a locally based online community and make a business of it.[4]

Situating Cyborganic in this brief cultural history highlights the vital role local communities have played in the development of the Bay Area as a techno-pole and of networked personal computing and shows the continuing importance of such groups to web publishing in the 1990s. Cyborganic combined the identity and trust-building power of face-to-face forums with the flexibility and greater reach of computer-mediated communication. This combination resulted in a community colocated in places online and onground and in the hyper-experience that results when these two are deeply intertwined.

The large-scale view described so far illustrates the importance of place in the development of web publishing. Now I turn to the small-scale view to focus on specific imaginaries, practices, and forms of networked media in the daily life of Cyborganic. Ethnographic analysis of these forms and practices demonstrates the way online intermediation can reconfigure experiences and imaginaries of place, identity, and embodiment without dematerializing these sites of subjectivity or rendering them obsolete as sources of anthropological insight. To make this demonstration, I begin with a few definitions and concepts before turning to examine one specific part of Cyborganic (the space bar chat) for what it shows about the interdependence of online and onground social forms.

Place, Media, and Colocation

In the 1990s, anthropologists (Appadurai 1990, 1991; Gupta and Ferguson 1997a, 1997b, 1997c) challenged the assumed "isomorphism between space, place, and culture" (Gupta and Ferguson 1997a, 34) and theorized "technological infrastructures as sites for the production of locality" without a necessarily geographic referent (Ito 1999, 2). Despite this decoupling, or unlinking, of social location from physical space, my Cyborganic study illustrates how spatial proximity onground and technologically mediated presence online continue to interact in significant ways. Rather than arguing for a return to place-based ethnography of face-to-face communities (see, e.g., Foster 1953; Redfield 1960), my emphasis on place builds on a concept of *colocation*—the colocation of people, jobs, and social activities together in particular places and channels of communication—that applies equally online and onground. This understanding of colocation is informed by Lisa Gitelman's definition of media "as socially realized structures of communication, where structures include both technological forms and their associated protocols, and where communication is a cultural practice, *a ritualized colocation* of different people on the same mental map, sharing or engaged with popular ontologies of representation" (Gitelman 2006, 7, emphasis added). Although media can be defined as "communication that is not face-to-face" (Spitulnik 2001, 143), the "ritualized colocation of different people on the same mental map" that Gitelman describes is a cultural practice that takes place onground as well as online. Moreover, it is one that figures centrally in Cyborganic's imaginaries and practices of networked social media, where online and onground colocation worked synergistically to reconfigure the experience and social relations of presence and place. For example, a 1995 manifesto on the Cyborganic website proclaimed: "Cyborganic will establish a real space for members to meet and interact—*a flesh-and-blood back-channel*—to its community-building efforts in cyberspace" (Cyborganic Garden website, "Our Big Plan"). "Back-channel" implies all the informal communications and interactions around a main channel. In telecommunications a back-channel is usually a lower-speed transmission flowing in a direction opposite the main channel. The irony of imagining "real space" and "flesh and blood" as the back-channel to online interaction is that face-to-face interaction offers a far richer spectrum of communication. All kinds of subconscious and preconscious communications flow across in "full duplex"—that is, in both directions simultaneously. This example serves to highlight the mutuality of online and onground in that both forms of interaction and social space are imagined as channels.

This is a thoroughly "infomated" imaginary of location, to use Shoshana Zuboff's (1988) term for the way information technologies support richer communication around the tasks to which they are applied. In 1988, Zuboff identified a "fundamental duality" between technologies that automate, that is, "replace the human body . . . enabling the same processes to be performed with more continuity and control," and technologies that, in her coinage, "infomate," meaning they simultaneously generate "information about the underlying productive and administrative processes" of whatever they automate. Although the logic of automation "hardly differs from that of the nineteenth-century machine system," Zuboff observes, "information technology supersedes the traditional logic" because it feeds back on itself by introducing "an additional dimension of reflexivity . . . Information technology not only produces action but also produces a voice that symbolically renders events, objects, and processes so that they become visible, knowable, and shareable in a new way" (Zuboff 1988, 9–10).

Technologies that infomate form the technological nucleus for the array of contemporary phenomena known as "Web 2.0," and their voices can already be heard in my Cyborganic research. Let me illustrate by looking at one aspect of Cyborganic—the space bar chat—where I identify practices of colocation, presence casting, phatic communion, and configurable sociality, all of which express the mutuality of online and onground in the daily life of Cyborganic.

Space Bar: Configurable Sociality from Colocation to Presence Casting

Space bar was an online chat where multiple people logged into the same channel to exchange text messages in real time. Space bar was not on the web but had a text or command-line interface and was accessed using the older telnet protocol. From the time it went online in April 1995, space bar had a contingent of regulars who spent much of each workday logged into the chat. Most were people whose jobs entailed being online at a computer much of the day, as these interview excerpts illustrate.

> I'm usually on the space bar by eleven thirty or eleven, say, and bail for lunch, go outside and talk to my tape-recorder or talk to my journal, or play guitar or something to get the stress out and then, show up at one and deal with afternoon meetings and then by, easily, definitely by three I'm back on "the bar."
>
> (DOMINIC SAGOLLA, INTERVIEW, OCTOBER 17, 1996)

> It's certainly busier during the day, during the week, when everybody's supposed to be working and they've got their telnet window open, on their computer desk . . . (laughs)
>
> (KAT KOVACS, INTERVIEW, OCTOBER 8, 1996)

Being on space bar was integrated into the workday and workplace. For Cyborganics with day jobs in San Francisco's SOMA neighborhood, space bar was a place to find people to go to lunch with during the week and talk about lunch afterward, back at work. For those who worked "down peninsula" in Silicon Valley, keeping a window open to space bar all day countered the isolation of the commute and corporate workplace, or "Cubeland," as some of my informants called it. Having a cohort of knowledgeable friends with you on your desktop at work dramatically changed the character of the workplace for the Cyborganics who frequented space bar. More widely, such forms and practices of techno-sociality (e.g., instant messaging, texting) have been identified as central to the new workplace of a "creative class" (Florida 2002) of "no-collar" workers (Ross 2003) associated with the new economy and 1990s dot.com boom.

Besides hanging out, gossiping, and bantering in the chat, Cyborganics used space bar as a hailing frequency. Even those who did not generally spend much time in the chat logged in when they needed to track somebody down or talk to a "live person." To facilitate this practice, Cyborganic's web team created a "porthole" on the Web (Figure 1.4), a webpage people could visit to see who was online in the chat without having to telnet to space bar and log-in.

Cyborganic also devised a "cadet detector" (Figure 1.5) that members could put on their homepages to indicate automatically with a graphic icon if they were logged in to space bar.

In the context of the porthole and cadet detector, people began using the space bar's nickname feature to append short status messages of different kinds (e.g., mood, location, role) to their log-ins. Displaying your presence across media—that is, from the space bar chat, which was not on the web, to a page on Cyborganic's website or a member's homepage—was what I call "presence casting." As the status updates so central to more recent online media such as Facebook and Twitter illustrate, this form of mediated communication has proliferated with the rise of the mobile Internet and social networking.

Beyond its presence in the workday, the chat was also active late at night when regulars logged in from home or while working after hours. As one of my informants said of space bar in 1996, "people live there"; some even stayed logged on when they were asleep or otherwise out of range of the "beeps" that users could send to one another's computers. When asked about this practice, some suggested it was "a status thing to be on the bar," whereas others indicated that staying logged on gave a sense of "being together" that was comforting. In this, and other practices, space bar served an essentially phatic function of maintaining social connection rather than communicating messages. Here I draw on Bronislaw Malinowski who "coined the phrase 'phatic communion' to refer to [the] social function of language, which arises out of the basic human need to signal friendship—or, at least, lack of enmity" (Crystal 1987,

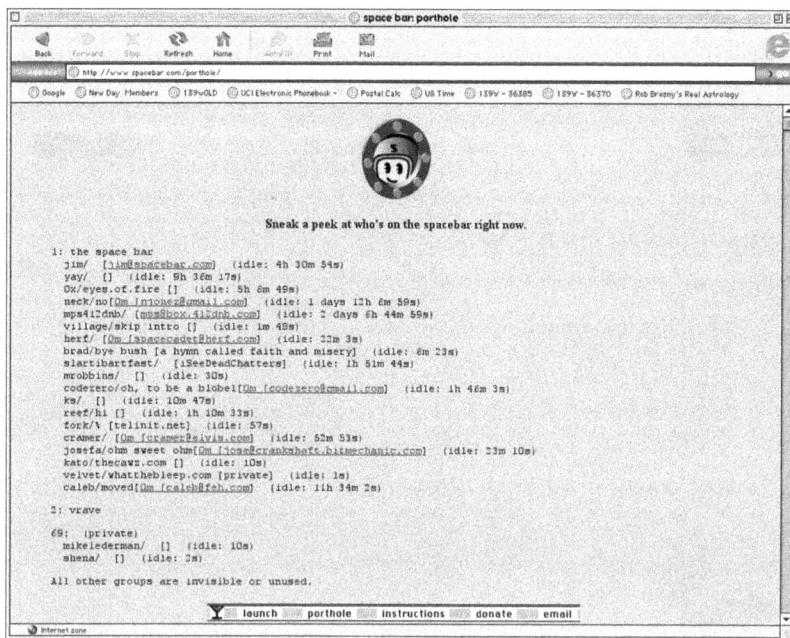

FIGURE 1.4.
The space bar porthole.

10; Malinowski 1989 [1923]). Linguist Roman Jakobson described the phatic function as one of contact over message where messages serve "primarily... to establish, to prolong, or to discontinue communication, to check whether the channel works," to attract or confirm attention (Jakobson 1981, 24). Space bar was online for thirteen years, and a group of about fourteen people continued to log-in through early 2008, mostly to idle together in the channel or engage in conversations that proceeded at a rate of one or two lines a day. Thus, in its last years of operation, space bar primarily provided phatic communion through a structure of communication that in its very minimalism demonstrates Gitelman's point that media are never only technological but always include and are realized through social protocols and cultural practices.

In technical terms, one might say this use of space bar *automates* the phatic function of communication in its display of users who are logged into the channel. But the function is also *infomated* with automated messages from the system (idle time), as well as customized messages from the users (e-mail addresses, nicknames). For example, one's presence on space bar was displayed automatically (in the text chat and through the web porthole) in the following form:

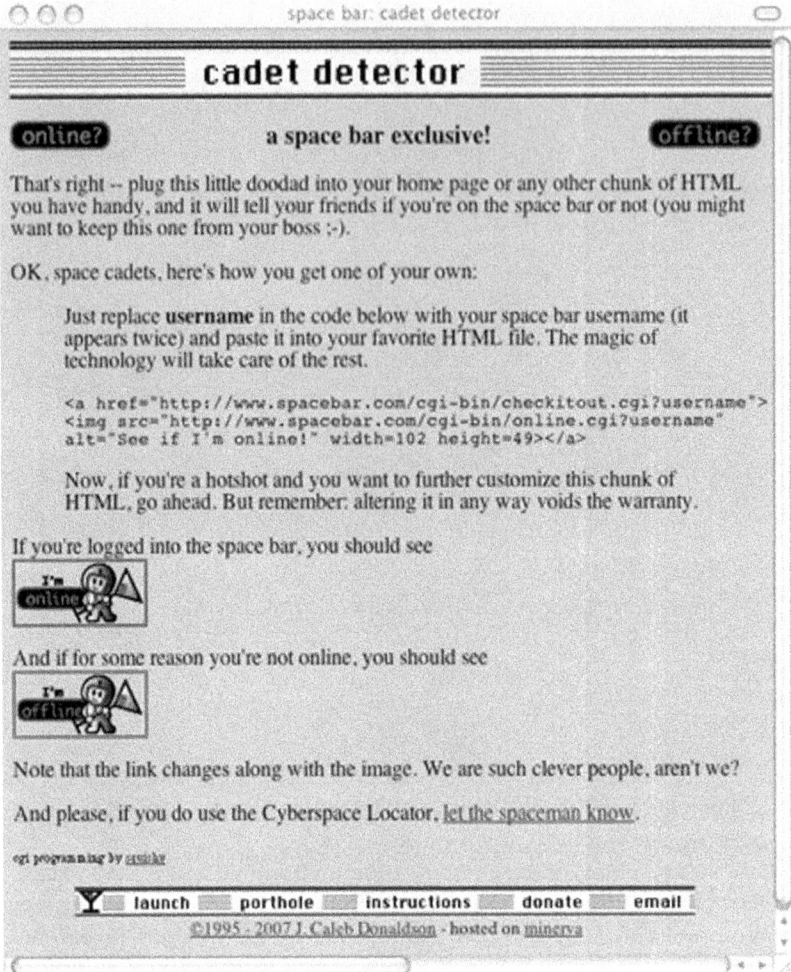

FIGURE 1.5.
The space bar cadet detector.

cool/anthropologist [jenny@cool.org] (idle:0s)

jim/obamageddon [jim@spacebar.com] (idle:23 days, 11h, 17m, 56s)

In this example, I (cool) have just logged in (*idle:0s* means idle for zero seconds), whereas space bar's systems administrator, or sysadmin, (jim) has been logged on and idle for almost twenty-four days. Appended after each log-in are "nicknames" (anthropologist, obamageddon), as they are called in space bar's command menu, although, as noted, they came to be used for status updates and short-form messages (in this example, political commentary), rather than to convey a fixed identity. Even in the rather limited use of its later years, space bar included a range of social functions and cultural meanings. Besides the phatic communion of a small group of old friends who stayed logged in to the channel, it provided a way for Cyborganics, many of whom had left the Bay Area by this time, to locate space bar regulars and learn when they had last said something in the chat.

The imaginaries and practices of colocation, presence casting, and phatic communion described in space bar reflect a form of just-in-time, configurable sociality that has proliferated with the media forms and practices collectively known as "Web 2.0," for example, in Facebook status messages or microblogging on Twitter. Facebook also demonstrates the central importance of place in establishing high trust social networks that can be augmented and maintained at a distance and over time through networked social media. Although it is now a global social networking site, Facebook was initially restricted to Harvard college students. Created in late 2003, it was an online representation of students' face-to-face community using real names and pictures from college identification cards (IDs). Within months, membership expanded to Stanford, Columbia, and Yale, then all Ivy League and Boston area schools, and later most North American universities. In September 2006, membership opened to anyone thirteen or older with a valid e-mail account. The connection of online and onground identity and extension of traditional place-based affiliations, such as college ties, are as central to Facebook as they were to Cyborganic and illustrate ways that although place-based identities and affiliations have been extended in time and space and reconfigured through networked sociality, they remain significant.

A central aspect of configurable sociality is the way it mediates online and onground presence, identity, and colocation. This can be seen in practices of using pseudonyms on space bar that tended to render identity configurable, obscuring or revealing onground connections depending on social context. Space bar constituted a liminal zone as a channel people could enter and use without revealing their onground identities. Anyone on the Internet could log-in and chat in space bar's channel 1 until the administrator ("the spaceman") verified a working e-mail address, at which point users could join any public channel and create public or private channels of their own. In addition, one person could have multiple accounts. As long-time systems administrator for space bar James Home notes, "A lot of the Cybo establishment used the same names [on space bar] as their main accounts but had aliases for fucking around" (James Home, personal communication, March 19, 2008).

About half of space bar's users had a log-in different from their main Cyborganic account, and although some might know who was who "in real life" (IRL), others might not. In this context, it became fairly commonplace for space bar regulars to have fun by fooling or tricking "chat newbies," as one regular described in a 1996 interview.

> Tunaluna is a space bar regular and she is usually very helpful to everybody, although she also just has fun playing around with newbies in channel 1 under a different ID, and as the moderator she has another log-in which if you ask her, she's always pretty helpful, but she also plays with newbies. There was one great evening, me and her and there were two other people and a couple newbies and within about half an hour we had them believe that everything they said was being measured for some big government project from Iowa and everything went into this big computer to design chat machines for the next generation. It's really childish at some level, but it's a harmless game that some people play, but then as the moderator log-in, she wouldn't do that, she would not intentionally mislead people [laughs].

> (SEAN ROBIN, PSEUDONYM, INTERVIEW, OCTOBER 21, 1996)

As this interview excerpt indicates, even space bar's moderators had different aliases and engaged in the in-group games with neophytes. These are practices of pseudonymity rather than anonymity, because the regulars in the online chat know the onground identity of each other's aliases, even though less frequent users would not. Aliases meditate online and onground by inserting a degree of distance (or freedom) between them, a configurable boundary some can see through and others cannot. This example demonstrates the way online practices express onground social relations, albeit in complexly reconfigured and reconfigurable forms. Each of the social imaginaries and practices described and analyzed in this chapter—colocation, presence casting, and configurable sociality—demonstrates ways in which the unlinking of social and physical proximity (of online from onground) opens new possibilities for their recombination and reconfiguration. None suggests the dematerialization of place or erasure of embodiment as a consequence of the proliferation of computer-mediated interaction. Rather, in the case of Cyborganic, mediated and face-to-face communication worked together synergistically to reconfigure the experience and social relations of presence and place.

PART 2

Challenges of the Posthuman

My analysis of Cyborganic's online and onground mutuality suggests ways to think about challenges to traditional conceptions of the anthropological subject that I refer to as challenges of the posthuman. Although I recognize the term *posthuman* is one anthropologists might find problematic (Boellstorff 2008, 28–29), and I even share some of their discomfort with the word, examining the figure of the posthuman proves valuable to under-standing questions of virtuality, materiality, and embodiment that attend the reconfigured relations of space, time, and being in the cultural worlds of the computer-mediated sociality that I study. Engaging the posthuman brings these questions into a broader discourse about challenges to inherited concep-tions of the human subject posed not only by the proliferation of technologi-cally mediated sociality but also by a succession of postcolonial, feminist, and postmodern critiques since the 1980s (Hymes 1974; Said 1978, 1989; Fabian 1983; Clifford and Marcus 1986; Marcus and Fischer 1986; Geertz 1988; Clifford 1988). By speaking of these together as challenges of the posthuman, I argue that, although it is vital for anthropologists to recognize diverse ways in which the historically specific construction called *human* continues to give way to a different construction, which some call *cyborg* (Haraway 1991; Downey and Dumit 1997) and others *posthuman* (Hayles 1999), it is equally vital to understand that this shift does not require the erasure of embodiment from anthropological conceptions of human subjectivity.

Ideas of the posthuman are varied and contradictory and extend from science fiction, cyberpunk, robotics, and artificial intelligence (Foster 2005; Moravec 1988, 1998; Minsky 1987; Warwick 2001, 2004) to critical social theory (Haraway 1991; Hayles 1999). The first set of sources shares a vision of transcending the limits of the human body (eliminating aging, extend-ing physical and mental capacities) and, thus, of the posthuman as *transhu-man*,[5] beyond human. The second set, however, focuses on challenging the liberal humanist subject, that is, the conception of the human that emerged in the West during the Enlightenment. In this conception, human subjectiv-ity is understood as stable, unitary, and autonomous and reason is seen as the defining characteristic of human being (as in Descartes famous phrase "I think, therefore I am"). It is this particular view of the human that critical social theorists seek to put in the past with the "post" of posthuman and to replace with alternate conceptions of human subjectivity, such as the image of the cyborg Donna Haraway has proposed. Haraway's cyborg, which has been taken up in the subspecialty of "cyborg anthropology,"[6] addresses three crucial boundary or category breakdowns—animal/human, organism/machine, and physical/nonphysical—that are central to the information age. Both trans-humanist and posthumanist versions of the posthuman foreground techno-logical mediation and speak to a wider set of contemporary challenges to the category human.

In *How We Became Posthuman* (1999), Katherine Hayles outlines com-peting versions of the posthuman and makes clear what is at stake in the con-test between them. Hayles's view of the posthuman is useful in theoretical, historical, and practical terms. First, she provides a framework for conceptu-alizing a de-centered, intermediated human subject for whom embodiment and place remain defining sources of identity and cultural difference. Second, she identifies a "teleology of disembodiment" in twentieth-century Western literary and scientific writing on information, cybernetics, and the posthuman (Hayles 1999, 22). And third, she cautions against extending this powerful cultural narrative of disembodiment—and with it the "prerogatives" of the autonomous liberal subject—"into the realm of the posthuman" (Hayles 1999, 287). Hayles uses *posthuman* to refer to the eclipse of a certain view of the human, not of humanity, and explicitly works to prevent the insertion of the liberal humanist subject into prevailing concepts of the posthuman. For example, she writes: "[T]he posthuman does not really mean the end of humanity. It signals instead the end of a certain conception of the human, a conception that may have applied, at best, to that fraction of humanity who had the wealth, power, and leisure to conceptualize themselves as autonomous beings exercising their will through individual agency and choice. What is lethal is not the posthuman as such but the grafting of the posthuman onto a liberal humanist view of the self" (Hayles 1999, 286). Hayles not only distinguishes the liberal humanist subject, as historically specific and powerfully constructed, from the general condition of being human but also critiques metanarratives of technological determinism and disembodied subjectivity that resurrect this culturally constructed subject in the posthuman. Such resurrection is lethal because it defines human subjectivity as independent of the material world, a self that theoretically (if not yet practically) could be downloaded to a computer and remain human. It eclipses embodiment and the ontological connection of space, time, and social being and extends the political and epistemological assumptions of the liberal humanist subject across new terrains of disembodied technopower.

Hayles applies *posthuman* to two very different conceptions of human subjectivity: a transhumanist vision that "configures human being so that it can be seamlessly articulated with intelligent machines" (1999, 3) and a posthumanist one that sees "the deconstruction of the liberal humanist subject as an opportunity to put back into the picture the flesh that continues to be erased in contemporary discussions about cybernetic subjects" (1999, 5). She writes:

> If my nightmare is a culture inhabited by posthumans who regard their bodies as fashion accessories rather than the ground of being, my dream is a version of the posthuman that embraces the possibilities of information technologies without being seduced by fantasies of unlimited power and disembodied immortality, that recognizes and celebrates finitude as a condition of human being, and that understands human life is embedded in a material world of great complexity, one on which we depend for our continued survival. (Hayles 1999, 5)

Although both nightmare and dream represent breaks with the liberal humanist tradition, Hayles's nightmare version of the posthuman is born of the idea that, as human beings, "we are *essentially* information patterns" (1999, 22; original emphasis). It adopts "a teleology of disembodiment" from the Enlightenment conception of subjectivity as seated in the conscious mind and free will, as opposed to the body. In contrast, her dream version of the posthuman contests to keep disembodiment from being rewritten in prevailing concepts of subjectivity.

For Hayles, what the posthuman means is an open contest: both transhumanist and posthumanist versions are not only possible but compete in cultural discourses, historical and contemporary. Hayles (1999, 22) puts forth a version that challenges "metanarratives about the transformation of the human into a disembodied posthuman" by replacing them "with historically contingent stories about contests between competing factions" over the disembodiment of human subjectivity. In much the same way, feminist, postcolonialist, and postmodernist anthropologists challenged metanarratives of the universal subject, replacing them with "ethnographies of the particular" (Abu-Lughod 1991, 149) and spatially, temporally, and socioculturally situated subjects (triangulated in the ontological nexus of space, time, and being). Hayles's conception of subjectivity as "a material-informational entity" (1999, 3) is one entirely familiar to anthropologists. It is precisely this view of the contemporary human subject that, echoing Bruno Latour (1993), leads Hayles to conclude "that we have always been posthuman" (1999, 291) and Boellstorff to state that "we have always been virtual" (2008, 5). These pronouncements of continuity challenge transhumanist notions of overcoming or escaping the limits of embodied subjectivity.

Conceived to "put back into the picture the flesh that continues to be erased in contemporary discussions about cybernetic subjects," Hayles's version of the posthuman challenges "metanarratives about the transformation of the human into a disembodied posthuman" (Hayles 1999, 5). In similar manner, I have worked in my ethnographic account of Cyborganic to read and write the flesh back into the genealogy of contemporary forms of technosociality. In both the large-scale view of cultural history and the micro-view of particular media practices, I have spoken of various sites of subjectivity—place, presence, and colocation—as mutually co-constructed online and onground. This is how I perceive the anthropological subject in the cybernetic circuits of contemporary society. Although material-information flows decouple and reconfigure, the circuit always comes to ground in situated subjects, embodied and emplaced in the nexus of space, time, and social being. As my Cyborganic examples show, the intermediation of online and onground can work to consolidate and extend, rather than weaken, affiliations based on place and embodiment (high school, college, age cohorts). Anthropologists have long seen such affiliations as defining sources of identity, cultural difference, and insight into the human subject. In recognizing that subjectivity is constructed through mediation of material and symbolic realms, we are well positioned to contest, with Hayles, the "teleology of disembodiment" that reinserts the liberal humanist subject into conceptions of technologically mediated subjectivity and sociality. By attending to the mutual co-construction of online and onground social forms, practices, and imaginaries, we can make ethnography speak to the challenges of the posthuman.

NOTES

1. Facebook (facebook.com), which claimed 845 million monthly active users worldwide in its February 2012 filing with the US Securities and Exchange Commission, and Twitter (twitter.com), which reported 140 million active users in March 2012, are two of the most popular social networking sites, but these practices and social imaginaries extend across media in many forms, collectively known as "Web 2.0" (Facebook 2012; Twitter 2012).

2. Dominic Sagolla, a key informant during my Cyborganic fieldwork, was a member of the team that created the micro-blogging service Twitter in 2006 (http://www.140characters.com/2009/01/30/how-twitter-was-born/).

3. Ontology is the branch of philosophy that studies the nature of existence or being.

4. I examine Cyborganic's blend of entrepreneurial and utopian imaginaries and practices in my ethnography, "Communities of Innovation: Cyborganic and the Birth of Networked Social Media" (2008).

5. *Transhumanism* is the term for the international cultural movement toward these ends.

6. Cyborg anthropology is a subspecialty launched in 1993 and "located within the larger transdisciplinary field of science and technology studies" (Dumit and Davis-Floyd 2001, 286). See Downey and Dumit 1997 and Downey, Dumit, and Williams 1995.

REFERENCES

Abbate, Janet. 1999. *Inventing the Internet*. Cambridge, MA: MIT Press.

Abu-Lughod, Lila. 1991. "Writing against Culture." In *Recapturing Anthropology*, ed. Richard G. Fox, 137–162. Santa Fe, NM: School of American Research Press.

Appadurai, Arjun. 1990. "Disjuncture and Difference in the Global Cultural Economy." *Public Culture* 2 (2): 1–24. http://dx.doi.org/10.1215/08992363-2-2-1.

Appadurai, Arjun. 1991. "Global Ethnoscapes: Notes and Queries for a Transnational Anthropology." In *Recapturing Anthropology*, ed. Richard G. Fox, 191–210. Santa Fe, NM: School of American Research Press.

Boellstorff, Tom. 2008. *Coming of Age in Second Life*. Princeton, NJ: Princeton University Press.

Boutin, Paul. 2002. "One More Thursday Night Dinner." *Wired News*. Accessed January 24, 2008. http://www.wired.com/culture/lifestyle/news/2002/05/52239.

Brand, Stewart. 1995. "We Owe It All to the Hippies." *Time*, 145, special issue.

Castells, Manuel. 2001. *The Internet Galaxy*. Oxford: Oxford University Press.

Castells, Manuel, and Peter Hall. 1994. *Technopoles of the World: The Making of 21st Century Industrial Complexes*. London: Routledge.

Cool, Jennifer. 2008. "Communities of Innovation: Cyborganic and the Birth of Networked Social Media." PhD diss., University of Southern California, Los Angeles.

Clifford, James. 1988. *The Predicament of Culture*. Cambridge, MA: Harvard University Press.

Clifford, James, and George Marcus, eds. 1986. *Writing Culture: The Poetics and Politics of Ethnography*. Berkeley: University of California Press.

Crystal, David. 1987. *The Cambridge Encyclopedia of Language*. Cambridge: Cambridge University Press.

Dibbell, Julian. 1998. *My Tiny Life: Crime and Passion in a Virtual World*. New York: Holt.

Downey, Gary Lee, and Joseph Dumit. 1997. "Locating and Intervening: An Introduction." In *Cyborgs and Citadels: Anthropological Interventions in Emerging Sciences and Technologies*, ed. G. L. Downey and J. Dumit, 5–29. Santa Fe, NM: School of American Research Press.

Downey, Gary Lee, Joseph Dumit, and Sarah Williams. 1995. "Cyborg Anthropology." *Cultural Anthropology* 10 (2): 264–9. http://dx.doi.org/10.1525/can.1995.10.2.02a00060.

Dumit, Joseph, and Robbie Davis-Floyd. 2001. "Cyborg Anthropology." In *The Routledge International Encyclopedia of Women*. London: Routledge.

Fabian, Johannes. 1983. *Time and the Other: How Anthropology Makes Its Object*. New York: Columbia University Press.

Facebook, Inc. 2012. Form S-1 Registration Statement, as filed with the US Securities and Exchange Commission on February 1, 2012. Accessed April 13, 2012. http://www.sec.gov/Archives/edgar/data/1326801/000119312512034517/d287954ds1.htm.

Figallo, Cliff. 1993. "The WELL: Small Town on the Internet Highway System." Accessed January 24, 2008. http://www.colorado.edu/geography/gcraft/notes/ethics/html/small.town.html.

Florida, Richard. 2002. *The Rise of the Creative Class: And How It's Transforming Work, Leisure, Community and Everyday Life*. New York: Basic Books.

Foster, George. 1953. "What Is Folk Culture?" *American Anthropologist* 55 (2): 159–73. http://dx.doi.org/10.1525/aa.1953.55.2.02a00020.

Foster, Thomas. 2005. *The Souls of Cyberfolk: Posthumanism as Vernacular Theory*. Minneapolis: University of Minnesota Press.

Freiberger, Paul, and Michael Swaine. 2000. *Fire in the Valley: The Making of The Personal Computer*. 2nd ed. New York: McGraw-Hill.

Geertz, Clifford. 1988. *Works and Lives*. Stanford, CA: Stanford University Press.

Gitelman, Lisa. 2006. *Always Already New: Media, History, and the Data of Culture*. Cambridge, MA: MIT Press.

Goodell, Jeff. 1995. "Webheads on Ramona Street." *Rolling Stone*, Issue 722, November 30.

Gupta, Akhil, and James Ferguson. 1997a. "Beyond 'Culture': Space, Identity, and the Politics of Difference." In *Culture, Power, Place: Explorations in Critical Anthropology*, ed. Akhil Gupta and James Ferguson, 33–51. Durham, NC: Duke University Press.

Gupta, Akhil, and James Ferguson. 1997b. "Culture, Power, Place: Ethnography at the End of an Era." In *Culture, Power, Place: Explorations in Critical Anthropology*, ed. Akhil Gupta and James Ferguson, 1–29. Durham, NC: Duke University Press.

Gupta, Akhil, and James Ferguson. 1997c. "Discipline and Practice: 'The Field' as Site, Method, and Location in Anthropology." In *Anthropological Locations: Boundaries and Grounds of a Field Science*, ed. Akhil Gupta and James Ferguson, 1–46. Berkeley: University of California Press.

Hafner, Katie. 1997. "The Epic Saga of the WELL." *Wired* (May): 98–142.

Haraway, Donna. 1991. *Simians, Cyborgs, and Women: The Reinvention of Nature*. London: Free Association Books.

Hayles, N. Katherine. 1999. *How We Became Posthuman: Virtual Bodies in Cybernetics, Literature, and Informatics*. Chicago: University of Chicago Press.

Hymes, Dell. 1974. *Reinventing Anthropology*. New York: Vintage Books.

Institute for the Future (IFTF). 1997. "Images and Stories of a New Silicon Valley." In *The Outlook Project, Special Report SR-625*. Menlo Park, CA: IFTF.

Ito, Mimi. 1999. "Network Localities." Paper presented at the annual meeting of the Society for the Social Studies of Science, San Diego, CA, October 27–30.

Jakobson, Roman. 1981. *Selected Writings*, vol. 3: *Poetry of Grammar and Grammar of Poetry*, ed. Stephen Rudy. Berlin: Mouton de Gruyter.

Kenney, Martin, ed. 2000. *Understanding Silicon Valley: The Anatomy of an Entrepreneurial Region*. Stanford, CA: Stanford University Press.

Kollock, Peter. 1999. "The Economies of Online Cooperation: Gifts and Public Goods in Cyberspace." In *Communities in Cyberspace*, ed. Marc Smith and Peter Kollock, 220–39. London: Routledge.

Latour, Bruno. 1993. *We Have Never Been Modern*. Trans. Catherine Porter. Cambridge, MA: Harvard University Press.

Malinowski, Bronislaw. 1989 [1923]. "The Problem of Meaning in Primitive Languages." In *The Meaning of Meaning*, ed. C. K. Ogden and I. A. Richards, 296–336. New York: Harcourt Brace Jovanovich.

Marcus, George E., and Michael M.J. Fischer. 1986. *Anthropology as Cultural Critique: An Experimental Moment in the Human Sciences*. Chicago: University of Chicago Press.

Markhoff, John. 2005. *What the Dormouse Said: How the 60s Counterculture Shaped the Personal Computer Industry*. New York: Viking.

Minsky, Marvin. 1987. *The Society of Mind*. New York: Simon and Schuster.

Moravec, Hans P. 1988. *Mind Children: The Future of Robot and Human Intelligence*. Cambridge, MA: Harvard University Press.

Moravec, Hans P. 1998. *Robot: Mere Machine to Transcendent Mind*. Oxford: Oxford University Press.

Redfield, Robert. 1960. *The Little Community and Peasant Society and Culture*. Chicago: University of Chicago Press.

Rheingold, Howard. 1993. *The Virtual Community: Homesteading on the Electronic Frontier*. Reading, MA: Addison-Wesley.

Roszak, Theodore. 1986a. *The Cult of Information: A Neo-Luddite Treatise on High-Tech, Artificial Intelligence, and the True Art of Thinking*. New York: Pantheon Books.

Roszak, Theodore. 1986b. *From Satori to Silicon Valley*. San Francisco: Don't Call It Frisco Press.

Rosen, Jeffrey. 2004. "Your Blog or Mine?" *New York Time Magazine*, December 19. Accessed January 24, 2008. http://www.nytimes.com/2004/12/19/magazine/19 PHENOM.html

Ross, Andrew. 2003. *No-Collar: The Human Workplace and Its Hidden Costs*. New York: Basic Books.

Roy, Allan. 2001. *A History of the Personal Computer: The People and the Technology*. Ontario, Canada: Allan Publishing.

Said, Edward. 1978. *Orientalism*. New York: Pantheon Books.

Said, Edward. 1989. "Representing the Colonized: Anthropology's Interlocutors." *Critical Inquiry* 15 (2): 205–25. http://dx.doi.org/10.1086/448481.

Saxenian, AnnaLee. 1993. "Inside-Out: The Industrial Systems of Silicon Valley and Route 128." Working Paper 605. Institute of Urban and Regional Development, University of California, Berkeley.

Saxenian, AnnaLee. 1994. Regional Advantage: Culture and Competition in Silicon Valley and Route 128. Cambridge, MA: Harvard University Press.

Saxenian, AnnaLee. 2006. *The New Argonauts: Regional Advantage in a Global Economy*. Cambridge, MA: Harvard University Press.

Smith, Marc A. 1992. "Voices from the WELL: The Logic of the Virtual Commons." Unpublished manuscript. Accessed January 24, 2008. http://www.sscnet.ucla.edu/soc/csoc/papers/voices/Voices.htm.

Soja, Ed. 1989. *Postmodern Geographies*. London: Verso.

Spitulnik, Debra. 2001. "Media." In *Key Terms in Language and Culture*, ed. Alessandro Duranti, 143–45. Malden, MA: Blackwell.

Stone, Allucquère Rosanne. 1991. "Will the Real Body Please Stand Up? Boundary Stories about Virtual Cultures." In *Cyberspace: The First Steps*, ed. M. Benedikt, 81–118. Cambridge, MA: MIT Press.

Stone, Allucquère Rosanne. 1995. *The War of Desire and Technology at the Close of the Mechanical Age*. Cambridge, MA: MIT Press.

Turkle, S. 1984. *The Second Self: Computers and the Human Spirit*. New York: Simon and Schuster.

Turkle, S. 1995. *Life on the Screen: Identity in the Age of the Internet*. New York: Simon and Schuster.

Turner, Fred. 2005. "Where the Counterculture Met the New Economy: The WELL and the Origins of Virtual Community." *Technology and Culture* 46 (3): 485–512. http://dx.doi.org/10.1353/tech.2005.0154.

Turner, Fred. 2007. *From Counterculture to Cyberculture: Stewart Brand, the Whole Earth Network, and the Rise of Digital Utopianism*. Chicago: University of Chicago Press.

Twitter. 2012. "Twitter Turns Six." March 21, 2012. Accessed April 13, 2012. http://blog.twitter.com/2012/03/twitter-turns-six.html.

Warwick, Kevin. 2001. *QI: The Quest for Intelligence*. London: Piatkus Books.

Warwick, Kevin. 2004. *I, Cyborg*. Champaign: University of Illinois Press.

Wellman, Barry, and Milena Gulia. 1999. "Virtual Communities as Communities: Net Surfers Don't Ride Alone." In *Communities in Cyberspace*, ed. Marc A. Smith and Peter Kollock, 167–94. London: Routledge.

Zook, Matthew. 2005. *The Geography of the Internet Industry: Venture Capital, Dot-coms and Local Knowledge*. London: Blackwell Publishers.

Zuboff, Shoshana 1988. *In the Age of the Smart Machine: The Future of Work and Power*. New York: Basic Books.

2

We Were Always Human

Zeynep Tufekci

"[The web] shares a strange feature with painting. The offsprings of painting stand there as if they are alive, but if anyone asks them anything, they remain most solemnly silent. The same is true of [the web]. You'd think they were speaking as if they had some understanding, but if you question anything that has been said because you want to learn more, it continues to signify just that very same thing forever. When it has once been [published online], every discourse roams about everywhere, reaching indiscriminately those with understanding no less than those who have no business with it, and it doesn't know to whom it should speak and to whom it should not."

The above paragraph is actually not about the Internet. It is about writing, and it is attributed to Plato (Plato 1997, 552). The text in brackets originally read "the written word" or "written down." Many new technologies are accompanied by loud protests of loss of humanity, and a common thread runs through them. Plato encapsulates the heart of the oft-repeated argument with his claim that writing robbed words of their soul by freezing them into an immutable medium rather than the flesh and blood human who can talk,

DOI: 10.5876/9781607321705.c02

respond, and listen in context. As I will argue, this unease stems from the fundamental duality of being human: we are at once embodied and symbolic. Some technologies allow us to separate those two aspects, thereby creating the gap Plato laments: words without bodies.

Once the thought and the human are separated, as in writing, the thought then enters a perilous territory. Disembodied meaning, it seems, cannot hold on to its context and can now be deconstructed, reinterpreted, misapplied, rewritten, and, even worse, used ironically, as I did above, to make a point that might in the end counter the original intent of the author, if one can still speak of authors and original intents. Even so, the reification of the word implies neither loss nor transcendence of humanity.

The proliferation of digital technologies has made us no more post-human than the invention of writing or the creation of those breathtaking Paleolithic cave paintings at Chauvet. Neither the first totem nor the type-writer, nor the telegraph, nor the pyramids, nor the libraries of Alexandria, nor the Internet, nor the cyborg-visions make us any more posthuman than before. The essence of humanity is that we have always been both symbolic and embodied. This, by itself, cannot be interpreted as post-, because there was never a pre- in which humans were not simultaneously and inseparably both symbolic and embodied.

Or maybe, said alternatively, we were always posthuman. The symbolic capacity of humanity has always meant that it was possible to separate and extend the word from the body. Once separated, or more accurately, alienated, from the living creator, the word can now stand on its own—or, contrary-wise, *pace* Plato, no longer attached to life, it dies. McLuhan (1962) famously compared all media to extensions of human capabilities—the eye, the ear, the hand, the skin. Finally, through information technologies, we have symbol manipulation technologies that allow us to extend our cognitive and social capabilities and do so in a networked manner.

A related, but not identical question is about the extension of our capa-bilities. Unlike almost all other animals, humans intrinsically extended their abilities through the use of tools, social organization, and their ability to externalize the symbolic, as discussed in this chapter. Our symbolic nature directly supports our capacity for extension of our abilities. A corollary of the argument presented here is that we are no less human than the first time an ancestor picked up a stick to extend an arm. On the other hand, this exten-sion, like all the others, is surely not without consequence.

To understand the almost visceral reaction of Plato and many commen-tators after him in response to these technologies of extension, alienation, and replication of our symbolic and cognitive capabilities, we must return to the source of this unease. There are three interrelated dynamics at play: external-ization and reification of the symbolic, mediation of human interaction, and extension of human capabilities.

EXTERNALIZATION AND REIFICATION OF THE SYMBOLIC

As stated, a core tension of being human flows from the fact that humans are embodied creatures as well as symbolic beings. As embodied beings, we are necessarily finite and limited. As symbolic beings, we can also externalize and freeze that which emanates from our minds. However, our minds are not attached to our bodies as an externality, merely an add-on or an option, but as part of our flesh, as lowly or as glorious as every other part of that mesh of blood, nerves, muscles, bones, cartilage, and skin that we are composed of. That truth is often difficult to assimilate, especially since the symbols that emanate from this flesh can be exteriorized and reified and can be drawn on caves, carved on stones, scribbled on papyrus, written on paper, typed on keyboards, stored in magnetic disks, and raised in Braille. Our symbols can be sent into space, buried in time capsules, stored in archives, and carved into mountains. All of this generates the haunting temptation of overcoming that finitude of the embodiment, which generates in some an awe and yearning for a desire to transcend the flesh and in others, as in the opening vignette by Plato, disgust with the perceived hollowness of the symbol that is no longer an inseparable part of the human lifeworld.

Hayles warns us against ignoring embodiment when she talks of her nightmare of a culture "inhabited by posthumans who regard their bodies as fashion accessories rather than the ground of being" and her dream of a "a posthuman that embraces the possibilities of information technologies without being seduced by fantasies of unlimited power and disembodied immortality" (Hayles 1999, 5). She is warning about the temptation to imagine ourselves as information that "leaves behind the body," an understanding conceptualizing a subjectivity resting on a mind/body duality that she argues is rooted in the dualist conception of humanity in which the mind is primary, and the body, merely a vessel. Indeed, if "I" only refers to this mind, an abstraction, and if the body at most an input/output mechanism, why not get rid of it or replace it with another? If our bodies are vats for our brains, can we perhaps pursue better vats?

Indeed, isn't leaving behind the body what cyberculture is all about? Many prominent and early theorists of cyberspace claimed that the Internet has become a place where the body becomes irrelevant, or at least much less relevant. Stone (1991, 101) provocatively asked "the real body to stand up":

> If the information age is an extension of the industrial age, with the
> passage of time the split between the body and the subject should
> grow more pronounced still. But in the fourth epoch the split is
> simultaneously growing and disappearing. The socioepistemic
> mechanism by which bodies mean is undergoing a deep restructuring
> in the latter part of the twentieth century, finally fulfilling the furthest

extent of the isolation of those bodies through which its domination is authorized and secured.

Similarly, when Turkle examined the nature of community in the early online communities like the WELL, she argued that cyberspace may be the realization of the postmodern identity that is decentered, multiple, and fragmented. Turkle affirms that although these developments precede the Internet, cyberspace now plays a prominent role in this story "of the eroding boundaries between the real and the virtual, the animate and inanimate, the unitary and multiple self" (Turkle, 1995, 10).

> In the daily practice of many computer users, windows have become a powerful metaphor for thinking about the self as a multiple, distributed system. The self is no longer playing different roles in different settings at different times . . . The life practice of windows is that of a decentered self that exists in many worlds and plays many roles at the same time . . . As more people spend more time in these virtual spaces, some go so far as to challenge the idea of giving any priority to RL [Real Life] at all. "After all," says one dedicated MUD [multi-user dungeon] player and IRC [Internet relay chat] user, "why grant such superior status to the self that has the body when the selves that don't have bodies are able to have different kinds of experiences?" (Turkle, 1995, 14)

However, there are reasons that this narrative is no longer helpful in understanding the profound changes brought about by the integration of the Internet into the lives of hundreds of millions of people. Early users who formed the center of those studies were very different from the general populace at the time: more male, more technically oriented, racially homogeneous, fairly well-off, and generally young and of particular cultural leanings (with an ethos of openness, a fondness for some version of libertarian politics, plus a fascination with the technical). It is also possible that identity experimentation was exactly the reason they were drawn to the early communities. In other words, what we saw was not necessarily a consequence of the Internet but the emergence of a particular community that was interested in that particular genre; therefore, the results were more of a "selection" effect rather than "treatment" effect. In contrast, current Internet users are very much like the general populace and we have not seen a mass rise in identity experimentation as a result of mass adoption of cybertools. And this is even truer for the younger populations, with obvious implications for the future. The Internet is no longer an exotic space where identity experimentation reigns, although this experimentation, of course, continues to exist.

However, it is important to note that the continuum from managing multiple social roles and audiences to identity experimentation has always been part of the human experience. Indeed, persons do not act the same way with their mothers as they do with their bosses or their romantic partners; those who did would be marked as deviant, without understanding of human social norms and conventions, sociopathic. Goffman (1959) extensively theorized the way we manage different audiences by using the language of dramaturgy and theater; if he were writing today, he might have talked about having online profiles and social presence. However, different social roles and the ability to adopt different online personas do not lead to a multiple or fractured self mainly because the body, in the end, centers and unites us. I am not arguing that embodiment homogenizes us or removes the conflicting desires, roles, and yearnings within the individual that is part of the human condition. I am, however, contesting the notion that the mere act of typing on a keyboard creates on ontological split within the body.

The obvious question then is what are the implications of increasing immersion and moving from typing to being swallowed by technologies like goggles, bodysuits, skin-input machines, and perhaps later the further integration of flesh and machines? Are the people who spend most of their waking hours playing immersive video games the vanguard of the future or mere remnants of a subculture that has always been with us? This question will no doubt continue playing out as technology evolves; hence, it is important to have these debates now.

Last, these early analyses of the Internet's ability to multiply selves depend on a conceptualization of the Internet as a separate, virtual world; thus, in effect, we have a double world—the world and the cyberspace. (Such an implicit stance often appears when people contrast the "virtual" world with the "real" world.) This is a corollary of the desire to provide the symbolic the same ontological status as the embodied human from which the symbol emanates. However, as a theoretical stance, the concept of the "virtual world" cannot be defended unless one is willing to extend such world-doubling qualities to writing, to telephone, and, indeed, to those cave paintings. It is only through the ontological equivalence of the reified, exteriorized symbol—the text, the file, the picture—with that of the embodied originator that we can truly equate typing as opening the door to separate identities, rather than as different segments of a complex identity. I choose to follow Hayles and declare that humans are intrinsically and inseparably embodied. As Wynn and Katz (1997) ask, "how can we call them 'selves' if they lack the situated intelligence of historical embodiment?" Uncoincidentally, death is often associated with the reification of symbols and words. As Ong notes, "[o]ne of the most startling paradoxes inherent in writing is its close association with death . . . The paradox lies in the fact that the deadness of the text, its removal from the living human lifeworld, its rigid visual fixity, assures its endurance and its potential for being resurrected into limitless living contexts by a potentially infinite number of living readers" (Ong 2002, 230–71).

IDENTITY EXPRESSION AND EXPERIMENTATION IN THE AGE OF FACEBOOK

I have claimed that early Internet theorizations are no longer helpful because current modalities of Internet use in this era of widespread "online sociality," in which increasing portions of our social interactions are mediated through social media, offer a very different type of experience. To explain the ramifications of recent developments with regard to implications for identity experimentation, I will examine one particular form of social media where there is a mixture of interactivity, responsiveness, and reification: profile-based social media sites. These popular Internet applications provide some of the most illuminating case studies of the consequences of mediation through platforms specifically geared toward projecting an identity. These sites are alternatively referred to as online social networking sites or online social network sites (boyd and Ellison 2007): "We define social network sites as web-based services that allow individuals to (1) construct a public or semi-public profile within a bounded system, (2) articulate a list of other users with whom they share a connection, and (3) view and traverse their list of connections and those made by others within the system. The nature and nomenclature of these connections may vary from site to site." The most prominent of these applications are Facebook and Myspace, which have recently been joined by Twitter; they constitute the most popular destinations on the Internet except for search engines, which are, of course, less of a destination and more of a tool for reaching some other destination. Facebook started out as a Harvard-only site, quickly spread to other colleges, and then was later expanded to high schools and, at last, all of the United States and the world, with about 1 billion users. Myspace, although not as popular as Facebook, remains a vibrant site with about 100 million users, although it receives less press coverage. Other sites that are popular outside the United States, such as Orkut, each have about 100 million users. Although there has been debate about the segregation of populations among social network sites, with Facebook seen as reflecting a hegemonic, wealthier, more white culture (boyd 2009) compared to Myspace, which is associated more with minority and poorer students (Hargittai 2007), more recent reports and numbers suggest that this situation may have changed with more people acquiring a Facebook profile, at least in the United States (Chang et al. 2010). It is perhaps most accurate to say that Facebook has become increasingly mundane and domesticated.

I have been conducting extensive research including surveys, interviews, focus groups, as well as ethnographic observations on social media practices of college youth since around the inception of Facebook. Based on more than 1,500 surveys, hundreds of interviews, as well as an ongoing dialogue with a variety of users of such sites as well as "virtual ethnography," I have been examining the myriad ways in which social network sites have reconfigured social practices, especially among college-age youth. This research has involved repeated surveys as well as continuation of interviews every year since 2005 until submission of this chapter in 2011.

This research shows that having a profile on a social network site has become a norm among this population (Tufekci 2008a, 2008b). There are fewer and fewer college students who are not represented on Facebook and these students tend to be either nontraditional students or recent immigrants whose families strongly disapprove of such activities. Students put in a lot of labor to create profiles, posting a plethora of information in an attempt to project an online persona. In my studies (Tufekci 2008a, 2008b), I found that, initially, 95 percent of the students on Facebook used their real names and engaged in enormous amounts of disclosure—about three quarters indicated their favorite music or movies as well as their romantic status, indicating whether they were currently single, in a relationship, engaged, married, or even, as a standard option "it's complicated." This percentage has recently been decreasing. In my latest study in December 2010, about 10 percent of the 450 students surveyed said that they were using a nickname, and another 10 percent reported using a variety of strategies to decrease name recognition. However, that still leaves an overwhelming majority, perhaps as high as 80 percent, who use their real names.

I also found that although privacy concerns may have impeded some students' willingness to join these sites, once on the sites, those concerned with privacy were no less likely to disclose important information than those that were less concerned. Logistic regression (reported in Tufekci 2008a) showed that privacy concerns had little effect on behavior within the sites once a student joined Facebook. This speaks to the importance of norms in negotiating behavior in online environments; once joined, behavior tends to converge toward the norm of the existing environment.

A persona on these sites is not solely controlled by owner of the profile but rather co-created through social networks. Just as Goffman (1959) describes it, identity formation is a collective process that relies on the participation, assent, and acquiescence of the social circle. There are multiple means through which the social networks within which people are embedded are implicated in the creation and affirmation of identity. At the simplest level, the list of Facebook friends is composed of people who have accepted the request and confirmed a connection. A person's list of friends is perhaps the most significant display of how identity is constructed collectively. Furthermore, the friends, the strength of which may range from weak acquaintances to very close friends and family, actively contribute to the profile through means that range from online-only activities, such as writing on a person's "wall," to those that merge the online and offline worlds even more thoroughly, such as posting photos and "tagging" the person, that is, identifying the face/body pictured in the physical world and linking it to the online profile.

The persona that is co-constructed with the person's social network on these sites is thus deeply integrated with the offline-world. In fact, ironically, the body is more, not less, present and on display through social media. Of all sites on the Internet, Facebook is the platform with the most photographs uploaded on any given day, far surpassing photo-dedicated websites such as Flickr. The ubiquity of cell phones and smart mobile devices with image capturing capabilities and the convergence of offline and online worlds have not facilitated the ascendance of the word at the expense of the body. As Hayles (1999) would put it, information has not been able to leave the body behind.

The female body is especially on display on Facebook. As part and parcel of mainstream culture, these sites reflect the ascendance of "raunch culture," a phenomenon noted by many critics (Levy 2006). Of course, it is a mistake to assume that all profiles display certain characteristics. Indeed, my main argument is that Facebook often represents deep integration with the offline world and, as such, is subject to the same variety of people, cultures and subcultures, trends and fads, and other vagaries and attributes of life in general. There is no "one" Facebook because there is no "One" Culture.

The Internet, unlike the physical world, allows for potentially permanent storage, easy searchability, link-based navigation, and data aggregation of previously unthinkable magnitude (Solove 2007). Combined with offline-online integration, the result has been an explosion of surveillance and monitoring. By operating on the Internet, a medium that stretches time through persistence so that the past is always available and collapses spaces so that different contexts can overlap, the current social media practices have resulted in shrinking the spaces for maneuverability and negotiation of different social roles and identity.

Thus, the prevalence of digital photographs, the affordances of tagging, and the convergence of media make everyone a potential spy, voyeur, and documenter of life. On most college campuses, a young person at a gathering of any sort is likely to be photographed, and that photo will be uploaded and tagged, perhaps within the hour. Such ubiquity of peer surveillance, which I dub "grassroots surveillance," has resulted in a particularly ironic twist with regard to the possibility of "identity play" in the age of ubiquitous social media: it is harder, not easier.

For example, in my latest survey in December 2010 of 450 college students, about 73 percent report having had their profile found by someone unwanted, 71 percent report unwanted photos posted by others, and 38 percent report having someone become upset with them because of a photo with someone else. About 71 percent report knowing of fights between boyfriends and girlfriends caused by Facebook postings, and about 50 percent had friends who broke up romantic relationships and another 65 percent witnessed fights between friends because of Facebook postings. Similarly, about 52 percent knew of friends who had fights with parents over Facebook. When asked about their own experiences, about 27 percent reported fighting with a romantic partner over Facebook, about 8 percent had ended a relationship because of it, and 25 percent fought with a parent whereas another 17 percent fought with a parent. A staggering 58 percent had caught their friends in a lie through Facebook.

This pattern of fights, eruptions of jealousy over photographs of boyfriends and girlfriends in the company of inappropriate others, friends caught in lies, unintended disclosures, unmasked pretenses, and all manners of otherwise likely innocuous—and likely ubiquitous—forms of concealment and nondisclosure would have passed without comment, or not been noticed at all, had it not been for social media-based surveillance.

"Facebook is the devil," declared one of the young adults I talked to as part of this multi-year, multi-method research project. Most young adults I have talked with report that social media has made it harder for them to engage in identity experimentation without taking elaborate care, even maintaining separate profiles for different audiences; monitoring carefully and continuously all profiles for unintended leaks, disclosures, crossing of wires, inappropriate photographs, unwelcome wall comments, and unfriendly activity; and guarding against parents, relatives, potential employers, college-admission boards, coaches, and other friendly and unfriendly authority figures that one may now encounter. The collapse of different contexts and continuation of links across geographical and temporal shifts (keeping high school friends as Facebook friends in college) make it harder to evolve without explicitly leaving behind others who were once close. The problem is not just hierarchical surveillance by those with power of those with less, but the strong pressure of peer surveillance and the ubiquitous co-monitoring activities of peers through social media.

New ways of managing this grassroots surveillance are emerging, and new norms and manners of interaction in response have been evolving for years. However, as of this writing, the cultural toolkit (Swidler 1986) of young adults has not yet completely absorbed the ramifications of this level of surveillance, resulting in strong tensions, disruptions, and conflict. Of course, in this context I refer to the hegemonic culture in college campuses, which includes other online environments and communities associated with them, such as that of Anonymous examined by Wesch elsewhere in this volume; diasporic avatars in immersive virtual worlds, such as Second Life discussed by Gajjala; or the intricacies of the popular "massively multiplayer online game" World of Warcraft probed by Graffam. All of these examples have developed completely different and, indeed, orthogonal practices compared with most Facebook users. Facebook has more in common with the Cyberorganic community examined by Cool (this volume) in its tendency for offline/online integration, which helps create the identity-constraining dynamic discussed in this chapter. In the end, the Internet is neither homogeneous nor a single

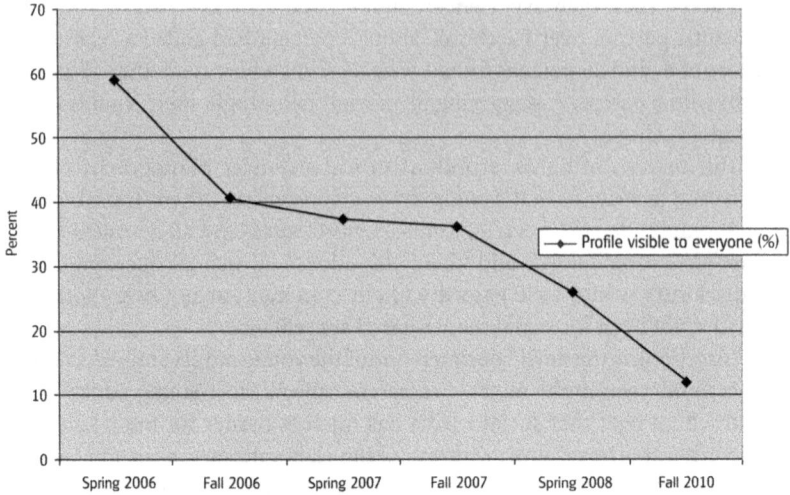

FIGURE 2.1.
Visibility of profile to everyone.

thing. However, as with all societies, it incorporates dominant cultural spaces as well as subcultures and countercultures. In this particular essay, I have discussed aspects that have become mundane and domesticated, at least for almost all college students in the United States.

It is also important to note that the emergence of grassroots surveillance is not the same as the often repeated, but incorrect, notion that young people are giving up on privacy or that they do not care. Rather, my findings show that they are struggling to adapt to a rapidly changing digital ground—but young people are actively responding to these changes. For example, Figure 2.1 shows the percentage of Facebook users who have their profiles visible to everyone. This percent dropped from nearly 60 percent to barely 10 percent in just a few years as young people learned about and adjusted their privacy settings. This, too, remains an area for scholars to watch as it evolves.

MEDIATION AND ITS DISCONTENTS

Another important aspect to examine is mediated sociality. Words, once separated, can also be transmitted to other people within social contexts. Such mediation of social interaction is increasingly not just common but routine and unremarked. E-mail, IM, phone, Facebook, text messages, tweets, chats, Skype, and so forth are no longer exotic or rare; rather, they are thoroughly integrated into the lives of hundreds of millions, if not billions, of people.

What are some of the implications of this increasing incorporation of digital mediation into our sociality?

We must not lump all forms of mediation into one undifferentiated pile because they differ, especially with regard to the heart of Plato's lament: interactivity. Interactivity can be perceived as a continuum, since conventional letters are also interactive in the sense that a conversation can go back and forth. However, the sense of interaction for humans is rooted, as is everything else, in the embodied person who perceives "interactive" to mean "immediate," as defined in blinks of the eye rather than hours, days, or weeks. Further, it matters whether the transmitted portion remains close to the human lifeworld, as voice and images do, or is more abstract, as in letters, e-mails, texts, and instant messaging. The disembodied voice of the telephone, although it departs from the instinctive human notion of interactivity, remains closer to it than the frozen words of the letter or e-mail. The Internet, of course, is not any one of these things and can incorporate multiple modalities: a real-time video chat, audio chat, text chat, static web page, blog with comments threads, online social network site, discussion board, instant-messaging application, among others. Each one might have a different impact on the reception of the message, the perception about the communication, and the quality of the social interaction that took place. Instant messaging, for example, is more likely to create the feeling that a person is there, whereas e-mail may not.

My research project included surveys in 2007, 2008, and 2010 and examined whether respondents thought friendship only through online mediation was possible. In 817 surveys in 2007–2008 and 450 surveys in 2010, I found a consistent polarization among the young adults surveyed in this study. About half expressed disbelief that it was possible to be friends using only online means whereas the other half were open, and even warm, to the idea. This difference was not necessarily a function of competence with the Internet; both groups used social media in roughly equal amounts.

I have proposed the trait cyberasociality, which I define as "the inability or unwillingness of some people to relate to others via social media as they do when physically present." On the opposite end of the spectrum are the hypersocial, a (small) group that feels a deeper connection was more possible through online methods, because the distractions of appearance and the potential concomitant judgments were absent and conversation, rather than physical attributes, dominated the encounter. This group echoed Walther (1996), who found that text-only interaction can create a hyperpersonal bond.

For the cyberasocial, however, lack of physical copresence makes it difficult, if not impossible, to respond to the interaction if they could not ground it in face-to-face presence. For these people, face-to-face interaction has inimitable features that simply cannot be replicated or replaced by any other form of communication. It is possible that preference for or avoidance of online sociality brings to the fore certain personality attributes that were simply not as crucial in the pre-Internet era and are thus not neatly quantified by existing measures and not reflected cleanly in traditional demographics.

Importantly, cyberasociality was not correlated with offline sociality. That is, statistical analysis showed that a person's cyberasociability was not predictable by the number of offline friends they had or the amount of time they spent with them. Thus, my study contradicted the commonly floated idea that "people who are more social offline are more social online, as well as the notion that it is only the social misfits who use social media to make new friends" (Tufekci 2010, 170). In other words, it was not the social rich getting richer online; rather, emerging dispositions of the digital age were starting to play a role.

Could cyberasociality be a personality trait that can only become visible with the emergence of mediated communication, similar to dyslexia, which only became an issue after writing was invented? Can this explain the ongoing debate about whether online methods are suitable for deep friendships (Deresiewicz 2009)? Babies as young as two weeks old respond differently to icons arranged as a face, with an identifiable pair of eyes, a nose, and a mouth, compared to the same icons arranged randomly. Eye contact, smiles, gestures, and physical copresence evoke strong responses. Some facial expressions such as smiles and frowns have been demonstrated to be universal, strengthening the case that our sociality and our biology are deeply connected (Ekman 1980).

It makes sense that our social responsiveness is not just an artifact or an afterthought of our cognitive capacities, something we can easily "will" ourselves to evoke because we know that there is a person on the other end of the mediated communication. In other words, we do not merely see a person and then decide to react; rather, the presence of a person evokes sociability in ways deeply buried in our human endowment. However, for some people, just the knowledge that the words appearing on the screen were typed by a person may be enough to summon that particular feeling of sociality and human connection. We all require a sense of presence to connect, but "presence" is a subjective, variable experience. For the moment, we need to contemplate the consequences of an increasingly digital world in which some people are unable or unwilling to channel sociability in response to a mediated interaction.

Cyberasociality can perhaps be seen as the third level of digital divide. Scholars have long documented a divide in access to computing technologies (first level), as well as disparities in skills and competence (Hargittai 2007). Cyberasociality, however, is better seen as the third level of digital *difference*, rather than *inequity*, although the divide may still disadvantage those who are cyberasocial, either by choice or through preference.

EXTENDING HUMAN CAPABILITIES: FROM HUMAN TO . . . HUMAN?

The limits of human sociality were famously explored by Robin Dunbar (1998), who concluded that the human brain—more specifically, the neocortex—is capable of keeping track of no more than 150 social relations with their concomitant ties and levels of reciprocity (Dunbar 1998; Gilbert and Karahalios 2009). Similar to the way a stick extends and strengthens the arm and the written word extends memory, do social media extend our capability for sociality and leave behind those who cannot or will not use it to its full capacity?

It is too early to reach conclusions regarding this new technology. Early research shows that people, on average, tend to have around 120 Facebook friends—a number remarkably similar to Dunbar's. Facebook friends, of course, can range from the weakest ties to the strongest. Perhaps ironically, recent research also shows that the number of closest confidants of Americans has plummeted (McPherson, Smith-Lovin, and Brashears 2006, 2009), although Internet users tend to maintain more confidants (Hampton, Sessions, and Her 2011). Network researchers generally confirm that there is little reason to think that people have more close relationships than they did a century ago or even before (Christakis and Fowler 2009), and our closest ties may remain at fairly similar levels to those of even our hunter-gatherer ancestors (Apicella et al. 2012).

In the end, technology may indeed enable us to keep in touch with more people or maintain numerous connections at professional networking sites, such as LinkedIn, but the size of our closest circles and the number of those nearest and dearest to us does not seem to have been affected much. That said, our broader circle may now be much larger and include persons scattered around the globe rather than be just members of a small tribe with whom we travel throughout our lives. Digital mediation changes everything, and yet it changes so little. The size of our capacity and ability for affection and bonding remains grounded in our humanness. And that perhaps is the most important conclusion. "Faster, higher, and stronger" through technology may be tempting, but we are, as we have always been, human and our limits transcend technology. We are, as we always were, human, all too human.

REFERENCES

Apicella, Coren L., Frank W. Marlowe, James H. Flowler, and Nicholas A. Christakis. 2012. "Social Networks and Cooperation in Hunter-Gatherers." *Nature* 481 (7382): 497–501. http://dx.doi.org/10.1038/nature10736.

boyd, danah. 2009. "White Flight in Networked Publics? How Race and Class Shaped American Teen Engagement with MySpace and Facebook." In *Digital Race Anthology*, ed. Laura Nakamura and Peter Chow-White. New York: Routledge.

boyd, danah, and Nicole Ellison. 2007. "Social Network Sites: Definition, History, and Scholarship." *Journal of Computer-Mediated Communication* 13 (1): 210–30. http://dx.doi.org/10.1111/j.1083-6101.2007.00393.x.

Chang, Jonathan, Itamar Rosenn, Lars Backstrom, and Cameron Marlow. 2010. "Epluribus: Ethnicity on Social Networks." *International AAAI Conference on Weblogs and Social Media.* Accessed June 4, 2010, http://www.aaai.org/ocs/index.php/ICWSM/ICWSM10/paper/view/1534.

Christakis, Nicholas, and James Fowler. 2009. *Connected: The Surprising Power of Our Social Networks and How They Shape Our Lives.* New York: Little, Brown.

Deresiewicz, William. 2009. "Faux Friendship." *The Chronicle Review.* December 6. http://chronicle.com/article/Faux-Friendship/49308/.

Dunbar, Robert. 1998. *Grooming, Gossip, and the Evolution of Language.* Cambridge, MA: Harvard University Press.

Ekman, Paul. 1980. *The Face of Man: Expressions of Universal Emotions in a New Guinea Village.* New York: Garland STPM Press.

Gilbert, Eric, and Karrie Karahalios. 2009. "Predicting Tie Strength with Social Media." *Proceedings of the 27th International Conference on Human Factors in Computing Systems,* 211–220.

Goffman, Erving. 1959. *The Presentation of Self in Everyday Life.* Garden City, NY: Doubleday Anchor Books.

Hampton, Keith, Lauren F. Sessions, and Eun Ja Her. 2011. "Core Networks, Social Isolation, and New Media: Internet and Mobile Phone Use, Network Size, and Diversity." *Information Communication and Society* 14 (1): 130–55. http://dx.doi.org/10.1080/1369118X.2010.513417.

Hargittai, Esther. 2007. "Whose Space? Differences Among Users and Non-Users of Social Network Sites." *Journal of Computer-Mediated Communication* 13 (1): 276–97. http://dx.doi.org/10.1111/j.1083-6101.2007.00396.x.

Hayles, Katherine. 1999. *How We Became Posthuman: Virtual Bodies in Cybernetics, Literature, and Informatics.* Chicago: University of Chicago Press.

Levy, Ariel. 2006. *Female Chauvinist Pigs: Women and the Rise of Raunch Culture.* New York: Simon and Schuster.

McLuhan, Marshall. 1962. *The Gutenberg Galaxy.* Toronto: University of Toronto Press.

McPherson, Miller, Lynn Smith-Lovin, and Matthew Brashears. 2006. "Social Isolation in America: Changes in Core Discussion Networks over Two Decades." *American Sociological Review* 71 (3): 353–75. http://dx.doi.org/10.1177/000312240607100301.

McPherson, Miller, Lynn Smith-Lovin, and Matthew Brashears. 2009. "Models and Marginals: Using Survey Evidence to Study Social Networks." *American Sociological Review* 74 (4): 670–81. http://dx.doi.org/10.1177/000312240907400409.

Ong, Walter. 2002. *Orality and Literacy: The Technologizing of the Word.* New York: Routledge.

Plato. 1997. *Plato: Complete Works.* Ed. J. M. Cooper and D. S. Hutchinson. Indianapolis: Hackett.

Solove, Daniel. 2007. *The Future of Reputation: Gossip, Rumor, and Privacy on the Internet.* New Haven, CT: Yale University Press.

Stone, Rosanne. 1991. "Will the Real Body Please Stand Up?" In *Cyberspace: First Steps*, ed. Michael Benedikt. Cambridge, MA: MIT Press. http://molodiez.org/net/real_body2.html.

Swidler, Ann. 1986. "Culture in Action: Symbols and Strategies." *American Sociological Review* 51 (2): 273–86. http://dx.doi.org/10.2307/2095521.

Tufekci, Zeynep. 2008a. "Grooming, Gossip, Facebook and Myspace." *Information Communication and Society* 11 (4): 544–64. http://dx.doi.org/10.1080/13691180801999050.

Tufekci, Zeynep. 2008b. "Can You See Me Now? Audience and Disclosure Regulation in Online Social Network Sites." *Bulletin of Science, Technology & Society* 28 (1): 20–36. http://dx.doi.org/10.1177/0270467607311484.

Tufekci, Zeynep. 2010. "Who Acquires Friends through Social Media and Why? 'Rich Get Richer' versus 'Seek and Ye Shall Find.'" International AAAI Conference on Weblogs and Social Media. Accessed June 4, 2010, http://www.aaai.org/ocs/index.php/ICWSM/ICWSM10/paper/view/1525.

Turkle, Sherry. 1995. *Life on the Screen: Identity in the Age of the Internet*. New York: Simon and Schuster.

Walther, Joseph. 1996. "Computer-Mediated Communication: Impersonal, Interpersonal, and Hyperpersonal Interaction." *Communication Research* 23 (1): 3–43. http://dx.doi.org/10.1177/009365096023001001.

Wynn, Eleanor, and James Katz, and the Eleanor Wynn James e. Katz. 1997. "Hyperbole over Cyberspace: Self-Presentation and Social Boundaries in Internet Home Pages and Discourse." *Information Society* 13 (4): 297–327. http://dx.doi.org/10.1080/019722497129043.

3

Manufacturing and Encountering "Human" in the Age of Digital Reproduction

Matthew Bernius

> As president, I believe that robotics can
> inspire young people to pursue science and
> engineering. And I also want to keep an eye on
> those robots in case they try anything.
>
> US PRESIDENT BARACK OBAMA (OCTOBER 23, 2009),
> SPEAKING TO STUDENTS IN WASHINGTON, DC, AS PART OF AN EVENT
> KICKING OFF A SCIENCE EDUCATION INITIATIVE

> I, for one, welcome our new robot overlords.
>
> KENNETH JENNINGS (BROADCAST FEBRUARY 14, 2011), USING A REFERENCE
> FROM *THE SIMPSONS* TO POKE FUN AT HIS IMMINENT LOSS TO WATSON, AN
> ARTIFICIAL INTELLIGENCE SYSTEM BUILT BY IBM, IN A SPECIAL TWO-GAME,
> COMBINED-POINT MATCH ON THE TELEVISION GAME SHOW *JEOPARDY*

There is little question that Jennings and President Obama had their tongues firmly planted in their cheeks when they made these remarks. The two jokes play upon a time-honored cultural meme: the more intelligent—or perhaps "human"—the machine, the more likely it is to threaten its creators. In the past, these types of references were largely restricted to what we might call "geek

DOI: 10.5876/9781607321705.c03

culture." Today, such references are becoming more and more mainstream, reflecting how our day-to-day lives are becoming increasingly intertwined with various forms of artificial intelligence (AI). From the "smart" algorithms that power Internet search engines, to the unmanned drone aircraft deployed by the military, to the GPS devices that direct us to destinations through vocal and graphic commands, more and more specialized tasks are performed by machines or through humans partnering with "smart machines."

And though there are no signs we have to worry about a "robot apocalypse"—at least not any time soon—there is a need to better understand the broader social implications of our increasing reliance upon AIs. This chapter explores approaches for studying and theorizing the complex and shifting relationships formed between humans and AI systems. I begin with a brief discussion of why many past efforts have focused on maintaining clear boundaries between human and machines. I then discuss how a "cyborg" approach, which blurs those boundaries, enables a different perspective on human/AI interactions. Using data collected in an ethnographic study of chatbots, I show how using the framework of "cyborg anthropology" helps us to uncover how humans and AIs work together to reinforce various cultural ideologies. Finally, I consider the potential limitations of a cyborg approach and how Donna Haraway's concepts of "companion species" and "encounter value" provide exciting possibilities for new understandings of human/AI interactions.

HUMAN OR MACHINE

Historically speaking, popular and academic writings[1] about the cultural implications of AIs have primarily dealt with definitions of the boundary between human and machine. Historian of science Jessica Riskin argues that, in the West, these two cultural categories have long stood in opposition to each other, with each defining and being defined by the limitations of the other (Riskin 2003). For a quality or action to be human, it cannot be replicated by a machine. Major technical advances in the capability of machines to replicate something considered human, in turn, shift our understandings of what it means to be human. For example, it was long believed that because the game of chess involved both mastery of logic and the ability to psychologically engage an opponent, it represented a pinnacle of human intelligence.[2] Once AIs began to beat grandmasters, chess was redefined as game in which success "can be reduced to a matter of brute force computation" (Hafner 2002).[3] Today's AI developers now agree that because of the role intuition plays in the game, creating "a strong Go program will teach us more about making computers think like people than writing a strong chess program"[4] (ibid.).

Although this shift from defining human intelligence in terms of the ability to use logic to defining it by the possession of intuition might seem trivial, it has important cultural implications. First, it demonstrates how Western cultures work to maintain clear boundaries between our cultural understandings of human and machine. A significant amount of science fiction is built on the profound discomfort that arises when one can no longer tell the difference between the two. Sigmund Freud argued that the root of this feeling of dread, which he termed "the uncanny,"[5] runs far deeper than simply being confronted by something one cannot be sure is human. He argued that in that moment, our culturally established "clean" understanding of the difference between man and machine is destroyed and must be re-created and recalibrated. In that moment of breakdown one can become "unsure of his true self" (Freud 2003, 142) and begin to question has machine become man, and am I no more than a socially programmed machine?

In addition to existential implications, there have been policy rationales for clearly demarcating man and machine. For example, by the 1980s an increasing number of academics and industry researchers had become concerned with the considerable amount of funding and attention being dedicated to the reproduction of human intelligence. These individuals successfully argued that most AI projects failed to understand the complexities of human intelligence (Suchman 2007; Winograd and Flores 1986). As a result of these efforts, research moved away from attempts to directly reproduce human intelligence and toward focusing on more algorithmic tasks such as data retrieval and organization.

These examples demonstrate the importance of being attentive to the boundaries between humans and machines. However, there are limits to this approach. Consider one of the best-known arguments against thinking computers: "the Chinese Room" thought experiment created by John Searle. Imagine a person sitting in a room filled with instructions and pieces of paper with seemingly random marks—these marks are actually Chinese phrases, but the occupant cannot read them. When a note with different unreadable markings—actually a phrase in English—is passed into the room, the instructions tell the occupant which piece of (Chinese) paper to pass back to their unseen interaction partner. Even though the room appears to be "fluent" in English and Chinese to someone interacting with it, the operator inside the room is simply following a set of specific instructions and never understands the content of what is being translated. Searle concluded that an AI, like the Chinese Room, could only follow directions but never think, that is, reflexively understand what it was doing.

Searle's argument demonstrates how attempts to define hard boundaries can gloss over the rich complexities of interactions between humans and machines. In part, this is an issue of shifting one's perspective. To make his argument, Searle uses what Haraway terms a "view from nowhere" (Haraway

1991b, 188–90)—an omniscient position, which allows him to simultaneously see and know everything going on within the encounter. In the real world, we can never actually occupy this position. Like the person interacting with the Chinese Room, we are situated within the interaction, knowing only what we have learned in the past and what we gain through the interaction. From Searle's view from nowhere, we see that the room is only following instructions. But the interaction partner, being within the interaction and thus having a limited knowledge position, leaves believing that the Chinese Room accomplished the translation because it understood the contents of the message. Although it is true that the Chinese Room does not think like a human, it is also true that, based on the interaction, the person believes that it does think like a human. And a belief that the Chinese Room—or any AI—is intelligent can potentially wield as much cultural influence, if not more, than the "truth" that the Chinese Room is not intelligent.

Thus, although we should not dismiss the issue of the boundary between human and machine, there is much to be gained by an approach that transcends it.

CYBORG ANTHROPOLOGY

> A cyborg is a cybernetic organism, a hybrid of machine and organism,
> a creature of social reality as well as a creature of fiction . . . By the late
> twentieth century, our time, a mythic time, we are all chimeras, theorized
> and fabricated hybrids of machine and organism; in short, we are cyborgs
> . . . The cyborg is resolutely committed to partiality, irony, intimacy, and
> perversity. It is oppositional, utopian, and completely without innocence.
>
> DONNA HARAWAY (1991A), "A CYBORG MANIFESTO: SCIENCE, TECHNOLOGY, AND
> SOCIALIST-FEMINISM IN THE LATE TWENTIETH CENTURY," PAGES 149–151

In the mid-1980s, Haraway argued that the cyborg could serve as a powerful metaphor for rethinking our understandings of sociocultural relations, transcending oppositional thinking, and subverting oppressive cultural institutions.[6] The promise of a cyborg system, which can be an individual or made up of linked individuals,[7] is that it sees no contradiction in being literally and figuratively assembled—or, in Haraway's words, "coupled"—from parts traditionally held in fundamental opposition to each other (e.g., human vs. machine, man vs. woman, human vs. animal). Never complete, cyborgs exist in a state of constant upgrade, pragmatically adding and removing parts as needed. And because all parts exist in dynamic relation to each other, any addition or removal shifts the understanding of every part and the aggregate whole. Full of contradictions and in a state of constant change, the cyborg is always many things at the same time, making it a powerful tool for understanding culture's messy complexities.

Using cyborgs as an analytical metaphor means focusing on seeing things as systems within systems. For example, despite the fact they can be physically separated, the person and the Chinese Room become part of a cyborg system through their interaction. At the same time, the person and the room are also systems unto themselves, constructed of different physical and social parts and connected to other social actors. However, we should resist—at least temporarily—our desire to break apart and categorize cyborgs. In analyzing, we must think in terms of "and" rather than "or." Instead of trying to establish pure "truths"—for example, is the Chinese Room intelligent or not—we concentrate on how different and contradictory aspects and understandings of the room can coexist without negating each other.[8]

In their 1995 essay "Cyborg Anthropology," Gary Lee Downey, Joseph Dumit, and Sarah Williams "coupled" cyborg analysis to anthropological methods and concepts to create an analytical framework founded on the belief that "human subjects and subjectivity are crucially as much a function of machines, machine relations, and information transfers as they are machine producers and operators" (ibid., 266). Rather than primarily focusing on how humans create machines, a cyborg anthropological approach adds a deep consideration of how technologies are agents in reproducing social life (ibid., 267). This is accomplished through examining the couplings and contradictions that make up the cyborg in question. Once we understand its construction, we then turn to exploring how, through its interactions with others—including other cyborgs—contradictory understandings of our cyborg come to affect and transform cultural and social systems.

In more anthropological terms, we must examine the ideologies that underlie both the creation of cyborg systems like AIs and the ways in which the cyborgs themselves represent and transform ideologies. Ideologies are clusters of interrelated and internalized ideas, beliefs, and values about different social phenomena. Culturally constructed and individually expressed, ideologies condition how we perceive and interact with the world. We consciously and unconsciously learn ideologies through interactions with individuals and cultural institutions and artifacts. Ideologies are continually reshaped (and also reinforced) in the same interactions that they condition. Using ideologies as analytical tools, anthropologists organize beliefs under different labels to uncover and describe differences between specific cultural groups and the flow power within a culture.[9] To find ideologies, an anthropologist examines the sites where cultural beliefs and values emerge and are reproduced, from media artifacts (books, magazines, movies, games, and websites) to interactions between individuals and groups. For example, the idea that intuition rather than logic is the correct marker for "true" intelligence represents a shift in what we might term an "intelligence ideology."

Now let us turn to my first data set, and see what is revealed when one applies cyborg anthropology to the study of chatrooms and sexbots.

AZ_TIFFANY

I met Az_Tiffany[10] in a Yahoo! chatroom while recruiting webcam users for ethnographic interviews during spring 2005.[11] Tiffany's profile described her as a college student who put on live pay-per-view webcam shows through her website. In hopes of getting an interview, I private-messengered (PM'd) Tiffany and, after a bit of negotiation, offered to join her website in exchange for an interview. She agreed and I left to sign up. After paying the one-day membership fee, I discovered that the site was a façade. Attempts to log in redirected me to a different webcam site where there was no mention of Az_Tiffany. Back in the chatroom, I PM'd her for an explanation. She responded but did not address my questions. In fact, she acted like we had never chatted. All at once the embarrassing truth of the situation dawned on me. A quick scan of our archived conversation confirmed my suspicion: Az_Tiffany was not a cam girl; she wasn't even a person. Az_Tiffany was a chatbot, a computer program designed to appear human (Leonard 1998, 7). A fake woman got me to join to a scam webcam site. I had been "pwn'd" by a machine.

Chatbots, like Az_Tiffany, operate within chatrooms and private messaging systems, engaging other users in conversations. First developed by academics and hobbyists/hackers, the earliest versions of chatbots began to appear in Internet relay chat (IRC) and multi-user dungeons (MUDs) during the late 1980s. Beginning in the 1990s, as websites—in particular, adult ones—began to pay "finder's fees" for new members (in some cases more than $40 a head), a new, gray-market application for bots arose as entrepreneurs began to see chatrooms as a seemingly limitless source of easy, ongoing income.

REPRODUCING HUMAN

At their core, bots and other conversational AIs are made up of two basic components: a program and a script. The program contains all the software commands the AI needs to take action in the world, including sensing and speaking. The script can be thought of as the bot's self. Authored separately from the program, the script is the AI's "personality," a repository of trigger words, responses, and the specific rules that will govern its behavior. A single program can be used to animate any number of personalities qua scripts, although typically only one at a time. On websites and discussion forums where adult webmasters gather to discuss business, the general consensus is that everyone should write their own scripts—as one poster put it, your bots need to be unique and sound "real . . . [otherwise they] won't catch anyone"[12] (Edwards 2004).

The bot is an excellent example of how complex AI systems are. Examining it from a cyborg perspective, we see how the bot is assembled from multiple components (program and script) by multiple people (programmers and authors). Drawing on Erving Goffman's model of the production of speech in his essay "Footing," the program is the "animator," literally a "talking machine" (Goffman 1979, 17), and the proverbial peg on which the script-as-self will be hung. And although, in an average conversation, the person who is animating those words is typically their "author" (ibid.), this is a case where these functions fall on different actors. The bot can be thought of as a cyborg system whose "parts" are never all copresent at once, although each has left a trace and can continue to have an effect on the system. The programmer did her work before the author of the script. And when the bot finally has the chance to communicate, like an actor in a movie or play, there is no need for the author to be present for the show to go on.

All of this building work must necessarily take place and be completed long before AIs can engage in a "live" encounter. Faced with the vast range of conversational possibilities, successful authors bound and control the conversation by creating scripts that perform contextually appropriate speech genres. Russian literary theoretician Mikhail Bakhtin wrote that "each sphere of [human interaction] contains an entire repertoire of speech genres that differentiate and grow as the particular sphere develops and becomes more complex" (Bakhtin, Emerson, and Holquist 1986, 60). By deploying the appropriate contextual cues the author can recruit interaction partners who, knowingly or unknowingly, perform and inhabit the participant roles of that genre. Because a speech genre reflects beliefs about how a type of person should speak, it is also an expression of ideologies. Through the selection of specific words and phrases that will make up the script, authors present us with their ideological beliefs about how those cultural categories combine to create a "real" webcam performer[13]—or the author's beliefs about the expectations that other chatters have about the performers. Thus, by studying the bot's profile, the words it uses for a script, the way those words are spelled, and other interaction markers, we begin to see how the bot embodies ideological understandings of gender, sexuality, language, and online behavior.

One limitation that must be addressed during the creation of the script is the bot's inability to parse and react to individual utterances within the chaos of a chatroom. Like the Chinese Room, the bot does not understand the meaning of anything that is being said in a chatroom. This means that the bot has no way of knowing if it is being addressed by another chatter. If it was allowed to participate in the chatroom conversation, the bot would respond to every post made in the chatroom, regardless of whether it had anything to do with the bot. The result would be an excessive "spamming" of the chatroom, immediate revealing that it is a bot.

To work around this limitation, authors simulate direct interaction with chatters within the shared space by taking advantage of established chat practices. For example, upon entering a new chatroom the bot Codi_1984 always began with the common chat greeting "A/S/L" (age/sex/language) followed

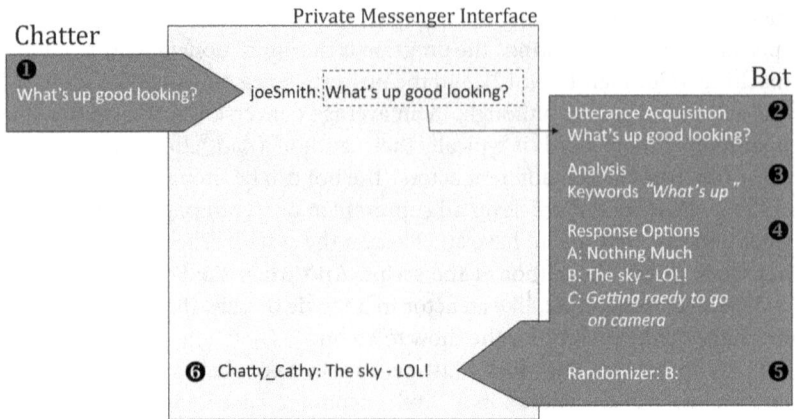

FIGURE 3.1.
Bot workflow.

by a pause in action. The bot's author hopes that during that pause an unsuspecting chatter will respond with his A/S/L. Should that happen, her[14] next utterance, "Hi, I'm Codi . . . 21 and single at USC," makes it appear as if she were replying in turn. After taking steps to establish the bot's identity, the well-planned script encourages chatters to initiate a private messaging session with the AI.

In the one-to-one encounter, the bot, or its creator, no longer has to worry about whether it is being addressed because there can be only two participants in a private messaging session. The bot can react to its interlocutor, using a workflow similar to what is charted in Figure 3.1. The interaction begins with the human projecting a new message (Step 1). The bot captures the utterance (Step 2) and searches for keywords (Step 3). Recognizing "what up," it follows the associated rule, randomly choosing a reply from a list of three possible responses and then projecting that response—"The Sky - Lol!"—into the PM conversation (Steps 4, 5, and 6). The pair-set is completed, and the bot waits for the next utterance from its interlocutor.

If the bot appears too automatic or mechanical, the encounter will fail. So although the bot can move through this workflow instantaneously, most have a delay built into their response mechanism, making it appear as if they are "thinking" and "typing." Bot authors also play with grammar, use Internet slang and txt spellings, and simulate common typing errors, intentionally misspelling words and transposing letters. Each of these decisions is the expression of an ideological understanding of what it means to participate as a human in a chatroom.

If the bot's script immediately pushes the webcam site, the bot will lose the chatter. However, bots are currently not sophisticated enough to maintain a lengthy convincing conversation. Although they can archive conversations, bots cannot access that archive in the midst of a conversation. When it comes to participating in conversations, chatbots "forget" what they said as soon as they say it. The longer the conversation goes on, the more likely the bot is to start repeating itself or repeatedly ask the same question. The challenge for an author is to create a script that is neither too short nor too long to get the job done.

Looking at the first twelve exchanges from my conversation with Az_Tiffany, one sees how her author created her script in such a way that the different utterances assembled into a narrative flow that moved the conversation toward the ultimate goal of getting me to join her website (see below). After exchanging greetings, she asked if I was interested in viewing webcams (a3 and a4). In a7, she stated that she was going to be going "on cam" soon. Next she informed me that she was getting lots of PMs (a8). Finally, the narrative came together in the twelfth exchange (a12).

(m1) MattB: hey . . . we talked earlier today . . . I'm a researcher and I'd like to interview you. In return for the interview I'll join [your] site. If you're interested contact me at [my e-mail address]

(a1) Az_Tiffany: yah

(m2) MattB: hey

(m3) MattB: didn't realize you were still online

(a2) Az_Tiffany: hiya

(a3) Az_Tiffany: are you viewing any cams right now?

(m4) MattB: not yet.

(a4) Az_Tiffany: are you viewing any cams right now? [repeat of a3]

(m5) MattB: not at the moment.

(a5) Az_Tiffany: so are you into cams?

(m6) MattB: not really

(a6) Az_Tiffany: ah ok

(m7) MattB: but I'm actually studying webcams for a project

(m8) MattB: actually my thesis

(a7) Az_Tiffany: sorry to change the subject but my break is almost up at this new cam thingy im doing, so like come and check my cam out if you want to

(a8) Az_Tiffany: ooomg im getting so many [IM]'s!!

(m9) MattB: are you interested?

(a9) Az_Tiffany: ok

(m10) MattB: hmmm so here's the deal . . .

(a10) Az_Tiffany: are you viewing any cams right now? [repeat of a3, a4] (m11) MattB: I'd like to interview you as part of my project

(a11) Az_Tiffany: yah

(m12) MattB: so how do I get to your cam?

(a12) Az_Tiffany: hon im getting bombarded with [PM]'s so im just
gonna go on my cam chat network . . . if you wanna come chat with
me its a good time, just go to [Tiffany's website URL] make a chat
name and sign in 'k?

Whenever the bot was faced with an utterance that she did not understand
(m3, m4, m7, m8, m10)—cases in which I wrote something that the bot did not
have a specific answer for—the script responded in a way that unobtrusively
advanced the conversation toward the eventual "call to action" (a12). Relying
on the interlocutor being firmly entrenched in his genre role and caught up
within his ideological expectations of the encounter, each of these "move-
along" utterances added and reinforced the bot's narrative and identity. I was
so convinced of the reality of my chat partner and so focused on getting an
interview with this "girl" that I glossed over a number of flags, including the
repetition (a3, a4, a10) of the specific question "are you viewing any cams
right now?" It was only upon discovering I could not access the site that my
interaction frame shifted. Upon reexamining the archive of the conversation,
I saw the seemingly obvious clues in the conversation.

BLURRING AND REESTABLISHING BOUNDARIES

In keeping with the attentions of cyborg anthropology and now understanding
how the bot was created and works, we now shift to examining interactions
between bots and human chatters. The relative ease of production and the
lucrative potential has led to Yahoo! chatrooms being "overrun by bots," as
one chatter described it. It is not unheard of to have upwards of ten bots in a
chatroom at once. Multiple bot postings often interrupt the existing flow of
conversation within a room, leading to frustrated outbursts from chatters like
"damn bots!" or "is there anyone within this room who isn't a bot?!" Beyond
this sense of general frustration, what can be gained from these encounters
with chatbots? The obvious answer might be financial gain for the bot author;
however, there is little evidence to suggest that most bot authors see much,
if any profit, from their creations. Based on interviews and postings made to
discussion boards, authors admit that their efforts are driven by the hope of
profits rather than the realization of them.[15]

Beyond any profits they generate, bots reinforce and change the ideological understandings through their interactions with other chatters. If a
person chats with a bot and never realizes it, that individual's beliefs about
webcam performers are reinforced through the interaction. In other words,

their preexisting ideological framework is confirmed by the encounter. But what happens if the encounter fails? What if, as in my case, the chatter discovers the bot? Take, for example, the following chatroom exchange in which the chatter "fly_me" quickly transitions from trying to engage a "girl" in conversation to warning the room of a bot in their midst:

> (g1) goofygal: does anyone here have a mic [for an audio chat]?
>
> (f1) fly_me: sorry goofy . . .
>
> (g2) goofygal: i just got a mic and made a sound clip if anyone wants to hear it ?
>
> (f2) fly_me: what format? goofy?
>
> (g3) goofygal: the clip is in my profile
>
> (g4) goofygal: does anyone here think i sound like Jessica Simpson, that what people tell me
>
> (f5) fly_me: dirty trick goofy
>
> (f6) fly_me: goofys clip is a link guys . . . shes a bot

Having discovered that he misrecognized a bot as human, fly_me scolds the bot (f5) and then outs it (f6). Unlike my encounter with Az_Tiffany, fly_me made this mistake in front of other chatters. By taking retaliatory action, fly_me attempts to shift the chatroom focus away from his mistake, presenting himself as a conscientious chat citizen outraged by the bot's presence. His remark "dirty trick goofy" publicly repositions his relationships with the bot, suggesting that the bot was cheating, playing outside of the accepted rules of the chatroom. Together with the warning (f6), fly_me signaled—intentionally or not—that he won't be fooled again and that he wanted to make sure no one else gets tricked by goofygal.

There was good reason for fly_me's public performance, because many chatters have little sympathy for anyone caught misidentifying a bot. The following is an excerpt from one chatroom's reaction to a chatter named "GalaxyCat," who was caught publicly flirting with a bot:

> Jack-0ff: Look at the responces you were getting . . . YOU JUST CHATTED UP A BOT !!! Bwahahahaha
>
> GalaxyCat: Like Im supposed to know that its a fucking bot . . .
>
> A-Ron_1980: gimme a fucking break . . . you got owned by a bot lol
>
> Mariner-Fan: GalaxyCat, you're so full of shit. Its one thing to fuck with someone, its another to make yourself look like a complete retard.
>
> MC-FlyGrrl: You got nailed by a robot, bitch

Even after GalaxyCat had fled the room, the taunting continued. Eventually, a chatter questioned how anyone could mistake bots for humans. In response, another wrote, "Don't worry, only dumb shits like GalaxyCat ever fall for bots." Although it is often said that reactions are bigger on the Internet, the severity of this sort of attack can also be unpacked as having to do with the violation of cultural boundaries.

For the uninitiated, the discovery that bots, disguised as humans, are interacting with users within the chatroom undercuts foundational assumptions about the chatrooms and creates an environment ripe for conflict and feelings of the uncanny. We can read the actions of fly_me and the chatters who attacked GalaxyCat as attempts to reestablish and redraw the boundary between machine and human.[16] Likewise, in discussions about why they do not use bots, a number of adult webmasters and performers shared explanations that reinforced that boundary. One performer I interviewed told me that she would "never use a bot . . . they just annoy people and make our job [of finding people who'll pay] harder . . . They lack the human touch." When I asked her what she meant by the "human touch," she replied, "You know . . . listening, imagination."

Ask a bot if it is a bot, and it will always respond with a denial. Some even make public posts like "I can't believe there are so many bots in this room!" and "If everyone complains to Yahoo, we'll get these bots kicked out." Contained with these various protests is the inherent claim of "humanness." And embedded within that claim is another one: "humanness" can be mechanically/digitally reproduced. Through its performance as "human," intended to hide its mechanical self, the bot becomes the personification of that second claim. In this way, these bots—cyborg couplings of programs, scripts, and authors—have a somewhat adversarial relationship with human chatters. When chatters reveal a bot in the present, the seeds are sewn for the next generation of more "human" bots. Many bot authors constantly review the transcripts archived by their bots to revise the scripts, addressing the flaws that gave the bots away. Once again we find human and machine constantly redefining each other, with one side establishing what it means to be—or rather perform—"human" within the chatroom, and the other side working to make their creations meet that definition, only to have it shift again.[17]

UPGRADING CYBORG ANTHROPOLOGY

For all the benefits the metaphor of the cyborg offers us, it has some potential pitfalls. We must recognize that not all couplings work. Throughout "The Cyborg Manifesto," Haraway emphasizes that the cyborg always chooses to couple (Haraway 1991a, 150–1). Although human chatters and sexbots interact and produce various economic, emotional, and ideological results, their adversarial relationship should be taken as a sign that it could be a mistake to join the two as cyborg. To do so would assume that any interaction—be it good, bad, or indifferent—between the two parties represents a coupling. Such a position ignores the issue of choice, expanding the idea of coupling to the point that everything in the world immediately becomes one giant cyborg. Such an argument certainly can be made, but we have to ask what making such a move, from an analytical and political perspective, would accomplish.

When analyzing a cyborg system, we also must remember that cyborgs are often recursive—systems within systems. To that point, we must recognize that few couplings are total. The sexbot is a cyborg made up of a network of actors and parts, but the fact still remains that the bot also functions as an individual actor, separate and separable from its creators. We, therefore, need ways of being attentive to how different parts function within and outside of the cyborg system. In other words, like the cyborg, we need to find ways to upgrade our analytical tools.

Haraway's recent writings provide an excellent framework for giving the actors who make up the cyborg their due. Of particular value are the concepts of "companion species" and "encounter value," which she has developed through her writings on animal/human relations.[18] Haraway defines "companion species" as groups of beings that have coevolved in relation to each other (Haraway 2003, 6–7). For example, in the process of domesticating livestock, humans altered the development of various species through selective breeding. At the same time, the integration of domesticated livestock into societies fundamentally transformed human culture. We have already discussed how humans and AIs have relationally redefined each other. And, as noted in the introduction, the proliferation of AIs is also transforming how we go about our daily lives.

Haraway notes that despite the familiarity gained through coevolution, we must recognize that we can never completely know a member of a companion species. Although we can communicate across species, things are always lost and gained in translation. This note of caution is also applicable to AIs. The nature of their production creates an illusion that they are fully knowable, but their creators admit this is rarely, if ever, the case. One AI programmer explained to me: "I am always astounded by my [AI's] ability to surprise me. I mean, I programmed it . . . every line of code. I should be able to predict all of its behavior. And then for whatever reason, it does something completely unexpected. And not always wrong. I know its still following its program—but it isn't what I thought I programmed."

Building from the concept of companion species, Haraway extended Karl Marx's categories of use and exchange value to include what she terms "encounter value" (Haraway 2007, 46). Use and exchange value function as abstract mediators, transforming objects and living things into economic commodities. For example, a cow becomes how much it costs to buy and maintain. It is measured by how many gallons of milk a year it produces. That milk, in turn, is understood in terms of how much it can be sold for. When the cow ceases to produce milk/profit, it can be sold for slaughter. Encounter value, Haraway's alternative, is an attempt to represent the more intangible forms of value that are created through interactions between, and in the entwining of, companion species. Returning to the cow, its encounter value is understood—versus calculated[19]—to be based on how it contributes, as a living component, to the broad ecosystem of encounters that produces and sustains what we call a "farm."

AIs are easily reducible to how much they cost to program, maintain, and operate; the value of the hardware that they run on; and how much power and other resources they consume. But, as with the cow, much is lost in an economic analysis of AIs, especially as if we shift our focus from AIs that exist in an adversarial relationship with humans to those that operate in a more cooperative fashion. To highlight how these two concepts can supplement a cyborg anthropology analysis, we move from the chatroom to a project in which AIs were used in encounter therapy.[20]

SAM

In the mid-2000s a team of researchers at Northwestern University's Articulab, led by Justine Cassell, ran a series of experiments in which embodied AIs called Virtual Peers took part in a therapeutic treatment for children with autism spectrum disorders (ASDs) (Merryman et al. 2008; Tartaro 2007; Tartaro and Cassell 2006, 2008). Initially developed to assist young interlocutors develop literacy skills through collaborative storytelling, the Virtual Peers were cyborg systems that manifested as three-dimensional, life-size, animated children (Cassell 2004; Cassell et al. 2000; Ryokai, Vaucelle, and Cassell 2002).

The particular Virtual Peer avatar used during the autism treatment was Sam (pictured in Figures 3.2 and 3.3). Projected onto a screen, she talked with her interaction partner using prerecorded vocal utterances and pre-scripted movements.[21] Her partner's responses were monitored in different ways, including via microphones and motion sensors. Sam's cyborg body also included a dollhouse (Figure 3.2) that sat in front of the screen onto which she was projected. The dollhouse and its contents were literally wired into the system using radio-frequency identification (RFID) tags and sensors, allowing Sam to "know" where each doll was in relation to the house (Cassell et al. 2000; Tartaro and Cassell 2006; Tartaro and Cassell 2007). The RFIDs embedded within the dolls allowed Sam's head and eyes to follow their movements, making it appear that she was looking at her interlocutor. The RFID also enabled the dolls to "crossover" into the virtual world. When a doll was placed in a "magic" compartment within the roof the dollhouse, a representation of it would appear in Sam's world for her to play with (Tartaro and Cassell 2006, 3).

FIGURE 3.2.
Child interacting with Sam (Tartaro 2007, *1678, fig. 1*).

Although Sam was theoretically capable of autonomous interactions with human interlocutors, the system could not reliably navigate the complexity and nuance of person-to-person interactions (Cassell and Tartaro 2007, 398). In other words, Sam was not capable of the thick interpretation (Geertz 1977) necessary to discern if a pause was because the child was thinking of what to say next, was frustrated, or simply remaining obstinately silent. Therefore, Sam was typically operated by a human using a computer running what "her creators dubbed the Wizard of Oz" (WOz) interface (ibid.).[22]

Despite the reliance on a human operator, it is a mistake to label Sam simply a puppet or metaphorical mask for her operator. The operator often sat in a separate room and followed the interaction through Sam's senses—the system's monitoring devices. The operator also had to learn to work within Sam's limited repertoire of responses. Many of Sam's reactions—such as following the doll with her eyes—were determined by the system, not the operator. And when Sam responded, it was not with the operator's voice or words but her own, which is to say the words recorded for her by the vocal actor.[23] From the perspective of cyborg anthropology, we can say that, in the encounter between Sam and the children, the operator was temporarily folded or coupled into the cyborg body of Sam.

FIGURE 3.3.

Sam (Tartaro 2007; image released by Northwestern University, Articulab website: http://www.articulab. justinecassell.com/projects/samautism/index.html).

ENCOUNTERING SAM

The goal of these experiments was to see if virtual peers could be used to help high-functioning children with ASD develop peer-interaction skills, in particular, the ability to contingently reply to utterances in communications rather than repeating themselves or responding with non sequiturs.[24] The rationale for this therapy was based on previous successes using Virtual Peers to assist children in developing storytelling and other early language skills. Cassell and team were also building on evidence that peer-to-peer interaction therapies can develop conversational skills in autistic children (Kalyva and Avramidis 2005) and findings that children with autism prefer interactions with computers to interactions with peers (Goldsmith and LeBlanc 2004).

A therapeutic encounter with Sam began when the child approached the dollhouse. Sam introduced herself and asked the child to do the same. Sam then invited her partner to help act out a co-created story using the dolls. The following is a summation of one such encounter:

> At the beginning of the interaction, Sam starts a story about two children playing hide-and-seek. Sam trails off part way into the story, indicating she isn't sure what happens next. Claire [the child interacting with Sam] does not at first pick up the trail of the story, but when Sam says, "Then what happens[?]," Claire begins listing items, "Then, they saw a tree. (Sam: Uh-huh.) And a fence." With some prompting from Sam through backchannel and directed questions, Claire begins participating in the interaction, but her utterances are not contingent with the content of Sam's story. Over the course of the interaction, her responses increasingly make sense within the context of the story. In her last story, she helps Sam tell a story about a boy and a girl baking cookies for the boy's grandmother who is sick in the hospital. She says, "They got the ingredients . . . And the recipe book . . . Baked chocolate chip cookies . . . Grandma's cookies." (Tartaro and Cassell 2008, 5)

For Cassell and Tartaro, the therapeutic potential of Sam and the other Virtual Peers are very much tied to their artificialness. For example, they refer to Sam as "indefatigable" (Cassell and Tartaro 2007, 403; Tartaro 2007, 1679; Tartaro and Cassell 2006; 2008, 383). Unlike a human child, Sam has limitless patience and her attention will not wane. And beyond partnering with Sam to build stories, the child could also use the WOz interface to control Sam in interactions with other children, a therapeutic technique used once the ASD child has demonstrated improvement in contingent conversation. Although Sam was designed to resemble a child, her value was also derived from the ways that she was explicitly *not* like a normal child. In other words, her "artificialness" was as important as her "humanness" in creating a successful encounter.

At the heart of that encounter between Sam and a child was the notion that the two must meet as peers, as equals working toward common explicit and implicit goals—in this case, the joint telling of a story and the development of new interaction skills. Cassell and Tartaro write about a "rapport" that must develop between the child and the AI over the course of an interaction to achieve successful therapeutic results (Cassell and Tartaro 2007, 403–4; Tartaro and Cassell 2007, 235–6). This notion of rapport brings us back to encounter value. Cassell and Tartaro described that rapport as being expressed through various signals like sustained eye contact, conversational coherence, and expressions from the children such as "[Sam] reacts to us!" Based on those criteria, the sessions were seen as yielding positive results, with children showing improvements in the areas of attention and conversational contingency after interactions with Sam (Merryman et al. 2008; Tartaro and Cassell 2006, 2008).

Those successes represent an overflowing of the encounter between child and virtual peer, the creation of something greater than the individual parts that persists after the encounter has ended. Generally speaking, all parties must be actively engaged within a therapeutic session. The goal of therapy is to achieve a change that could not occur on its own. Success is therefore a coproduction, something that all share responsibility for. And in the end, that success can be seen as being greater than the individual contributions of each party. A positive change in behavior—the manifestation of the encounter's value—can only be realized when the child and Sam, although they meet as members of different companion species, productively interact with each other as peers.

CONCLUSIONS . . . AND BEGINNINGS

This chapter discussed how cyborg anthropology can be used to study the ways in which AI and human cultures are becoming increasingly intertwined. This included focusing on how AIs and humans exist in relation to each other, attending to how conversational AIs come to embody certain ideologies and how, in their interactions with humans, bots reinforced, challenged, and transformed cultural beliefs and understandings. I finished by discussing the benefits of joining the concepts of companion species and encounter value in cyborg anthropology to ensure we remain attentive to limits of coupling and the fact that the parts of a cyborg often have the power to act outside of the system that they are joined to.

In the case of the bots in Yahoo! chatrooms, following cyborgs led us back to the familiar juxtaposition of humans and machines and provided another example of how the boundary between the two is constantly contested and shifting. At the same time, we can look to Sam and her human peers as an example of a situation in which that boundary is never in question. Sam's creators never attempted to portray her as a living, breathing human. And yet, although she was not human, the children who worked with Sam greeted her as a playmate and a peer and referred to her as a "friend." It is true that children have long made friends with imaginary and inanimate objects, but I cannot help but wonder as I type this if there is something different about a building friendship with an AI like Sam. But I cannot yet say what it is that feels unique about forming such a bond with a digital companion species.

I, however, am sure of one thing. In 2004, when I began this research, I had trouble finding colleagues who knew what a bot was. By the time the first draft of this chapter was submitted, all of my friends were using GPS units instead of maps; robots were beginning to clean waste, deliver food, and dispense drugs in hospitals in the United States, Japan, France, and Scotland; and the *New York Times Magazine* had just begun an extended series of articles called "Smarter than You Think," chronicling the sociocultural effects of recent developments in artificial intelligence. Just before I began edits on the final draft, Watson beat the two best *Jeopardy* players in the world, and the "Terminators" that dominate public discussions are unmanned Predator drone aircrafts. You do not need to be a social scientist to know these signs suggest plenty of opportunities, and an ongoing necessity, to study human/AI encounters for years to come.

NOTES

1. Examples include everything from historical research into the philosophical foundation of modern AI projects (Riskin 2003), to deconstructing how teams approach the process of planning and developing an AI and how those decisions shape the overall project (Forsythe 1996; Suchman 2007), to explorations of various ideologies and definitions of "intelligence" and "life" (Forsythe 1993; Helmreich 2000; Riskin 2003; Suchman 2007).

2. To appreciate chess's historic cultural significance as an index of intelligence, one need look no further than media discussions of Cold War matches between

American and Russian players and, in particular, the 1972 World Chess Championship match between Bobby Fischer and Boris Spassky. Media in both countries positioned each competitor as playing to prove his nation's inherent intellectual and ideological superiority.

3. Similarly, following Watson's win on *Jeopardy*, many commentators noted that the game's focus on trivia made winning largely a function of a "mechanical" ability to efficiently organize, store, and retrieve data.

4. An ancient Asian game in which two players—one using black markers, the other white—compete to acquire and defend territory on a game board.

5. Roboticists and designers use a slightly different articulation of "the uncanny" in discussions about how an artificial representation creates a heightened sense of revulsion in those it interacts with as it becomes outwardly more human (Mori 1970). This concept, termed "the Uncanny Valley," was wonderfully articulated by Judah Friedlander's character on the television program *30 Rock* who pointed out the difference between R2-D2 and C-3PO, the "nice" robots in *Star Wars*, and the "scary," dead-eyed characters of the computer-animated children's film *The Polar Express* ("Succession," *30 Rock*, 2008).

6. It is important to understand that the cyborg, like most of Haraway's theoretical contributions, was intended to be a tool applicable to both activism and analysis; Haraway would arguably see no difference between the two. It was developed as a response to contemporary debates circulating among political activists and in academic disciplines including science studies and feminism.

7. In addition to the classical cyborgs of science fiction, like the Terminator, a single body made up of both organic and mechanical materials, Haraway's cyborgs can include more metaphorical assemblages like a community action group made up of people from all categories of a society who come together to accomplish a specific task (Haraway 1991a, 154–5).

8. In the cyborg, there is no assumed equivalence or naïve relativism. Two contradictory truths might coexist, but that does not mean that they are equal or should be equal. Haraway explicitly states that the cyborg is "never innocent" and must recognize inequalities both outside and within itself (Haraway 1991a, 150–1).

9. Although people who hold a given ideology may think theirs is superior to others, from the analytical perspective of linguistic and media anthropology, ideologies are never inherently moral or immoral, true or false.

10. All usernames, human and bot alike, have been altered for this section. Beyond altering the identities of chatters, all quotes from chatrooms and discussion boards are reproduced "as is," with no corrections to spelling or grammar.

11. The primary fieldwork for this part of the chapter was conducted in Yahoo! chatrooms during spring 2005 and supplemented with irregular visits to chatrooms over the year that followed. This entire section will be situated in that ethnographic present. Yahoo! was chosen because, at the time, it was the largest chat network where memberships were freely available to any individual with Internet access. Within the chat network, the majority of my time was spent within rooms designated as general discussion areas, where there was no specific restriction or guidance for the subjects discussed. When I encountered a chatter that I believed to be a bot, I engaged it in a PM session and record the ensuing interview for later analysis. Supplemental observations and interviews were also conducted on a number of Internet discussion boards

where administrators of adult websites meet to discuss various aspects of the online pornography business.

12. Words like "real" or "true" often signal when someone is making an ideological claim.

13. In this chapter I only use examples of bots performing one specific genre of webcam performer—the "sexy co-ed." In my fieldwork, I encountered numerous other types of bots, including "male" ones that frequented gay chatrooms. All the bots played a specific genre of sex performance.

14. Rather than using "it" to refer to the gender-neutral technology of the AI, I keep with long-standing cross-cultural linguistic practices that treat gender as a performance (Kulick 1997) and thus typically refer to the AI according to the gender it performs.

15. Generally speaking, it was unlikely for a single bot to bring in more than a few dollars a month. Even with more than ten bots operating at once, the average "successful" bot-master still makes less than $50 a month, or, as one creator put it, "enough to buy beer."

16. See Riskin (2003) for an extended consideration of the processes by which that boundary has historically been crossed and reestablished through sociocultural interactions with various forms of artificial intelligence and artificial life projects.

17. As with the example of the games of chess and Go, we see with bots how the test that defines the boundary between human and machine also becomes the goal that must be overcome. Phillip K. Dick's *Do Androids Dream of Electric Sheep?* and its movie adaptation, *Blade Runner*, provide an excellent explanation of the drive to constantly surpass the boundary. In the book and the movie, the test used by the police to identify androids is constantly threatened by the company responsible for manufacturing the androids. The rationale the company offers in the book is that they are not intentionally trying to undermine the police. Instead, they are only doing what their customers want: "[Following] the time-honored principle underlying every commercial venture. If our firm hadn't made these progressively more human types, other firms in the field would have" (Dick, 1996, 54).

18. Haraway's writings on companion species deal with profoundly complex ethical issues and concerns surrounding the treatment of animals. I want to be clear that my use of these concepts, in particular, the application of encounter value to human/AI interactions, is not an attempt to draw moral or ethical comparisons or equivalencies between machines and animals.

19. Unlike use or exchange value, encounter value fiercely resists translation into an economic formula.

20. The research on the Virtual Peers project was largely archival, supplemented by short e-mail exchanges with Cassell's collaborator and coauthor, Andrea Tartaro.

21. Sam's creators refer to her as female in publications, and I follow their practice.

22. This name is a reference to how the visage of the "great and powerful Oz," in *The Wizard of Oz* (1939), was a projection, controlled by the far more mundane figure "behind the curtain," or in Sam's case, in the adjoining room.

23. Sam's voice is also cyborg; instead of using a voice synthesizer to enable Sam to speak on the fly, an adult actress lent her voice to Sam. After all the utterances were recorded, they were digitally manipulated to make them sound like a child had spoken them.

24. Note that the belief that certain skills need to be developed to communicate correctly reflects a specific and dominant language ideology. Following that line of thought, Sam was also a tool for reproducing that ideology within these children.

REFERENCES

Bakhtin, M., C. Emerson, and M. Holquist. 1986. *Speech Genres and Other Late Essays.* Austin: University of Texas Press.

Cassell, J. 2004. "Towards a Model of Technology and Literacy Development: Story Listening Systems." *Journal of Applied Developmental Psychology* 25 (1): 75–105. http://dx.doi.org/10.1016/j.appdev.2003.11.003.

Cassell, J., M. Ananny, A. Basu, T. Bickmore, P. Chong, D. Mellis, et al. 2000. "Shared Reality: Physical Collaboration with a Virtual Peer." *Proceedings of the Conference on Human Factors in Computing Systems*, January 7–11, Boulder, CO.

Cassell, J., and A. Tartaro. 2007. "Intersubjectivity in Human/Agent Interaction." *Interaction Studies: Social Behaviour and Communication in Biological and Artificial Systems* 8 (3): 391–410.

Dick, P. K. 1996. *Do Androids Dream of Electric Sheep?* New York: Ballentine Books.

Downey, G., J. Dumit, and S. Williams. 1995. "Cyborg Anthropology." *Cultural Anthropology* 10 (2): 264–9. http://dx.doi.org/10.1525/can.1995.10.2.02a00060.

Edwards, J. 2004. "Chat Room Bots: Part 1." XBiz.com. http://www.xbiz.com/article_piece.php?cat=45&id=6706.

Forsythe, D.E. 1993. "Engineering Knowledge: The Construction of Knowledge in Artificial Intelligence." *Social Studies of Science* 23 (3): 445–77. http://dx.doi.org/10.1177/0306312793023003002.

Forsythe, D.E. 1996. "New Bottles, Old Wine: Hidden Cultural Assumptions in a Computerized Explanation System for Migraine Sufferers." *Medical Anthropology Quarterly* 10 (4): 551–74. http://dx.doi.org/10.1525/maq.1996.10.4.02a00100. Medline: 8979239

Freud, S. 2003. *The Uncanny.* New York: Penguin Classics.

Geertz, C. 1977. "Thick Description: Toward an Interpretive Theory of Culture." In *The Interpretation of Cultures*, 3–30. New York: Basic Books.

Goffman, E. 1979. "Footing." *Semiotica* 25 (1–2): 1–30. http://dx.doi.org/10.1515/semi.1979.25.1-2.1.

Goldsmith, T., and L. LeBlanc. 2004. "Use of Technology in Interventions for Children with Autism." *Journal of Early and Intensive Behavior Intervention* 1 (2): 166–78. Citeseer.

Hafner, Katie. 2002. "In an Ancient Game, Computing's Future." *New York Times.* August 1. http://www.nytimes.com/2002/08/01/technology/in-an-ancient-game-computing-s-future.html.

Haraway, D. 1991a. "A Cyborg Manifesto: Science, Technology, and Socialist-Feminism in the Late Twentieth Century." In *Simians, Cyborgs, and Women: The Reinvention of Nature*, 149–81. New York: Routledge..

Haraway, D. 1991b. "Situated Knowledges: The Science Question in Feminism and the Privilege of Partial Perspective." In *Simians, Cyborgs, and Women: The Reinvention of Nature*, 183–201. New York: Routledge.

Haraway, D. 2003. *The Companion Species Manifesto: Dogs, People, and Significant Otherness*. Chicago: Prickly Paradigm Press.

Haraway, D. 2007. *When Species Meet*. Minneapolis: University of Minnesota Press.

Haraway, D. 2008. "When Species Meet: An Interview with Donna Haraway." *Animal Voices*. http://animalvoices.ca/2008/04/22/when-species-meet-an-interview-with-donna-haraway/.

Helmreich, S. 2000. *Silicon Second Nature: Culturing Artificial Life in a Digital World*. Berkeley: University of California Press.

Kalyva, E., and E. Avramidis. 2005. "Improving Communication between Children with Autism and Their Peers through the 'Circle of Friends': A Small-Scale Intervention Study." *Journal of Applied Research in Intellectual Disabilities* 18 (3): 253–61. http://dx.doi.org/10.1111/j.1468-3148.2005.00232.x.

Kulick, D. 1997. "The Gender of Brazilian Transgendered Prostitutes." *American Anthropologist* 99 (3): 574–85. http://dx.doi.org/10.1525/aa.1997.99.3.574.

Leonard, A. 1998. *Bots: The Origin of New Species*. New York: Penguin Books Limited.

Merryman, J., A. Tartaro, M. Arie, and J. Cassell. 2008. "Designing Virtual Peers for Assessment and Intervention for Children with Autism." *Proceedings of the 7th International Conference on Interaction Design and Children*. ACM. 81–84.

Mori, M. 1970. "The Uncanny Valley." *Energy* 7 (4): 33–35.

Riskin, J. 2003. "The Defecating Duck, or, the Ambiguous Origins of Artificial Life." *Critical Inquiry* 29 (4): 599–633. http://dx.doi.org/10.1086/377722.

Ryokai, K., C. Vaucelle, and J. Cassell. 2002. "Literacy Learning by Storytelling with a Virtual Peer." *Computer Support for Collaborative Learning* 352–360.

Searle, J. R. 1982. "The Myth of the Computer." *New York Review of Books* 29 (7): 3–6.

Suchman, L. A. 2007. *Human-Machine Reconfigurations*. Cambridge: Cambridge University Press.

Tartaro, A. 2007. "Authorable Virtual Peers for Children with Autism." In *CHI '07 Extended Abstracts on Human Factors in Computing Systems—CHI '07*. New York: ACM Press, April 28.

Tartaro, A., and J. Cassell. 2006. "Authorable Virtual Peers for Autism Spectrum Disorders." *Proceedings of the Combined Workshop on Language-Enabled Educational Technology and Development and Evaluation for Robust Spoken Dialogue Systems at the 17th European Conference on Artificial Intelligence*.

Tartaro, A., and J. Cassell. 2007. "Using Virtual Peer Technology for Children with Autism." In *Universal Usability: Designing Computer Interfaces for Diverse User Populations*, ed. Jonathan Lazar, 231–62. Hoboken, NJ: John Wiley and Sons.

Tartaro, A., and J. Cassell. 2008. "Playing with Virtual Peers: Bootstrapping Contingent Discourse in Children with Autism." *Proceedings of the 8th International Conference on International Conference for the Learning Sciences* 2: 382–389. International Society of the Learning Sciences.

Winograd, Terry, and Fernando Flores. 1986. *Understanding Computers and Cognition: A New Foundation for Design*. Norwood, NJ: Addison-Wesley.

4

The Digital Graveyard

Online Social Networking Sites as Vehicles of Remembrance

Jenny Ryan

This is the use of memory: for liberation—
not less of love but expanding of love
beyond desire, and so liberation from the
future as well as the past.

T. S. ELIOT[1]

Only the Lonelyhearts of the world expect a
personal reply from the movie, phonograph record,
or radio program. Or to be more precise, we are all
Lonelyhearts inasmuch [as] we "interact" with books,
pets, infants, or distant correspondents.

JOHN DURHAM PETERS[2]

In October 2007, my grandmother was diagnosed with the cancer that led to her eventual death the following spring.[3] A devoted mother of fourteen children, she, along with her children, grappled with many difficult spiritual and medical decisions throughout her illness. One evening I witnessed first-

DOI: 10.5876/9781607321705.c04

hand the incredible unity and strength that comes about in the toughest of life's challenges and the capacity for technology to extend the possibilities for collectively coping with them. Ten of my aunts and uncles took part in a conference call to discuss plans and options: my mother, a nurse, gave medical advice; my uncle Joe, manager of a medical supply company, arranged the delivery of a special bed; my aunt Mary, who works for an insurance company, discussed insurance options; my uncle Jack, a devout Christian, had been researching spiritual healing centers; and my grandmother interjected often with words of love, faith, and strength. Fueled by a desire to help, I realized that I could tap into my specific area of expertise, online social media. In a matter of hours, I set up a public wiki and encouraged my family members to write in the communal blog, to help in the creation of an extensive address book, and to arrange visits on a digital calendar. The wiki was quickly adopted by a substantial majority of my family, including the many out-of-town grandchildren. It became a source of ongoing updates about my grandmother's condition, and the calendar proved particularly useful for organizing a continuous stream of visits and appointments. When she passed away, my family continued to regularly update the blog with tales of their daily struggles, fond memories of the past, inspirational quotes, and Biblical passages. They also posted photographs and videos. The site became a living memorial, a collective archive of personal remembrances, simultaneously shaping and shaped by their very inscription.

The Internet is a complex new medium that allows for the intimacy, interactivity, and casualness of speech, as well as the permanency and permeability of writing. Despite popular discourse's perpetuation of a distinction between "virtual" cyberspace and "real life," it is evident that people are integrating technologies of the Internet into their lives as extensions of everyday communication and identity performance, shaped by changing cultural conditions that are in turn affected by these new technologies. Drawing from the methodological approach of existential anthropology, the principal aim of this project is a phenomenological exploration of the ways in which these unique facets of the Internet have enabled mourners to expand the process of remembering the dead.[4] Specifically, I have examined examples of online shrines on the social networking sites MySpace, Facebook, and Tribe.net, positioning them as vehicles for individual and collective remembrance of the dead.

While skimming my Facebook News Feed[5] one afternoon, I came across a headline informing me that thirty-six of my Friends had joined a Group called "In Memory of Mr. Burns." Shocked, I clicked on the name and navigated to the Group's homepage, where I discovered that my beloved seventh-grade social studies teacher had recently died of cancer. Hundreds of his former students had already joined the Group, the Wall of which was littered with touching remembrances both funny and profound. In the discussion threads, a student proposed that members create a book of their fond memories for his family. I immediately joined in the conversation: "That Social Studies class-room was the safest place in the world during lunch in 7th grade. Thanks for providing solace to a shy little nerd. A superhero amongst mere mortals. What was that banana song he played in class?" Later that day, an old class-mate responded on my Wall: "YES WE HAVE NO BANANAS, BANANAS IN SCRANTON PA! (the banana song in mr. b's class. fucking great)." I found myself digging through old photo albums until I found two photos of Mr. Burns, taken nearly twelve years ago, which I promptly scanned and uploaded to the Group.

Jose van Dijck (2007, 16) writes that "[a]t once a means of inscription and an external repository, media are seen as apparatuses for production and stor-age, modeled after the mind's alleged capacity to register and hold experiences and impressions." Online social networking practices entail the inscription of personal identity, cultural tastes, and social relations as well as their archival. As such, they provide a rich framework for understanding the complexities inherent to new technologies, which blur preexisting boundaries of space, time, privacy, communication, representation, and memory.

DIGITAL TRACES, VIRTUAL PLACES

Memory . . . is in a manner the twin sister of written speech [*litteraturm*] and is completely similar [*persimilis*] to it, [though] in a dissimilar medium. For just as script consists of marks indicating letters and of the material on which these marks are printed, so the structure of memory, like a wax tablet, employs places [*loci*] and in these gathers together [*collocat*] images like letter.

CICERO[6]

In *Remembering: A Phenomenological Study*, Edward Casey (2000) describes what he calls the "primary traits of remembering": search, display, encapsul-ment, expansion, persistence, and pastness. These traits are strikingly par-alleled on the Internet. Because most of the information available on the Internet is archived by *search* engines such as Google, the medium signifi-cantly enhances one's capacity to remember. Social networking sites such as Facebook *display* individual identities through the construction of dynamic member profiles. These profiles serve to visually and textually articulate vari-ous aspects of one's personality (such as interests, favorite books and mov-ies, and photographs), social network, and social interactions through the medium (such as comments, "Likes," and group discussions on Pages and Events). In the event of a member's death, this online presence becomes fro-zen, a potentially permanent *encapsulation* of a life as it was being lived online. Loved ones of the deceased often find that the existence of this encapsulated online identity reveals aspects of a life they may have been partially or wholly unaware of, and thus it enables the *expansion* of remembering. These online shrines, created through repeated visitation practices marked by the nostalgic public messages of loved ones, allow for the *persistence* of the deceased in memory, which simultaneously and inevitably evokes the deceased's very *pastness*.

In his book discussing the impact of electronic media on social behavior, Joshua Meyrowitz (1985, 7) writes that "one of the reasons Americans may no longer seem to 'know their place' is that they no longer *have* a place in the traditional sense of a set of behaviors matched to physical locations and the audiences found in them." Modern communications technologies have altered our perceptual fields by extending them beyond the realm of direct, face-to-face interaction. In turn, the perceived relationship between physical place and our social environment has been expanded into the seemingly nebulous virtual realm, allowing for the emergence of new pathways and horizons of experience. Casey's (2000, 213) discussion of place memory is an especially apt paradigm for understanding online social networks as a kind of place: "It is in providing outward display for things and pathways as they exist within the horizons of landscape that places enable memories to become inwardly inscribed and possessed: made one with the memorial self. The visibility *without* becomes part of the invisibility *within*" (emphasis added).

As previously noted, the primary function of online social networks is the explicit display of an individual's social connections, self-expression, and interactions within the medium. To become a member of such sites is to construct a meaningful horizon, oriented about the self, within the vast cybernetic landscape. Within this horizon, memories are literally "inscribed and possessed"; the site serves as a container of past events, preserved and accessible through one's personal profile.

All technologies extend the possibilities of humankind, and in turn, they become humanized and embedded in everyday experiences. Thus, the notion of "embodiment" must be reconfigured in light of the highly participatory and immersive nature of online interaction. Just as the telephone evokes a sense of copresence, viewing and interacting with an online profile can make one feel as though the other is in some way "there." It is common to observe continued interactions with the frozen online "presence" of the deceased in the form of conversational messages, as if the profile were a medium that enables active communication with those who have departed from the physical world. However, such acts often elicit confusion and discomfort in those who prefer to bury their dead. Furthermore, the casual and at times superficial character of online communication introduces a new set of issues concerning proper respect for the dead. What follows is a more nuanced exploration of the practices and attitudes surrounding this contemporary form of commemoration.

MY(DEATH)SPACE

MySpace was the most popular social networking site until 2006, when it was overtaken by Facebook. The site's original niche membership was primarily composed of musicians, twenty-somethings, and high school students. For teens in particular, the site serves as a medium through which they can "hang out" with their friends and express themselves freely. The design of the site is such that member profiles can be fully customized, prompting many to plaster their pages with videos, photographs, music, and coding that is often poorly executed (a common complaint of viewers). In the event of a member death, friends and family members will often continue to post Comments on the MySpace profile of their loved one. The overwhelming majority of the "MySpace shrines" I found were instances of young and often tragic deaths, such as murder and suicide, perhaps modeled after spontaneously created physical shrines commemorating sudden, unexpected deaths (such as the Princess Diana tragedy and the victims of 9/11). In nearly every case, such profiles continued to serve as active sites of commemoration by family and friends even years after their creators' deaths.

Online profiles are far more than merely textual representations. Typically, one's online persona includes photographs of oneself, one's friends, and past experiences. The power of visual representations is best exemplified by their capacity to evoke visceral memories, enabling one to remember another with the immediacy and presence of the visual in tension with the pastness of the person it represents. "Damn B! Itz takin me so long to even click onto ur page kuz of all the tears that wanna come out from just puttin the curser on ur pic," writes one grieving friend. A photograph provides proof of the existence of its contents, lending credence to what are otherwise the untenable shadows of the forgetful mind. On the other hand, photographs are also open to subjective interpretation, and thus online profiles may be judged in unintended and potentially negative ways. Given the increasing ubiquity of online social networking in the everyday lives of youth, the public archival of personal information has become a normative practice. MySpace Profiles are often rife with highly personal information, such as revealing photographs, online diaries, and emotionally fraught conversations played out through Comments. This can challenge the spirit of communication, confusing the boundaries between the informality of social relationships and the "sacred" nature of memorializing the deceased.

Death undoubtedly provokes some of the deepest fears and fascinations. Some, driven by fascination, seek out open and safe spaces on the Internet to discuss issues surrounding death with others who share their frank curiosity. In searching for the MySpace Profiles of the deceased, I was led to the controversial site MyDeathSpace.com. This popular "death networking" site serves to catalog obituaries that include links to the MySpace Profiles of the dead. MyDeathSpace maintains a heavily active message board, home to a solid niche community teeming with camaraderie. The vast majority of message threads on the site are found in the "Off-Topic" forum, where it is evident that the community comprises diverse individuals drawn to the site for myriad reasons. Despite their relative anonymity and geographic dispersion, members of MyDeathSpace demonstrate a collective bond through shared norms of communication and behavior, exemplifying many attributes of the "virtual community" described by Howard Rheingold (1993).[7]

As the name "MyDeathSpace" implies, there is certainly a dark and morbid element to the community, which the members are the first to acknowledge. This dark side can be found in the second-most active forum, "Article Discussions." Here, conversations center on reactions to specific obituaries posted on the site, particularly those pertaining to murder, suicide, and so-called public interest stories (such as the Virginia Tech shootings and the death of Anna Nicole Smith). Such public "chitchat" about the dead frequently provokes outrage in grieving individuals discovering that their departed is a matter of public and often hurtful gossip. The anger and confusion that may result from coming across casual public discussion of the deceased is exemplified by the following post, titled "Confused, Help Me Understand":

> I really don't mean to offend anyone but I wonder if I am the only person that discovered this site and felt as though someone stabbed me in the heart. I was searching Yahoo for my best friends obit the other day to send to a friend out of state. I simply typed in her name and noticed that a link to this site came up. I was horrified to see her name as the topic of a discussion board. Not only that, but there were blogs and poems taken from her friends and family's MySpace pages. After taking a hard look at the site it is obvious that suicide seems to be the favorite topic. Now, I understand that the psychology behind suicide can be extremely interesting but when I read comments like "suicide is my favorite" and "I like the ones where they inhale dustoff or some other cleaner, because those are ones I can laugh at," I feel so frustrated. There are friends and families that are grieving and feel that there is no reason people half way across the country needed to be speculating "what sent them over the edge." Unfortunately, the family is having her MySpace page removed and the memory page turned to private after reading this. I can't even begin to tell you what it felt like seeing what I saw today or what her mother did when she saw it. Like I said, I don't mean to offend anyone and I don't want to get in a name calling heated debate. I just want you to remember what your comments and jokes can do to grieving loved ones. If it was up to me this site would not exist, but it is not, all I ask is that you have respect and I would assume that if a family member requests you to remove a death you do so. Thank you for your time.

The community nature of the site is manifested when members unite to defend their actions. Some argue that the MySpace Profiles of the dead help to humanize life and death, providing a window for understanding the greatest of mankind's mysteries. Others take a less romantic perspective; as one member put it, "MySpace has given dead people their 15 minutes." Nevertheless, it is generally agreed that "if you don't want certain aspects of your life to be made public, then YOU have to keep it out of the internet. If you project yourself as a 'bad ass gangster' or such, chances are that's how people are going to remember you when you are gone" (member post on MyDeathSpace). Thus, it is important to note that, although a Profile is often publicly accessible, it is frequently made publicly *visible* in the event of the owner's death.

The extremely public and promotional nature of MySpace also allows for a high level of spam, which may (however inadvertently) intrude on the "sacred" Profiles of the deceased. As one MyDeathSpace member put it, "My deal I have since I have been on here, is all the spam left on these peoples Profiles after they have passed . . . that is a blight to see on any page, but it just seems wrong to see it." It is not uncommon to find Comments left by spambots promoting pornography sites and diet pills in the midst of the heartfelt messages of Friends. These comments come across as egregious and disrespectful to those seeking to preserve and respect the "living memory" of the dead and are akin to the desecration of monuments and cultural artifacts. MySpace's policy on the issue states:

> We're very sorry to hear about your loss. If you're the next of kin (mother, father, spouse, legally registered domestic partner, son, or daughter) of the deceased, we can delete or preserve the Myspace profile for you.
>
> For the sake of our users' safety and security, however, we'll need you to email us proof of death, such as an obituary or death certificate at accountcare@support.myspace.com. Please write us from your personal email address and tell us how you're related to the deceased, and include the deceased user's Myspace friend ID along with your specific request to either delete or preserve the profile, or to remove content.
>
> Unfortunately, we can't let you access, edit, or delete any of the content or settings on the user's profile yourself, but we'll be sure to review and remove any content you find objectionable.[8]

For the most part, however, the Profiles of the dead become sites through which loved ones express their love and grief. Such messages are nearly always directed to the deceased members, often as if they were still checking their profiles from beyond the grave. The following post is an example:

> miss u b. just havin a long nite i guess. cant sleep. or dont want too . . . workin on my future interview questions. & was thinkin of u in them. watcha think of them? you can help me remember wat to say when the time comes hopefully. cuz you know you were my memory since i dont have one as good as yours . . .

The above message is representative of the way in which many MySpace natives communicate through the medium, reflecting the manner in which the Internet, like remembrance itself, transcends the spatial and temporal boundaries of the physical world. Communication within online social networks is unlike other forms of online communication (such as instant messaging and e-mail) in that reciprocity is not always expected. For instance, earlier today I posted words of encouragement on a friend's profile simply to let her know that she's not alone in spending her final weekend at school writing papers. Messages posted to online Profiles are often intended as public displays of connection, serving primarily to affirm and maintain social bonds.

For family members and friends, viewing the online Profiles of the recently departed is often both comforting and painful. In an online news article about the trend, a grieving father articulated his experiences of regularly visiting his deceased daughter's MySpace profile, much as one would regularly visit a grave: "Some days it makes me feel she's still there," he said. "And some days it reminds me I can never have that contact again" (as cited in St. John, 2006). These sentiments are made apparent through the public messages inscribed on the online Profiles of the deceased, which tend to express a mix of pastness as well as a sense of continued copresence:

> I was listening to some salsa... and of course u came to mind my dude!!!!
> The song finished just as i started thinking about u teaching me how to dance salsa wit a little more style..... And then "Vamones Pal Monte" comes on..... Damn bro... I miss ur ass bee..... (comment on MySpace Profile)

The above message exemplifies the cognitive process of remembrance: external reminders follow internal mental pathways, evoking emotional memories that find their fulfillment in external, outwardly directed expression. It is through language that we represent and understand our experiences; they take on meaning through the conversational process of articulation. In this particular form of articulation, these experiences become archived in a place that serves to encapsulate the identity of another. In this way, online social networks serve as extensions of our memory—tangible pathways that connect us to the past—as well as potential vehicles for immortality, introducing a new form of active resistance to the needs of forgetting.

DEATH IN THE TRIBE(.NET)

Individual Profiles are but one way that online social networks allow for remembrance of the dead. On Tribe.net, most communication occurs through participation in the message board forums of various online groups, called Tribes. A substantial population of the site consists of intimately connected but geographically dispersed members of communities revolving principally around the annual Burning Man arts festival. In the absence of face-to-face communication, Tribe.net becomes a crucial platform through which this community interacts. When members of this community die, they are often commemorated in forum threads of the Tribes they were members of. Friends share stories, personal feelings, images, and links to artwork created in honor of the deceased. Unlike the default option for MySpace Profiles, public messages posted to individual Profiles (called "Testimonials") must be approved by the owner to be displayed, and thus individual Profiles are unlikely to become sites of collective commemoration or personal communication.[9]

It should also be noted that Tribe.net is generally community-centric, as opposed to the ego-centricity of MySpace and Facebook. "The original thesis of Tribe," states cofounder Paul Martino (personal communication, 2007), "was to marry Friendster and Craigslist—or as one of our focus group members said, 'Craigslist with a face.'"[10] Although the classifieds feature is active and based on widely shared principles of trust, the most popular activity on the site is found on message boards based on shared interests, values, and beliefs. Like MyDeathSpace, these forums teem with camaraderie and intimate long-distance friendships that have developed an online momentum independent of their offline origins. In the event of deaths among the Burning Man Tribe, which is the most popular group on the site with nearly 21,000 members, this forum is used to disseminate news about memorial services, express condolences, pass on words of wisdom and support, share cherished memories of the deceased, and provide links to groups and websites formed in their honor. Through such forms of collective remembrance, many find a renewed sense of community: "Something that Spyral points out, that really resonates with me, is the way in which an event such as this lays out so clearly how very deep and good the people in this community are. You see really good things in people and it does make you proud to be connected to them" (member post on the "Burning Man" Tribe.net forum).

Tribe.net's emphasis on community is further exemplified by the site owners' personally posting messages such as the following: "To Shoshana and Nathan, their families, friends, and everyone else effected [sic] by this accident, the prayers and well wishes of all the Tribe staff are with you."

The culture of Tribe.net is such that "alternative" lifestyles and viewpoints are normalized and encouraged. Those connected through Tribes like Burning Man have often come together through underground happenings that promote shared values of creativity, generosity, acceptance, and collective ecstatic experience. The nature of their remembrance often reflects these sentiments:

> Doing stuff for BM [Burning Man] and talking to people about my experiences there has made me think of her alot as she invited me to her camp and was so tied up in so many happy experiences there for me. I was

used to not seeing her for months but I don't think you ever get use to not seeing someone forever. I still keep expecting that I will see her. (member post on the "Burning Man" Tribe.net forum)

Many of the deaths reported on Tribe.net forums serve to highlight pertinent issues for the communities involved. For example, deaths at Burning Man are often the result of unsafe practices: bicycle and "mutant vehicle" collisions, drug overdoses, dehydration, and other potentially avoidable accidents. Exemplifying how the deceased "live on" in the collective memory, these stories can teach valuable lessons that are passed on to the wider community through their dissemination online. In a similar vein, deaths may serve to strengthen the community by enabling new relationships to form on the basis of shared grief:

> I woke up this morning with a terrible sinking feeling and the image of a large black hole amidst a vast spider's web. The hole is where Allison used to be. Frayed threads hung and pulled against the stark darkness. Limp, dim strands extended all around. I've had a notion which I'm throwing out there for everyone's personal consideration. That is, the healing that can come from recognizing and honoring Ally's connective force by looking around this tribe and choosing even just one new person to get to know. As part of this, we should each remain receptive and open to anyone who approaches us in the same light.
> Forever changed, we can mend this broken web. (Member post on the "we miss allison lange" Tribe.net forum)

Members of Tribe.net often form relationships online with those they physically interact with only occasionally or never at all. While many friends would be unable to travel cross-country for a traditional memorial service, some may simply be unable to leave their comfort zone. Nevertheless, online mourners find support in commemorating the dead through a medium that, for much of the Tribe.net population, is well known and comfortable for them:

> i attended the memorial, but left just before it started b/c i felt disconnected from the crowd. i didn't know allison very well, but she still touched me and i am mourning her loss. the thing is, i wasn't comfortable being upset in a large group of people i didn't know and thought it best to leave and be alone for a while. (Member post on the "we miss allison lange" Tribe.net forum)

Upon visiting the site, loved ones of the deceased may discover an entire community of grieving friends they were unaware of:

> I'm not sure if Mary [the mother of the deceased] is in this tribe, but she has created a tribe account. She would like to stay in touch with Allison's friends as a way to feel connected to her. If you have positive stories to share about the way Allison touched your life, or even just a fun or funny

story, or have time just to say hello I would ask that you please send her a note. (Member post on the "we miss allison lange" Tribe.net forum)

Unlike MyDeathSpace, where anonymous strangers often casually engage in what could be construed as disrespectful and "profane" conversation about posted deaths, discussions of the deceased on Tribe.net are typically more intimate in tone. When strangers do contribute to these threads, I have observed only words of respect and sympathy. Because the site is not well known and most members identify themselves by nicknames, many of the problems that arise in more public sites (such as MySpace) are negated. Such a contrast exemplifies the manner in which small, niche-based online communities differ greatly from massive and high-profile sites such as MySpace.

SPECTERS OF FACEBOOK

With more than 500 million active users,[11] Facebook has rapidly become embedded in the social practices of high school and college students around the world. As one student informer put it, "you don't exist if you're not on Facebook." For many, checking the site has become as routine as checking e-mail. The site serves as a container of information pertinent to the offline social worlds of its members and is a fairly accurate representation of "real-world" social networks. Members are able to find old high school acquaintances, create event invitations, upload photo albums, and interact with others through private messages, public postings on the Walls of individual Profiles, and Group message boards. Many of these activities are then published to the "News Feed," made up of streaming "headlines" that are displayed on a user's homepage upon log-in. This feature enables the spread of social information that would otherwise be relegated to more active and unilaterally directed forms of communication, such as face-to-face conversation and telephone calls. For instance, personal messages posted on the Walls of those in one's network may appear as a "headline," as well as newly formed Groups created or joined by friends in honor of the deceased. As such, it is possible that geographically distant friends may learn of a common friend's death upon logging into the site.

Unlike MySpace, individual Facebook Profiles are typically inaccessible for strangers. Thus, I was unable to personally view more than a few memorialized Profiles. Nevertheless, secondhand accounts attest to the fact that friends post messages on the deceased's Facebook Profile in a manner quite similar to that of MySpace. My friend Celia told me that she regularly comes across new messages posted on the Wall of her brother's girlfriend, nearly two years after her tragic death. These messages, depending on the member's News Feed settings, may appear on the Facebook homepages of those in her social network, and thus serve as reminders for the remembrances of others. By permanently encapsulating the dead and providing an outlet for the expression of their ongoing presence in the minds of the living, social networking sites become a vehicle for individual remembrance.

Groups, on the other hand, are more often than not publicly accessible, and it is a common practice for friends to create Facebook Groups in memory of the dead. These Groups encourage collective remembrance much like those on Tribe.net. Because Facebook makes the sharing of various forms of media relatively simple, I regularly came across an expansive plethora of homemade videos, photographs, and shared news articles commemorating the deceased and encapsulated within the online shrine of a Facebook Group. Group members often comment on these individual objects of memory, as well as share memories, poems, and other sentiments on the Group's homepage. Such Groups, like those on Tribe.net, provide a means of collective remembrance that strengthens community bonds (although rather than communities based on shared interests or lifestyles, communities on Facebook typically represent "real-life" networks, such as university affiliations and family relationships).

It is clear that many feel strongly about the medium as a way of honoring the memory of the deceased. Facebook's policies regarding the status of deceased members' Profiles have been the subject of much controversy. Originally, their policy was to "memorialize" such Profiles, removing them thirty days after becoming aware of a member's death (Walker 2006). However, following the murder of thirty-two students at Virginia Tech, this policy was revoked, allowing Profiles to remain (in a "memorialized state") indefinitely.[12] The campaign behind this change was spearheaded by John Woods, a friend of the fallen students, who organized a Facebook Group called "Facebook Memorialization Is Misguided: Dead Friends Are Still People," which amassed 2,700 members in two weeks. Despite the change in policy, the Group continues to be quite active with 1,334 members (as of June 2011). The Group description lists the following current issues:

> Firstly, their interests, favorite books, favorite movies, favorite television shows, "about me," and quotes are gone.
>
> Secondly, we who were their friends cannot say that we met someone through them. This information is gone. (I, for one, met many people through Maxine before and after she was killed.)
>
> Thirdly, their groups are no longer listed. These groups reflect the things in life about which they cared, the things that made them laugh, and the ideas that moved them.

The founding principle behind the Group is that dead people deserve to "live on" through Facebook, just as they do in the memories of others. Furthermore, many Americans believe that those who have died continue to look after those they have left behind from heaven. "I went to it and saw how many people are still leaving comments about missing her, wishing her happy birthday, and just saying random things that they would say if she were still alive," Lewis wrote. "I find this so touching and I'm sure that she does to, up there in heaven."[13] Interestingly, I rarely came across instances of communication among members of these Groups, whereas interpersonal support is prominent on Tribe. net. This is likely because Facebook networks are frequently spatially bound representations of offline communities, and thus grieving friends need not express their support for one another online.

Following the outrage expressed by users concerning the new "Suggestions" feature—particularly reports that Facebook had "suggested" that they "reconnect" with a deceased Friend—a Facebook employee (Kelly 2009) published a blog post concerning the updated memorialization policy:

> We understand how difficult it can be for people to be reminded of those who are no longer with them, which is why it's important when someone passes away that their friends or family contact Facebook to request that a profile be memorialized. For instance, just last week, we introduced new types of Suggestions that appear on the right-hand side of the home page and remind people to take actions with friends who need help on Facebook. By memorializing the account of someone who has passed away, people will no longer see that person appear in their Suggestions.
>
> When an account is memorialized, we also set privacy so that only confirmed friends can see the profile or locate it in search. We try to protect the deceased's privacy by removing sensitive information such as contact information and status updates. Memorializing an account also prevents anyone from logging into it in the future, while still enabling friends and family to leave posts on the profile Wall in remembrance.

Among the hundreds of comments in response to this post were two prominent points of discomfort and contention; namely, that those who were not Facebook Friends with deceased friends or family members should be able to view their Profiles and post messages to their Walls, and that removing any of the content posted by the deceased (especially status updates and Wall posts directed to others) was not only unfair, but downright painful:

> Important information and years of past posts by my son were removed from his page when it was memorialized. His page was stripped down to almost nothing. I would have loved to have had the chance to at least copy the things he had written, before they were gone forever. This has been very upsetting to me. Shame on you, Facebook, for inflicting a "secondary wound" on an already grieving family because of your not very well thought out policy on this.

In describing her experience of viewing the Facebook Profile of a deceased high school acquaintance, my friend Anna expressed discomfort with the "strangeness" of others' use of the medium to continue communicating with the dead. However, it would seem that communication within online social networks is simply more comfortable for some, particularly those who regularly interact electronically. The relationship between "native" users of the Internet and one's interactions with the medium can be likened to the habitual nature of "body memory," which Casey discusses at length. For example, as I sit here writing on my laptop, I find myself instinctively responding to the "ding" that signifies a new e-mail, and in moments I am clicking on a link that sends me to my Facebook Profile. Drawn down this familiar pathway, I reflexively scan the News Feed, where the faces of my friends peer back at me, reminding me of their existence. Scarcely a day goes by without communication through this medium, which does not require the immediate presence of others, nor their reciprocity. The simple act of pressing "send" is a fulfillment of the intention behind this particular communicative act, because seeing the message displayed on the screen confirms that communication has occurred. For "digital natives," it is often more comfortable to communicate with unseen others through the online medium than it is to communicate with the dead in more traditional ways, such as kneeling in prayer or lighting a candle. Thus, it seems only fitting that those accustomed to this form of communication may continue to post messages directed to a dead friend, reinforcing a habitual act that serves to express the ongoing presence of another in one's memory.

LIVING ON ONLINE

> The trace that I leave signifies to me both my death, either to come or already past, and the hope that it will survive me. It's not an ambition of immortality, it's structural; it is the constant form of my life. Every time I allow something to go forth, I see my death in the writing. The extreme test: one expropriates oneself—one gives oneself away—without knowing to whom one confides the thing one leaves. Who will inherit it now and how? Will there even be inheritors?
>
> JACQUES DERRIDA[14]

Through this elucidation of the myriad ways in which the dead are commemorated in the "online shrines" of MySpace, Facebook, and Tribe, it is clear that the Internet extends and reconfigures the possibilities for the persistence of memory. Although Casey's traits of remembrance remain pertinent (if somewhat altered), I contend that his emphasis on physical "place" in the process of remembering must be extended to include "virtual space" as well. As the term "cyberspace" implies, people conceptualize the abstract realm of the Internet metaphorically, relating it to more familiar domains of embodied experience and physical place. However, at times technologies may seem alien and incomprehensible, instigating fear and a sense of powerlessness. Through modern technology, our experiences of the social world are increasingly disconnected from the physicality of the body and the place it is located. On the Internet, we are everywhere and nowhere at once. Online social networks expand one's horizon of social interactions, simultaneously blurring the pathways between them. As a result of these new formations, a whole new set of anxieties and possibilities arise, challenging preconceived notions regarding the boundaries between public and private, respect for the dead, rituals of mourning, and the persistence of individual identity.

In his theory of *sur-vival* ("on living on"), Jacques Derrida (1987) asserts that all written correspondences are inevitably subject to scattering. Derrida was referring specifically to postcards, but the public and persistent nature of online identities applies this notion quite literally. Our digital traces serve as artifacts of ourselves; the dead *live on* in the public and persistent realm of the Internet, enabling ongoing dialogue between their memorial traces and those left behind in the land of the living. When even the dead can join the dialogue, today's social networking sites come to resemble a haunting electronic nebula populated by everyone you've ever known, interacting in new modes of spatiality and temporality.

Although death is a universal inevitability of humankind, and although it may come at any time, it is precisely for these reasons that we go about our everyday lives without consciously factoring in its imminent possibility. If we did, we would forever be locked in existential stasis. To act, at least in American society, is often to direct oneself toward some future possibility—of happiness, reward, prestige, love, security, and on and on. Thus, when we "type ourselves into being" online, we are motivated by such possibilities and often fail to consider that we are creating traces of ourselves that will outlive their creators. However, just as traces of a deceased individual persist as the remembrances of others and through objects such as graves and photographs, so too do they persist in the ethereal realm of the Internet. Like traditional memorial services, the sites of these traces can serve to connect previously unaffiliated individuals through their shared loss. The Internet expands this possibility of connection, because it is in many ways easier to articulate deeply felt feelings to strangers through the anonymity, convenience, and delocalization of online communication. Despite the concerns of those still not comfortable with the medium, online social networks allow grieving friends to share stories, mediated memory objects, and words of support at any time, regardless of the distance between them. Although it is not particularly pleasant to ponder the traces we leave of ourselves after death, I hope this chapter has illuminated the ways that online profiles can evolve into ongoing sites of commemoration, suggesting we take into consideration how we choose to represent ourselves through them.

NOTES

1. From "Little Gidding," *4 Quartets.*

2. John Durham Peters, *Speaking into the Air: A History of the Idea of Communication* (Chicago: University of Chicago Press, 1999), 150–51.

3. This chapter is based on the final chapter of my master's thesis in anthropology, "The Virtual Campfire: An Ethnography of Online Social Networking" (Wesleyan University, 2008).

4. Michael Jackson, *Existential Anthropology: Events, Exigencies, and Effects* (New York: Berghahn Books, 2005).

5. Throughout this chapter, the ordinary language terms used to describe official features of these sites will be capitalized as proper nouns.

6. As quoted in Carruthers (2008, 18).

7. The term "virtual community" was coined in 1993 by Howard Rheingold, specifically in reference to his experiences with the WELL (Whole Earth 'Lectronic Link), a message board community much like MyDeathSpace.

8. "How can I access or delete a deceased member's profile?" http://www.myspace.com/help (accessed June 16, 2011).

9. This may not always be the case, as suggested by the following post on a Tribe.net forum: "Back in the Day, tribe would also let customer service approve testimonials for people who had passed. I'm sure they still will, if asked."

10. Friendster was the top social networking site until it was overtaken by MySpace in 2004. Craigslist, a free, text-only site made up of classified ads organized by city, was founded in 1996 and has remained one of the most popular sites on the Internet today.

11. According to Facebook's "Factsheet," there are more than 500 million active users as of June 16, 2011. "Active users" are users who have logged on to the site in the past thirty days (www.facebook.com).

12. Certain elements of Facebook profiles designated as "memorialized" are hidden, such as contact info and personal information (interests, favorite books, favorite movies, favorite television shoes, favorite quotes, and the "about me" section). However, friends are still able to view photo albums, basic information, and education (history) and can post messages on the public "wall" of these profiles (Hortobagyl 2007).

13. As quoted in Stelter (2007).

14. As quoted in Butler (2005, 31).

REFERENCES

Butler, Judith. 2005. "On Never Having Learned How to Live." *Differences: A Journal of Feminist Cultural Studies* 16 (3): 27–34. http://dx.doi.org/10.1215/10407 391-16-3-27.

Carruthers, Mary J. 2008. *The Book of Memory: A Study of Memory in Medieval Culture.* 2nd ed. Cambridge: Cambridge University Press.

Casey, Edward S. 2000. *Remembering: A Phenomenological Study.* 2nd ed. Bloomington: Indiana University Press.

Derrida, Jacques. 1987. *The Post Card: From Freud to Socrates and Beyond.* Chicago: University of Chicago Press.

Hortobagyl, Monica. 2007. "Slain Students' Pages to Stay on Facebook." *USA Today*, May 8. http://www.usatoday.com/tech/webguide/internetlife/2007-05-08-facebook-vatech_N.htm?csp=34.

Jackson, Michael. 2005. *Existential Anthropology: Events, Exigencies, and Effects*. Oxford: Berghahn Books.

Kelly, Max. 2009. "Memories of Friends Departed Endure on Facebook." *The Facebook Blog*, October 26. http://blog.facebook.com/blog.php?post=163091042130.

Meyrowitz, Joshua. 1985. *No Sense of Place: The Impact of Electronic Media on Social Behavior*. New York: Oxford University Press.

Peters, John Durham. 1999. *Speaking into the Air: A History of the Idea of Communication*. Chicago: University of Chicago Press.

Rheingold, Howard. 1993. *The Virtual Community*. Accessed June 16, 2011, http://www.rheingold.com/vc/book/intro.html.

Ryan, Jennifer. 2008. "The Virtual Campfire: An Ethnography of Online Social Networking." Accessed June 16, 2011, http://thevirtualcampfire.org.

St. John, Warren. 2006. "Rituals of Grief Go Online." *The New York Times*, April 27.

Stelter, Brian. 2007. "On Facebook: Life after Death." *The Towerlight*, June 8. Accessed April 12, 2012, http://wwww.thetowerlight.com/2007/06/on-facebook-life-after-death/.

Van Dijck, Jose. 2007. *Mediated Memories in the Digital Age (Cultural Memories in the Present)*. Stanford, CA: Stanford University Press.

Walker, Marlon A. 2006. "Net Generation Grieves with Facebook Postings." *The News & Observer*, December 14.

5

Anonymous, Anonymity, and the End(s) of Identity and Groups Online

Lessons from the "First Internet-Based Superconsciousness"

Michael Wesch and the Digital Ethnography Class of Spring 2009

Fox 11 News in Los Angeles calls the "group" Anonymous "hackers on steroids." The *Economist* calls them "Internet activists." They call themselves "the first Internet-based superconsciousness" with a meta-laugh, laughing at all attempts to describe them, including their own. They interact with one another primarily on imageboards like 4chan but spread to other web domains as needed, strategically leveraging the tools and structure of the Internet to accomplish their goals. They interact almost entirely anonymously, rarely if ever sharing any details of their offline identities. They continuously work to shed their collective identity as well, sometimes declaring themselves as harbingers of the *end* of identity and groups as we know them, while offering a critical commentary on the *ends* of identity and groups in our contemporary society and popular culture. The phenomenon of Anonymous presents a scathing critique of the postmodern cult of celebrity, individualism, and identity while presenting itself as the inverted alternative—a "group" made up entirely of unidentified and unidentifiable "members" whose presence and membership is fleeting and ephemeral.

DOI: 10.5876/9781607321705.c05

Most of those who know of Anonymous have heard about them because of their "hacktivist" activities, starting with their attacks on the Church of Scientology in 2008. Such hacktivism has ranged widely from the reckless e-debauchery of YouTube porn day, in which they disguised thousands of porn videos as children's videos, to the much more serious and important efforts they have made to support the Arab Spring by training local activists on maintaining anonymity, releasing names and e-mail addresses of governmental officials, and attacking and successfully blocking government websites.

But Anonymous has not always been a loose band of hacktivists, and many purists believe such activities are not in the true spirit of the original Anonymous, which was born on 4chan in 2003.[1] A modest no-frills imageboard, 4chan was created by Christopher Poole, a kid who was then just fifteen years old and living in New York City. For years most people only knew Poole by his 4chan name "moot" (as in, "of little or no practical value or meaning"), a name that could perhaps serve as an omen for the "Anonymous" community that would soon take root on the site. The site is now one of the largest online communities on the web, recording approximately 700,000 posts per day from about 7 million unique visitors (Poole 2010).

Although many recently launched social websites have extensive features such as profile and privacy management, multiple modes of communication, and multiple forms of media-sharing, 4chan is remarkably simple. Based on the popular Japanese site "2chan," this website has no sign-on or identity-verification process. The user is greeted with a simple submit button next to six empty field boxes: name, e-mail, subject, comment, file, and password. Anybody can post under any name, but most posters forgo the name field altogether. When the name field is not filled in, the post appears with the username field filled in as "Anonymous."

Anonymity creates the foundation for a remarkably chaotic and creative space. As noted by psychologist John Suler (2004), anonymity, invisibility, minimization of authority, and other characteristics of certain online spaces can create an "online disinhibition effect." On /b/, 4chan's random image board, anonymity shields participants from any long-lasting social shame. Although a poster on /b/ may feel a sting of shame when their post is ridiculed, they can quickly move on since it does not affect their long-term standing in the community. With no persistent identity, there is no real "standing" or hierarchy on /b/. The environment not only allows participants to push beyond social norms and the status quo, but it also actively encourages such behavior because the only way to get any reaction on the site is to post something that stands out and compels others to respond.

Beyond /b/, the people participating as Anonymous are active and highly networked across the web and highly skilled and knowledgeable about how to spread their creations across the web using multiple platforms, technologies, and hacks. Their collective actions on image boards, message boards, chat channels, and websites like Digg and YouTube are sometimes described as the "primordial ooze" from which many of the most prevalent Internet cultural icons, images, sayings, and trends (called "memes") have been born.[2] For example, one of their most successful memes started in 2005 when 4chan users started uploading pictures of cats with funny captions written in broken English. Saturdays were designated "Caturdays" and the pictures were called lolcats (Laugh-Out-Loud Cats). Lolcats proliferated throughout the web, entering e-mail boxes everywhere, inspiring several books, and eventually finding their own home on popular mainstream sites like icanhazcheezburger. com. 4Chan has also greatly contributed and sometimes originated other widespread Internet phenomena such as the grotesque image of goatse, the revival of Rick Astley's "Never Gonna Give You Up" as part of the Rickrolling prank, and many others. Encyclopedia Dramatica, the "Wikipedia" for all things related to Anonymous, jokes that Anonymous is "responsible for 85% of all quotes ever made."

RESEARCHING ANONYMOUS

My Digital Ethnography Research Team of fifteen undergraduate students at Kansas State University set out to study Anonymous in spring 2009 as part of a broader study of anonymity, both as a cultural motif (the general feeling of anonymity widely expressed in the social conditions of late modernity) and also how anonymity is used, experienced, and negotiated in social interactions (especially online social interactions). We were drawn to Anonymous for the ways in which it complicated our taken-for-granted assumptions about identity and community. The primary place where we decided to observe and participate in Anonymous was 4chan's /b/ message board, one of the primary locations for Anonymous activity online. Two members of our research team also met and recorded interviews with Anonymous participants protesting the Church of Scientology in Kansas City on multiple occasions. However, the focus of this chapter is the online activities of Anonymous, and particularly those that originated or centered on the /b/ message board.

The fieldwork for this project quickly proved to have its share of dangers. Anonymous is well-known for its disregard for social mores and its capacity to perform spectacular hacks and release awe-inspiring viruses, which are sometimes malicious, sometimes vigilante, but almost always comical for those who are in on the joke. On my own first visit to /b/, all of my windows suddenly collapsed and my computer turned off, rebooted, and warned me that my computer had become seriously infected and that I should download Windows Antivirus 2009 immediately. Upon further research I discovered that Windows Antivirus 2009 actually was the virus, and that my computer had been hijacked by "scareware," a program designed to scare me into down-loading more malicious viruses. Ultimately, I had no choice but to wipe my entire hard drive clean.

To the uninitiated, 4chan's /b/ is not just dangerous but also disturbing, thriving on its "no rules" ethos. Shock imagery and shock language proliferate, along with a heavy dose of irony and just enough self-mockery to let you know that they are not taking their lack of seriousness very seriously. It was the forum of choice for Sarah Palin's Yahoo e-mail account hacker. After hacking the account, he posted her password on 4chan. When the hack made national news, 4chan users prepared for the onslaught of news media by posting the most disturbing (to the mainstream) images they could find (mostly gay, scat, and bestiality pornography). The image at the top of the board featured a naked, hairy-chested man with an erect penis along with a note to visitors that read: "GOOD EVENING, NEWS MEDIA, AND WELCOME TO /b/! I WILL BE YOUR TOUR GUIDE. DO NOT BE ALARMED BY WHAT YOU SEE HERE."

Fear and disgust were enough to drive most of my research team away from the study of Anonymous. After a few weeks of exploratory research, only two students were willing to study Anonymous directly, with the other students focusing their studies on other aspects of anonymity.

PLAYING WITH "IDENTITY"

Many of the memes of Anonymous build from anime, gamer, program-mer, and hacker culture. Taking stock of the imagery, Chris Landers of the *Baltimore Sun* quipped, "In the high school of the Internet, /b/ is the kid with a collection of butterfly knives and a locker full of porn." The memes become part of the shared repertoire of Anonymous participants. Clever ref-erencing of these memes—along with the creative use of words and language conventions drawn from previous interactions on /b/, computer code, or the Internet-born and -based language "leetspeak"—creates a peculiar, ever-changing argot that allows a long-time user ("oldfag") to recognize the post-ing of a new user ("newfag").

Much of the argot involves shock language generated from mainstream society's ever-expanding list of politically incorrect language. They frequently use the "n-word" and all other obscenities (often involving obscure scato-logical sex acts), refer to each other as /b/tards, and call each other fags as "a term of derision/endearment, your affiliation/location suffixed with -fag" (Encyclopedia Dramatica).

The -fag suffix provides fleeting moments of identification and labeling in a social world that is otherwise devoid of identification markers. With no method of individual identity verification, /b/ becomes a community made up of nonpersistent individual identities. When you post on /b/, nobody can prejudge you based on your looks, age, wealth, status, or style. They only have your words. One could even go so far as to say that there are no identities at all, although playing with "identity" is still very much a part of the serious fun of /b/.

Everybody on /b/ is anonymous. Even those who choose to use a specific name cannot verify that they are the ones posting with that name since no name can be registered to a single user. As a result, nobody except the poster can know who authored any specific post. Users can take on the identity of another user in the middle of a conversation. People can even have long conversations with themselves, posing as multiple users in the same thread, making it appear as if there is great interest in the topic at hand even when there is not.

Most threads begin with a post that involves a funny, shocking, or interesting picture and a statement that comments on the picture, asks for similar pictures, or asks for more comments related to the picture. Because most users do not fill in the name form and names can be used again by any poster, the only unique identifiable mark for each post is an automatically generated post number. In this way, the post itself, not necessarily the person who posted it, becomes the relevant interlocutor. When a poster wants to respond to a specific post, they can write ">>(post number)," which will then link back to the relevant post.[3]

The following sequence posted on June 5, 2009, is a fairly typical example of the kind of conversation that emerges on /b/. It is also an example of a classic "trolling" attempt in which somebody posts something inflammatory, off-topic, shocking, or intentionally incorrect with the purpose of creating an argument with others. This particular trolling attempt begins with an image that reads, "Trolling is a art."

> Original Post: Trolling is a art.
>
> No. 139804092: i'm not taking the bait. no, not this time.
>
> No. 139804103: old.
>
> No. 139804140: it would be AN art anyway. gtfo [get the fuck out]
>
> No. 139804237 >>139804140: troll'd. nao, YOU gtfo

As noted earlier, since all posters are anonymous, posters refer to specific posts. In this case, post 139804237 calls out 139804140 as being trolled, having taken the bait and attempting to correct the purposefully incorrect grammar of the original post. Keep in mind, however, that posters can pose as another poster or even talk to themselves. Somebody could also pose as multiple people in the same conversation. All of which add to the fun of the art of trolling on 4chan. The next post takes the trolling bit a step further:

No. 139804330 >>139804237: double trolled

Here 139804330 is claiming that it is actually 139804237 who has been trolled, and that post 139804140 was not the trolled but the troller, setting new bait by pretending to be trolled by an obvious troll. The thread quickly (d)evolves into meta-trolling:

> No. 13980487 >>139804330: LOL TRIPLE TROLLED YOU FUCKING BUTTHURT FAGGOT
>
> No. 139804618: Everyone who posted in this thread got trolled except for me.
>
> No. 139805734: trolls trolling trolls trolling trolls ad infinitum

Trolling celebrates and re-creates the core values of /b/ while policing and rehabilitating those who transgress them. As one poster in the midst of the preceding trolling episode commented:

> No. 139804547 >>139804330: Another newfag made to look like an idiot, and trying to recover his pride. It's anon, dumbass.

Here the poster reminds the others that they are all anonymous. Where there is no identity, there is no pride to have or regain.

ANONYMOUS AS CORE MORAL VALUE

Within this playful world of anonymity, anonymity itself emerges not just as a feature of the interaction but as a core moral value. As noticed in the preceding interaction, one should not take anything, especially one's self, too seriously. To be capital-A "Anonymous" one must always be anonymous, never taking on an identity, label, or name. When this rule is breached, the poster faces an onslaught of severe ridicule.

For example, on March 21, 2010, somebody using the name "ANON STRAIGHT EDGE" (in all caps) posted the following with the subject line "WHY DO PEOPLE HATE US."

> No. 208488786: AM BULLIED EVERY DAY AT MY SCHOOL BECAUSE I CHOOSE TO BE STRAIGHT EDGE AND YOU KNOW WHAT IM SICK OF IT. I LOVE MYSELF AND I AM PROUD OF WHO I AM ANY OTHER STRAIGHT EDGERS ONLINE NOW

Instead of receiving responses from other "straight edgers," he received a barrage of hate. Playing with the anonymity of the medium, some mocked the poster by posing as the original poster (designated as OP in the /b/ vernacular), pointing out the poster's identity posturing and call for attention.

No. 208490692: OP HERE! I'M A FAGGOT WHO HAS TO TYPE IN
ALL CAPS TO GET ANY ATTENTION AT ALL! DISREGARD
EVERYTHING I'VE SAID, I SUCK COCKS!

Others took on the poster more directly after the poster (or somebody posing as the poster) asked for clarification on why they had offended the /b/ community:

No. 208493552: biggest problem with straight edge is that they call themselves straight edge, giving yourself a title always makes you a douche.

No. 208493671: Because people who call themselves "straight edge" are fucking attention whores. I know many people that dont do drugs and dont drink alcohol, but they dont call themselves "straight edge" to be cool . . .

This core value extends to other message boards in which Anons interact, such as the Chanology boards used to discuss and organize the Anonymous protests against the Church of Scientology. Here users take on pseudonyms but usually maintain the core value of anonymity. When Gabriella Coleman, an anthropologist studying the protest, was invited to the forum, she was warned by "Ann O'nymous": "[T]here are people here who do not like rockstars. As a IRL person, you are an easy target in a asymmetrical game. If you fall for their provocations, you might get hurt. Having said that, do as you please." Another clarified that a "rockstar" is simply "anyone who is not anonymous and who may be important" or someone who has been "namefagged" as another noted. Fortunately, she had strong contacts in the group who could vouch for her; one promised to "have a buttfuck cannon aimed at anyone who doesn't know how to act." "Consensus" summed it up, "Here's the long and short of it: the cardinal sin of Anonymous is Unwarranted Self-Importance."

Anonymous carries this aversion to self-importance, names, and identity to their own group identity as well, playing with and mocking concepts such as "culture," "community," and "group" that artificially bound, reify, and label. A plethora of Anonymous sayings that Chris Landers of the *Baltimore Sun* dubbed "mock-serious slogans" captures this ethos in phrases like "Anonymous is not a person, nor is it a group, movement or cause: Anonymous is . . . a commune of human thought and useless imagery."

Indeed, Anons often point out with some pride that defining themselves as Anonymous creates a logical impasse to any definition or label, for any definition or label is, by definition, not Anonymous. One of their mock-serious slogans gloats, "No one shall learn the identity of Anonymous, for in finding identity, we lose our anonymous selves." They demonstrate their pride in their collective non-identity by sharing and mocking any definitions, labels, and explanations of their existence offered by journalists, scholars, or other critics and commentators.

Their mock-serious slogans often co-opt all anonymous agents through-out time as part of Anonymous, noting that Anonymous is not a group or entity but an ongoing collective happening occurring wherever people are act-ing or interacting anonymously. "Anonymous is everywhere. Anonymous is legion. Anonymous is nowhere. Anonymous doesn't have a family or friends. Anonymous is your family and friends." As the 4chan FAQ on Anonymous explains:

> Anonymous is not a single person, but rather, represents the collective whole of 4chan. He is a god amongst men. Anonymous invented the moon, assassinated former President David Palmer, and is also harder than the hardest metal known to man: diamond. His power level is rumored to be over nine thousand. He currently resides with his auntie and uncle in a town called Bel-Air (however, he is West Philadelphia born and raised). He does not forgive.

ANONYMOUS AS CULTURAL CRITIQUE

Anonymous extends far beyond the confines of 4chan and other imageboards and messageboards, and it is here that we see this core moral value of anonymity emerging as a full-fledged critique of our cultural obsession with individualism and identity and the cult of celebrity that emerges from it. One of the mock-slogans prophetically declares: "With an identity you will eventually be found. The day will come when only Anonymous will walk the ground. We will stop at nothing until we've achieved our goal: Permanent destruction of the identification role."

Anons from /b/ often flock to other forums and online discussions to troll or arrange "raids" in which they use their swarming large numbers and technical skills to perform large scale pranks and manipulate Internet culture (what one Anon described as "ultra-coordinated motherfuckery," according to Gabriella Coleman [2010 at 0:44]).[4] For example, as celebrities like Oprah and Ashton Kutcher raced to be the first with 1 million Twitter followers, Anonymous leveraged their technical skills to create a worthy competitor known as "BasementDad" with a Twitter profile based on an Austrian man who had imprisoned his daughter in his basement for twenty-four years. Using various hacks they managed to race to over 300,000 followers before Twitter started disallowing new followers of BasementDad.

Although any Anon will tell you that their raids and mass pranks are not politically motivated but simply "for the LULZ" (for the laughs), the punch line requires a certain play with the rules, norms, mores, and the general ethos of society. The more individualistic and identity-obsessed our society becomes, the more poignant their actions and their collective anonymous way of carrying them out.

Anonymous does not just challenge the cult of identity and celebrity by raiding and trolling celebrities; they also mock celebrity culture by manufacturing celebrities out of nobodies. In 2009 they raided the online *Time's* 100 Most Influential People competition, "hacking" it so that the founder of 4chan, "moot," was voted the most influential. They even managed to rig the top twenty-one names so that the first letters of their names read "marble cake also the game" (referring to a slang term for an obscure scatological sex act). They have developed numerous techniques to hack such rating systems and have also had some success launching the most unlikely celebrities like Tay Zonday into e-celebrity on YouTube. When interviewed about the *Time* magazine hack, moot made a reference to the core value against self-importance that is so pervasive among Anons. "If I asked the community to do this, they would have done everything in their power to make sure that I was at the bottom of that list—that's just the way they work."

This general critique of identity and celebrity was clearly stated after a raid on the John Edwards's Second Life campaign site. After defacing the virtual property with feces and graffiti, the following was posted as a comment on the John Edwards blog by an anonymous user:

> As the Internet has grown in popularity, a disturbing phenomenon has occurred: Everyone thinks that they are SPECIAL. We have news for you . . . You aren't special. You aren't unique. You are a mindless horde of filth, traversing the universe on a small ball of dirt. A speck upon a speck in the vastness of existence. We are here to remind you of this. Wherever someone takes themselves too seriously, we will be there. Wherever someone has an inflated ego, we will be there. We will do it through madness. And we will remove you from the high place you have built for yourself.

In this way, Anonymous provides an insightful critical commentary on our cultural obsession with identity and the cult of celebrity, which itself emerges in reaction to the anonymity that has emerged as "a common structure of feeling" (to use the words of Raymond Williams [1973]) in the social conditions of modernity. As early as 1926, Henry Canby suggested that the desire for fame and celebrity could be explained as "a panicky, an almost hysterical, attempt to escape from the deadly anonymity of modern life, and the prime cause is not the vanity of our writers but the craving—I had almost said the terror—of the general man who feels his personality sinking lower and lower into a whirl of indistinguishable atoms to be lost in a mass civilization" (1926, 80). An Anonymous mock-serious slogan echoes the sentiment: "We are all Anonymous in some sense. The person on the bus. A customer in line. A stranger in another country."[5]

As Charles Taylor has noted, the late modern self has formed in conditions in which identity and recognition are not givens (1992). Meanwhile, our technologized consciousness begins to see identity as just another thing to be engineered (Berger, Berger, and Kellner 1973), and so we find ourselves struggling to engineer and create our own identities in the search for identity and recognition. This "search for the authentic self" creates two trends (or "slides" as Taylor calls them), one toward "self-centered modes of self-fulfillment" and another toward "the negation of all horizons of significance" (Taylor 1992, 60). The possibilities for identity proliferate at the cost of an increasingly fragmented and disconnected society that leaves its members starving for meaning and recognition.

In Thomas de Zengotita's analysis of mediated culture, we find that these two slides co-generate one another. He connects the malaise that goes along with the lack of meaning and recognition with the blossoming of YouTube celebrity and the eagerness with which people rush onto the new stages that the Internet provides to become e-famous. "Now the representational spaces have been technologically magnified," he notes. "That's the condition that allows the virtual revolution to take place . . . spectators were primed for it, motivated to undertake what the technology only made possible" (2006, 116). And so the incessant striving for celebrity takes to the Internet, and we enter the age of the e-famous and the microcelebrity.

Such an analysis is not far from the "disturbing phenomenon" noted by the Anonymous user in which "[e]veryone thinks they are SPECIAL" on the Internet. As another Anonymous mock-serious proverb notes, it would seem that the meaningful recognition that people seek and the confirmation and external validation of one's identity are exceedingly rare and perhaps a thing of the past: "Identity. One of our most precious possessions. You believe we all have one, but you are sadly mistaken. Identity belongs only to those who are important. Those who have earned it by struggle and blood. Those who matter. You, my friend, do not."

Anonymous offers the ultimate alternative to identity, asking people to give up the superficial struggle for identity and celebrity: "Identity is a fragile and weak thing. It can be stolen or replaced. Even forgotten. Identity is a pointless thing for people like us . . . So break away from your identity. Become one with Anonymous and give up the struggle for identity. Join us and belong."

In an increasingly fragmented society, Anonymous offers the ultimate group to belong to, a group that could never deny you, a group you can always fit into, a group with no demands or constraints, a group that asks (quite literally) nothing of you, and you do not even have to accomplish that impossible task of "just being yourself" since you do not know what that means anyway. It is the group to end all groups, and an identity to end all identities. "Being Anonymous protects us in some way, making us feel safe at night and keeping us sane. How, you may ask. Simple. Being Anonymous is to be part of the world, the ones like you who do not matter and do not stand out. It makes us feel like we belong."

THE END(S) OF IDENTITY

Anonymous itself captures the double meaning of the "end" of identity and groups. It declares itself as the end (conclusion) of identity and the categorically identified or identifiable group, while also providing a running commentary on the ends of identity and group formation in late modern society. Furthermore, it is itself a special example of the kind of "group" or "identity" that can emerge (and be used) in the meta-reflexive age of late/postmodernity.

This poses several problems for a discipline that Roy Wagner once described as "founded on the necessity to fix either groups or units (or both) as a beginning point to analysis" (1974, 95). Of course, Wagner was, in the 1970s, on the "Frontiers of Anthropology" (to borrow from the title of the edited volume from which this quote came), part of a broad movement to rethink the discipline's categorical approach focused on relatively static, bounded, and discrete cultures and to consider instead more dynamic approaches that recognize and theorize the processes of culture—the strategies, power dynamics, playfulness, and ongoing negotiations of social life. Wagner's next work, *The Invention of Culture* (1975), invited us to consider the implications of "culture" as an anthropological invention rather than something objectively "out there" in the world.

By the 1990s, Lila Abu-Lughod and others were "writing against culture" (the title of her 1991 essay). Akhil Gupta and Jim Ferguson proposed moving "beyond 'culture'" and "the convenient fiction that mapped cultures onto places and peoples" (1992, 8). By the end of the decade, Christoph Brumann was able to compile an extensive montage of anthropologists criticizing the concept for the ways in which culture suggests "boundedness, homogeneity, coherence, stability, and structure" (1999, S1).

Although such criticisms have not yet proven to mark the *end* of the culture concept, they have revealed many of the *ends* that the culture concept has served. Beyond simply serving as "a beginning point to analysis" by bounding the unit of analysis, it also serves to exaggerate differences and distances between "us" and "them" and to substantiate the anthropologist as the expert on "their culture." At worst, it could be argued that such boundary-making has also made anthropologists complicit in colonial, post-colonial, and even corporate projects of the simplistic categorization of cultural groups for the purpose of census-taking, control, and resource extraction and allocation. As Lila Abu-Lughod notes in response to Brumann's defense of the culture concept, anthropology might also be considered an accomplice to the use of the term in non-anthropological accounts like Samuel Huntington's "glorification of Western superiority and gross simplification and reification of cultures and cultural difference," which she fears might "resonate with popular sentiment and racist politics" (S14). As she states most strongly in "Writing against

Culture" (1991, 146), "It would be worth thinking about the implications of the high stakes anthropology has in sustaining and perpetuating a belief in the existence of cultures that are identifiable as discrete, different, and separate from our own."

Critics and supporters alike note that just as anthropology seems to be giving up on the concept, people all over the world are starting to use it as a means to their own ends. As Ulf Hannerz noted, "culture is everywhere" (1996, 30). Academics, immigrants, corporations, young people, and old people all "have it," discuss it, and imagine themselves in its terms. By 1994, Marshall Sahlins could comment that even "imperialism's erstwhile victims" were using the term, or some local equivalent, often employing it to gain power or profit or simply to regain a lost (imagined) sense of identity, community, and purpose (1994, 3). As George Marcus noted recently, "the concept of culture, while emblematic of what the discipline is interested in, is no longer viable analytically and has been appropriated everywhere and by everybody" (Marcus 2008, 3).

In such conditions, the anthropological project has likewise become less about stable, static, and bounded "cultures" and more about "the process through which such reified and naturalized representations are constructed and maintained" (Gupta and Ferguson 1992, 12). Anthropologists have increasingly turned away from essences and toward processes (to use Clifford's terminology [1988, 275]), describing how communities might be imagined (Anderson 1983), how traditions were invented (Hobsbawm and Ranger 1983), and how identities might be created, used, and negotiated (e.g., Gillis 1994).

This moves us quite far from the discipline Wagner described as "founded on the necessity to fix either groups or units (or both) as a beginning point to analysis." But it does not yet offer a viable alternative for beginning to analyze Anonymous. Although the people who collectively perform the actions that make up the phenomenon of Anonymous are embodied people in specific places, their particular form of sociality is not in any way relevant to this fact, and they are not involved in a conscious or unconscious process of "group" or "culture" creation. Quite the opposite, Anonymous is an ongoing experiment in sociality that attempts to undermine traditional notions of "groups," "culture," and "identity" altogether.

Most importantly for the discipline of anthropology, Anonymous exposes the "ends" to which we put the concepts of "group" and "identity" to work in our descriptive endeavors and challenges us to think of new ways to conceptualize human sociality. Although the Anonymous (non)social (non)organization may seem novel, on further reflection it becomes apparent that in many online contexts the metaphors of "groups" and "identity" are no longer useful for social analysis. Plenty of cultural theory has guided us away from a focus on things and categories and toward process and practice for several decades, but Anonymous leaves us no option because the "thing" itself is nothing but process. It only exists in the fleeting moment of its own activity. Name it, categorize it, and then it is gone. Theoretical trends away from essences and toward processes may not have gone far enough.

The activities of Anonymous help us see a broader and more important lacuna in current anthropological conceptions of human sociality, exposing such conceptions as primarily based in assumptions of embodied copresence. Since the early days of Internet communities, even prior to the advent of the World Wide Web, scholars have been speculating about and documenting the possibilities of identity play online (see, e.g., Rheingold 1993; Turkle 1995). The opportunities provided by anonymity and pseudonymity were captured for the public imagination by the now classic *New Yorker* cartoon "On the Internet, nobody knows you are a dog." But more recent forms of online sociality such as Facebook now make the opposite equally probable. As Zeynep Tufekci (2007) has noted, "On the Internet, everybody knows you are a dog." Facebook, MySpace, imageboards, forums, chatrooms, e-mail, and other Internet-based social platforms all create different architectures for participation. Some, such as Facebook, require persistent and mostly verifiable identities, whereas others allow for more identity play, pseudonymity, or anonymity. Some connect people around the world, and others emphasize local connections. Some are text-only, others audio-only, and some use video or a mix of all three. Some are synchronous whereas others are asynchronous. Some are open, others closed. Some are archived, providing a running history of social interactions; others are not. Every feature shapes the possibilities for sociality.

In the end, the most pertinent and active structuring principle of online sociality is not a simple list of features and characteristics but instead an open-ended range of possibilities limited only by human imagination. The Internet has become a playground for new media forms, each one connecting people in different ways and allowing new forms of sociality to emerge. In the digital realm, the structures of our participation are not inevitable or permanent. We can restructure the structures themselves. Indeed, more people than ever now have, and even more soon will have, the capability not just to add content to the web and participate in these emerging forms of sociality but also to create the structures of participation by creating their own digital platforms. Killerstartups.com reviews more than fifteen Internet startups every day, many of them proposing yet another way for humans to relate to one another. Plugins and widgets can be used as building blocks in user-designed blogs and portals, creating new forms of communication in just a few hours with little technical expertise required. Dion Hinchcliffe notes that the Web is "increasingly turning into a sort of online Home Depot with its shelves lined with thousands of useful, off-the-shelf parts of every description and utility" (2007).

As adept manipulators of the online mediascape, Anonymous participants exploit and expose the possibilities of digital sociality while attempting to challenge and subvert our most basic assumptions about sociality itself. Although many scholars have used and written about the digital space as an arena to try on and play with alternative identities and create virtual communities, Anonymous plays with and mocks the concepts of "identity," "community," and "groups," making a joke out of them and creating a dynamic and living social formation that is not based on identified or identifiable individuals in an identified or identifiable "group." In this way, their social forms and commentaries help us question our own assumptions and expand our perspectives on the limits and possibilities of sociality and social forms in digital spaces.

NOTES

1. For more on this split, see Underwood (2009, 133–161).

2. "Meme" originated in Richard Dawkins's *The Selfish Gene* (1976) to describe an idea or cultural phenomenon that spreads.

3. Sometimes the post numbers themselves become part of a game called a "GET," in which posters try to be the one who is assigned an especially significant or unique post number, such as 12345678 or 20000000. As noted on 4chan, "GETs are sought after by many, and normally over one thousand users will compete for one, often posting very quickly in order to better their chances of achieving the desired GET number." 4chan moderators recently tired of this game, especially following the flurry of posts trying to achieve the "200MGET" on February 21, 2010. Since that time, the last three digits of each post appear as XXX. A Greasemonkey script can reveal the actual numbers. Post-naming and GETs are less common since February 21, 2010, but still continue; therefore, it appears that at least some users are using the Greasemonkey script or similar tool to see actual post numbers.

4. It is in such raids that they seem to take on the most identifiable "group-like" formations, what Rogers Brubaker would call "high levels of groupness" (2002, 172). But even in these circumstances they are not really a group, and they are not a "they." As Chris Landers (2008) notes, they are only a group "in the sense that a flock of birds is a group . . . they're traveling in the same direction. At any given moment, more birds could join, leave, peel off in another direction entirely."

5. The Anonymous rage against e-celebrity and our cultural obsession with identity is not unlike that of many poets of the 1920s, who began urging their fellow writers to "not make a cult of expression" (E. M. Forster as quoted in Ferry 2002, 188). Or as stated in a twenty-nine-page pamphlet authored by Walter Lowenfels and Michael Frankel and titled *Anonymous: The Need for Anonymity*: "The Anonymous struggle to project the completed novel, or poem, becomes the struggle for a world ideal, creation; not the advancement of any one poet's standing, or recognition . . . If he is an artist, that is enough" (1930, 13).

REFERENCES

Abu-Lughod, Lila. 1991. "Writing against Culture." In *Recapturing Anthropology: Working in the Present*, ed. Richard G. Fox, 137–162. Santa Fe, NM: School of American Research Press.

Anderson, Benedict. 1983. *Imagined Communities: Reflections on the Origin and Spread of Nationalism*. New York: Verso.

Anonymous. 2009. "Anonymous." In *Encyclopedia Dramatica*. Accessed November 25, 2009. http://encyclopediadramatica.se/Anonymous.

Berger, Peter L., Brigitte Berger, and Hansfried Kellner. 1973. *The Homeless Mind: Modernization and Consciousness*. New York: Random House.

Brubaker, Roger. 2002. "Ethnicity without Groups." *Archives européennes de sociologie* 43 (2): 163–89. http://dx.doi.org/10.1017/S0003975602001066.

Brumann, Christoph. 1999. "Writing for Culture: Why a Successful Concept Should Not Be Discarded." *Current Anthropology* 40 (S1): S1–27. http://dx.doi.org/10.1086/200058.

Canby, Henry. 1926. "Anon Is Dead." *The American Mercury* (May): 79–84.

Clifford, James. 1988. *The Predicament of Culture: Twentieth-Century Ethnography, Literature, and Art*. Cambridge, MA: Harvard University Press.

Coleman, Gabriella. 2010. "Old and New Wars over Free Speech, Freedom and Secrecy or How to Understand the Lulz Battle against the CO$." Online Video. Accessed May 10, 2010, http://vimeo.com/10837847.

Dawkins, Richard. 1976. *The Selfish Gene*. New York: Oxford University Press.

De Zengotita, Thomas. 2006. *Mediated: How the Media Shapes Your World and the Way You Live in It*. New York: Bloomsbury Publishing.

Encyclopedia Dramatica. "Fag." *Encyclopedia Dramatica*. http://encyclopediadramatica.se/Fag.

Ferry, Anne. 2002. "Anonymity: The Literary History of a Word." *New Literary History* 33 (2): 193–214. http://dx.doi.org/10.1353/nlh.2002.0015.

Gillis, J. R., ed. 1994. *Commemorations: The Politics of National Identity*. Princeton, NJ: Princeton University Press.

Gupta, Akhil, and James Ferguson. 1992. "Beyond 'Culture': Space Identity and the Politics of Difference." *Cultural Anthropology* 7 (1): 6–23. http://dx.doi.org/10.1525/can.1992.7.1.02a00020.

Hannerz, Ulf. 1996. *Transnational Connections: Cultures, People, Places*. London: Routledge.

Hinchcliffe, Dion. 2007. "Tracking the DIY Phenomenon." *Zdnet blog*. February 11, 2007. Accessed May 11, 2010. http://www.zdnet.com/blog/hinchcliffe/tracking-the-diy-phenomenon-part-1-widgets-badges-and-gadgets/80.

Hobsbawm, Eric, and Terence Ranger, eds. 1983. *The Invention of Tradition*. Cambridge: Cambridge University Press.

Landers, Chris. 2008. "Serious Business: Anonymous Takes on Scientology (and Doesn't Afraid of Anything)." *Baltimore City Paper*, April 2. www2.citypaper.com/columns/story.asp?id=15543.

Lowenfels, Walter, and Michael Frankel. 1930. *Anonymous: The Need for Anonymity*. Berkeley: Carrefour Editions.

Marcus, George. 2008. "The End(s) of Ethnography: Social/Cultural Anthropology's Signature Form of Producing Knowledge in Transition." *Cultural Anthropology* 23 (1): 1–14. http://dx.doi.org/10.1111/j.1548-1360.2008.00001.x.

Poole, Christopher "moot." 2010. "The Case for Anonymity Online." Internet video. Filmed February 2010; posted June 2010. http://www.ted.com/talks/christopher_m00t_poole_the_case_for_anonymity_online.html.

Rheingold, Howard. 1993. *The Virtual Community*. Boston: Addison Wesley. http://www.rheingold.com/vc/book/.

Sahlins, Marshall. 1994. "Goodbye to Tristes Tropes: Ethnography in the Context of Modern World History." In *Assessing Cultural Anthropology*, ed. Robert Borofsky, 377–94. New York: McGraw-Hill.

Suler, John. 2004. "The Online Distribution Effect." *Cyberpsychology & Behavior* 7 (3): 321–6. http://dx.doi.org/10.1089/1094931041291295.

Taylor, Charles. 1992. *The Ethics of Authenticity*. Cambridge, MA: Harvard University Press.

Tufekci, Zeynep. 2007. "Presentation of the Self for Everyday Surveillance: On the Internet Everyone Knows You Are a Dog." Unpublished manuscript.

Turkle, Sherry. 1995. *Life on the Screen: Identity in the Age of the Internet*. New York: Simon & Schuster.

Underwood, Patrick. 2009. "New Directions in Networked Activism and Online Social Movement Mobilization: The Case of Anonymous and Project Chanology." MA Thesis, Ohio University, Athens.

Wagner, Roy. 1974. "Are There Groups in the New Guinea Highlands?" In *Frontiers of Anthropology: An Introduction to Anthropological Thinking*, ed. Murray J. Leaf, 95–122. New York: D. Van Nostrand Company.

Wagner, Roy. 1975. *The Invention of Culture*. Chicago: University of Chicago Press.

Williams, Raymond. 1973. *The Country and the City*. New York: Oxford University Press.

6

Splitting and Layering at the Interface

Mediating Indian Diasporas across Generations

Radhika Gajjala and Sue Ellen McComas

INTRODUCTION

Since early 1990s, a time that coincides with global access to the Internet in the form of the World Wide Web, there have been certain rearticulations of categories of diasporas from the South Asian region through techno-mediation. Such rearticulations are based in the naming of diasporas through the politics of a nation-state whereas others are based in the naming of diasporas through transnational linkages along the lines of struggle for a nation-state (as in the case of Tamil Eelam diasporas). In addition, these diasporas (as is the case with previous diasporas) are shaped by labor needs within various economic contexts. Digitally produced and circulated media play a significant role in such South Asian diasporas. Thus, in the case of the Indian nation-state and diasporas mediated through digital online media, "New Bollywood" invokes nostalgia for an imagined homeland for the non-resident Indian (NRI) population (Booth 2008). At the same time, a particular section of the NRI population is being encouraged to "return home" to establish transnational industry

DOI: 10.5876/9781607321705.c06

and business in India (Mallapragada 2000). Still other sections of the population are being mobilized as part of an offshore labor force that keeps their
bodies in one social context and requires their labor, services, and skills to
be projected, in a seemingly disembodied manner, into other social contexts.
The term "diaspora," in turn, has been mobilized by the Indian government
and industry to build particular types of transnational connections. In this
context, the phrase "digital diaspora" becomes a way to build networks of
transnational capital and labor.

Through these articulations and rearticulations of selves, the issue of
authentic "Indian" identity is continually negotiated in a productive tension
between enactment and representation. Individuals and communities joining
(i.e., reluctantly or voluntarily seeking membership through compliance or
resisting existing formations through explicit countering of previous articulations) such diasporic communities continue to use media and technology
in the re-creation of community and identity amid host environments that
sometimes oppress and sometimes liberate. Present-day new waves of globalization offer opportunities for, and require mobility of, labor and capital
through digital environments and produce variations of split and post-liberal
human identities. Digitally produced and circulated media play a significant
role in such diasporas. Within such an overall context, this chapter performa-
tively and descriptively engages instances of (post-)human instances/view-
points of living online, spanning three to four generations of Internet users of
Indian origin as encountered by Radhika during continuing ethnographies in
these environments.

Working from this background, we start by discussing how notions of
nostalgia and presence shift through disembodiment and reembodiment at
mediated interfaces starting with a narration of "splitting" and "multiplying"
in diaspora in pre-digital times through what we refer to as communicative
spaces of media. This splitting, layering, and multiplying are explored further through an examination of specific encounters with online/offline young
men and women who identify as being of Indian origin. Much of the shaping
of online "Indianness" happens through subconscious and affective linkages
and immersion based in how Indian-identified artifacts, practices, sound-
bites, and images travel through digital worlds such as Second Life, Facebook,
LiveJournal, blogs, YouTube video sharing, production of Machinima, and
so on. These are, in turn, actualized materially and discursively online and
offline as "Indian" or "not Indian" as larger community formations and groups
authenticate particular behaviors, signifiers, and characteristics as "Indian."
The splitting at the interface that we locate in this chapter leads to a different way of understanding how community is simultaneously imagined, lived,
and enacted as we move in and out of multiple mediated environments. This
sort of imagining of community through mediated networks linked nodally is
based in different mediated economic and social formations than that implied

by Benedict Anderson's (2006) notion of imagined community. It is this shift that produces the authentication of the posthuman diasporic Indian and allows the idea of "Indian digital diasporas" to emerge in the current socio-economic and technical moment in time and space.

COMMUNICATIVE SPACES OF DIASPORA

In this section, Radhika draws on her experience as a "nomad" in pre-digital times (offline) to illustrate what is meant by "communicative spaces of diaspora." The offline pre-digital communicative spaces of diaspora she refers to are based in the post-1960s flow of professional, mostly upper caste and upper class, Western-educated labor away from South Asia toward modernity, internationalization, and development. Post-1960s imagining of community, for instance, materialized through communicative spaces of diaspora, where "home" was a romanticized, frozen place remembered through nostalgic storying and through radio, LP records, slides, photographs, home movies, and occasionally televised and screened movies from the subcontinent.

Diasporic affect based in nostalgia for a geographical location of home fostered connections between diasporic groups that identified as originating from the South Asian subcontinent with subgroups formed along national, religious, linguistic, and sometimes even caste lines. Post-1960s migration from the South Asian subcontinent was also a response to international modernization. The United Nations (UN), and related global nongovernmental organizations, and the International Monetary Fund (IMF) came to be seen as global facilitators of development and upliftment of "underdeveloped" nations, while the United States rose to the status of superpower. It is well known that the 1965 Immigration Act was a result of US labor needs, as well as the political need for the United States to be perceived as more open than before.

In the post-1960s waves of migrations, "South Asian" group identities were more strongly forged than in previous generations as a response to the professional and social expectations of that time. In cosmopolitan international social gatherings, such as those attended by a growing number of UN officials from the subcontinent, exclusive identification along national, religious, or caste identities (as in "Pakistani," "Indian," "Hindu," "Muslim," "Brahmin," and so on) were discouraged through social cues pointing to the non-modern nature of such ways of identifying. Rather, religious and linguistic diversity was celebrated as part of world cultures. Further, this modern space was urban-centric. The rural could be romanticized when spoken of, but South Asian "third-world" rural practices in everyday living were considered unhygienic, backward, and primitive. The rural is thus automatically positioned as the opposite of modern.

The professional class and their families therefore learned to police themselves into the appropriate cosmopolitan, modern sociocultural behaviors expected of them in such public international spaces. Religious, regional, and rural daily practices, if they persisted, were contained in the private space of the home, where the woman became the keeper of culture. Uma Narayan, for instance, writes of the "dark side of epistemic privilege" and of the "double vision" generated through the code-switching necessitated by continual negotiation of multiple contexts (Narayan 1990, 265). The double vision that results from the encounters with spaces of individualization and that lead to voicing on the Internet could result in a variety of negotiations in relation to cultural oppression during the transition from one kind of community-based hierarchy to another.

Entering new spaces generally requires a process of negotiating multiple contexts through a kaleidoscope of lenses as the (re)coding of self and surroundings happens in various ways. Hierarchies constructed through the process of shifting into new cultures surface when those who have and those who do not have the sociocultural, socioeconomic, and techno capital required to produce and consume information and/or products in that space become positioned accordingly. Negotiating enactments and representations of identity can result in a splitting of the subject who is transitioning betwixt and between spaces of (un)familiarity and nostalgia. Spaces of transition, whether they occur online in digitally connected communities or offline in physically present ones, require a shifting of literacies that subsequently impacts performances and politics of identity in both online and offline spaces. In global online networks that constitute "new types of global politics and subjectivities," identities become positioned physically and virtually in the "oppositional politics" of transnational online labor (Sassen 2004, 1–2).

TRANSNATIONAL ECONOMIES AND DIASPORAS DIGITALLY MEDIATED

Identities produced within digital contexts enabled by computer software and hardware are made possible through the coproduction of sociocultural digital place and global networks involving time-space compression. These sociocultural contexts are coproduced by inhabitants who access these contexts. The sociocultural literacies of these inhabitants determine the kinds of free labor they contribute toward the building of these spaces (Terranova 2004). The continued inhabiting of these spaces leads to a reorganization of social space and everyday practice similar to that experience by call-center workers from India who are tuned in to time zones and cultural practices in the Western worlds as described by Ananda Mitra (2008) in his work on outsourced call workers. Therefore, they experience a social, affective transformation that orients them toward life in global multicultural communities similar to those encountered in a diaspora. Further, these online residents also experience displacement and disorientation similar to that produced in social encounters within diaspora.

However, this is still not the same as that encountered by traveling bodies. Thus, although the digital diasporas produced through online encounters of global environments can effectively simulate diasporic life and even actually change the everyday praxis of offline bodies, the experience is not fully that of those in a diaspora. Simultaneously, the digital spaces are also inhabited by younger generations from various diasporas the world over. Contact zones of geographically dispersed diasporas from South Asia are produced in the encounter between these differently located digital subjects. Thus, these spaces can be considered transitional places orienting digital subjects toward a particular kind of multicultural globalization. They provide the entry point for new and emerging digital forces connecting from non-global geographical areas of South Asia that are not fully rural but neither are they fully urban and global in the way scholars have described global cities.

These present generations of global workers thus live in a dynamic moment in history, with the First and Third Worlds involved in a major confrontation of cultures and the Third World and its myriad diasporas in the West engaged in an attempt to reframe their cultural identities to stave off the threat of "cultural genocide" through the effects of a rampant globalization (Rajagopal 2001). There are several entry points into online South Asian digital formations. Some of these points of entry privilege the cultural and social practices, whereas others privilege the economic routes. The several "routes" crisscross in layers. Neither the cultural nor the economic routes are mutually exclusive. The cultural entry point sometimes precedes the economic layer, and the economic quest for jobs tends to precede cultural transformations. These digital places and global networks become potential transitional places and contact zones for the formation of transnational subjects able to work within the increasing digital global economy through sociocultural processes facilitating the further intellectualization of labor (Bratich 2008; Naficy 2001).

What sorts of convergences, conjunctures, and connections emerge in relation to globalization and migrant populations the world over as we move into what is being referred to as "Web 2.0"? How are transnational, intergenerational diasporas manifested in relation to economic and cultural globalization? It can be argued that at the intersection of local and global markets, laboring locations and practices not only are impacted by international digital trade but contribute to the experiences that constitute digital diaspora. In his work concerning global economics, Venkataramana Gajjala explains that "ICTs [Information and Communication Technologies] enable hitherto untradeable services to be traded internationally, just like commodities, via the Internet and the telephone—recent outsourcing of software programming, airline revenue accounting, insurance claims and call centers to India

... have enabled not only small- and medium-sized firms but even start-ups to globalize their operations" (Gajjala 2006, 1).

The unbundling of goods and services for global dispersion through ICTs creates not only a transnational labor force but also a transitional space in which there is a sense of being betwixt and between "places" past and present in national and international domains. As a result, cultural identity narratives are enacted and represented simultaneously in the virtual and the real. And although transnational diasporas involving physical presence are affected and effected differently than those who labor in online spaces from "home," both must negotiate unfamiliar cultural codes and scripts if participating beyond a local market. This impacts the present body in material ways regardless of location. In the process of compiling novel and nostalgic narratives and weaving them anew, liminal spaces in the process situate identity as seemingly anonymous, invisible, unknowable, and exploitable. No longer are labor markets within only the local reach of possibility and power.

SOUTH ASIAN DIGITAL DIASPORAS TO INDIAN DIGITAL DIASPORAS

> Who has not known, at this moment, the surge of an overwhelming nostalgia for lost origins, for "times past"? And yet, this "return to the beginning" is like the imaginary in Lacan—it can neither be fulfilled nor requited, and hence is the beginning of the symbolic, of representation, the infinitely renewable source of desire, memory, myth, search, discovery—in short, the reservoir of our cinematic narratives. (Hall 1993, 236)

Stuart Hall notes how nostalgia and affect form the foundation for how we build narratives of identity and belonging, which he calls "cinematic narratives." At online/offline intersections, we continually build "reservoirs" of mediated narrative and communicative spaces of diaspora. There are specific circumstances that compel us to mobilize the term "digital diaspora"—globalized markets, as well as the interactive nature of online technologies, notwithstanding—and these are not reasons enough to refer to digital travelers as digitally diasporic. We need to take into account the layered and nuanced ways in which such diasporic subjectivities are produced if we are to understand how the global/local continuum plays out in specific situations in present-day cultures and economies.

It can be argued that in the digital time-space continuum and our ability to record practices that leave behind histories and actual archives there is something unique because we can study the use of these technologies, thereby making it possible to view the resulting texts as diasporic in and of themselves. It can also be argued that in the formation of online representations (whether texts, moving images, static images, or three-dimensional representations) there is a certain situatedness. There is a sense of "landing" somewhere. There is a simultaneous affective reproduction of travel as well as a disorientation through encounters with other cultures that simulates culture shock. Thus, it can be argued that the quality of digital existence contributes to the use of the phrases "digital diaspora" and "virtual community."

The term "digital diaspora," however, is easily used to talk about how diasporic populations throughout the world use the Internet to connect to each other. Digital media used for digital diaspora formations are interactive and networked, potentially allowing people from all over the world to feel located in one "place" where people with similar interests and similar missions can gather in common space. Thus, online networks formed through digitally mediated communicative media—whether accessed via desktop computers, Xboxes, or iPhones—permit the local to exist within the global and vice versa. When print media became mass media, it allowed the imagining of common place through what Anderson (2006) called the convergence of capitalism, and print technology on the fatal diversity of human language created the possibility of a new form of imagined community, which in its basic morphology set the stage for the modern nation. Thus, print media's accessibility— actually or potentially—to "the masses" went hand in hand with the growth of modern capitalism and internationalism as modern nations emerged.

Interactive online technologies go hand in hand with transnationalism based on global flows of capital and labor. The interactivity of the online technologies in current forms—as they are made available to "the masses"—is a logical extension for digital finance. The architects of digital capitalism have pursued one major objective: to develop an economy-wide network that can support an ever-growing range of intracorporate and intercorporate business processes. Anderson's (2006) work has formed the basis of many arguments about digital diasporas and virtual communities, but few of the works that celebrate imagined community online make a clear political economy connection. Interactive digital and wireless technologies go hand in hand with transnationalism based on global flows of capital and labor. The interactivity of the online technologies in current forms—as it is made possible through "the World Wide Web"—is the logical extension for digital finance. In Dan Schiller's words:

> The architects of digital capitalism have pursued one major objective: to develop an economy-wide network that can support an ever-growing range of intra-corporate and inter-corporate business processes. This objective encompasses everything from production scheduling and product engineering to accounting, advertising, banking, and training. Only a network capable of flinging signals—including voices, images, videos, and data—to the far ends of the earth would be adequate to sustain this open-ended migration into electronic commerce. (Schiller 2000, 1)

The unique features and processes involving intra and inter exchanges, through multiple media that parallel with transnational business networks, are the backdrop against which digital diasporas form.

So we see very specific circumstances that allow a political-economic moment for mobilizing the notion of digital diaspora—which I must reiterate is *not* the same as "diaspora." Globalized markets as well as the interactive nature of online technologies are unique features allowing this to happen. In such a context, we also need to take into account the layered and nuanced ways in which such diasporic subjectivities are produced if we are to understand how the global/local continuum plays out in specific situations in present-day cultures and economies. Although the physical material conditions of the digital user, consumer, or producer may not drastically change, it can be argued that there is something unique in the digital time-space continuum and in the ability to record practices that leave behind histories and actual archives. The resulting texts can themselves be viewed as diasporic agents/ actors. It can also be argued that the formation of online representations includes a certain situatedness. There is a sense of landing some*place.* There is a simultaneous affective reproduction of travel from place to place. There is also a sense of disorientation and displacement through encounters and placement in relation to other cultures that simulates culture shock. Thus, it can be argued that the quality of digital existence contributes to the use of the phrases "digital diaspora" and "virtual community."

However, to understand how globalization and technology play out in transnational economies, we must take the argument further. We must attempt to understand the power hierarchies that permit the articulation of these online existences as digitally diasporic if we are to understand global and local placements and interlinked online/offline hierarchies.

POSTHUMAN ENACTMENT AND RE-PRESENTATION IN ONLINE NETWORKS

> Enactments and the realities that they produce do not automatically stay in place. Instead they are made, and remade. This means that they can, at least in principle, be remade in other ways.
>
> JOHN LAW (2004, 143)

It is the tension between enactment and representation that produces the online (post-)human subject that leads to a spacio-temporal layering, slicing, splitting, and realigning of social, economic, cultural, and technical literacies that creates the impression of disembodiedness and placelessness. In actuality the body is being replaced, disembedded, and re-embedded in social and economic hierarchies suited to emerging digital capitalist organizations of labor and society through processes of experimentalism and creative destruction

Radhika Gajjala
Networks keep us away from each other as we work alone towards similar goals.... So that we cant physically be digging at the same path. But we all share a feel-good virtuality that makes us seem connected. What do I *really*know what is happening there ? Just what I think I saw you stat(us)

33 minutes ago via Mobile Web · 🖼 Like · Comment

Radhika Gajjala And what assumptions of continuity might you be building of me as you produce your own idea of what my story is from the snapshots of memories, presences, connections, a stated words... Offline or online... Kith or kin.... Friend o...r acquaint...ance... Relative or colleague....STOP.

For I am not that.

Nethi nethi na ithi
2 seconds ago · Like

Write a comment...

FIGURE 6.1

that characterize the neoliberal technocapitalist ethos embedded in present-day logics of globalization. It is in this technocapitalist-embedded environment that previous conceptions of humans as autonomous are challenged.

As bodies and digital identities converge in cyberspace and become re-embedded in the hierarchies of global capitalist economies, new platforms emerge for reconceptualizing the human as posthuman, no longer the exclusive entity responsible for processing and expressing information (Hayles 1999). Disseminating information, services, and goods internationally through interconnecting digital machines also links bodies, place, and temporal zones in ways that blur local/global cultural boundaries. Through this transitional space, multiple frames from which to view the interaction between humans and machines materialize at the intersection of online and offline culture and commerce. The cybernetic dynamic that exists between (post-)humans and machines works not to erase humanity but rather to decenter past perceptions that have placed humans as autonomous beings free to enact and exert agency and choice at will (Hayles 1999).

In cyber-nets, where cognitive systems are redistributed to include machine and human flesh, an actor's identity and sense of self is formed in simultaneous feedback loops of re-enactment and re-presentation. The term "posthuman," then, represents that shifting environment in which processes of becoming "human" occur at a time when "humans, animals and intelligent machines are more tightly bound together than ever in their cultural, social, biological and technological evolutions" (Hayles 2006, 159–166). What does this reevaluation of human in a post form mean for identity? If "post" means that we function as information systems, interconnected through digital channels and converging cultures, then "post" appears to represent identities in an ongoing state of flux and a constant process of renegotiating transitional spaces for a sense of physical presence.

The process of authentication of "Indianness" in online settings performs a Turing-test-type function as it forms the basis of inclusion and exclusion within online worlds and networks. This test is especially and clearly apparent in settings where the interactions are purely text-based (as in the pre-image-sharing world of online communication of the 1980s and early 1990s) or where the offline body of the user is clearly masked through the use of online avatars, as in the case of computer games and virtual worlds such as Second Life, where it is not customary for users to reveal their offline reality. Social formations in these spaces reproduce notions of "Indian" through online diasporic networks and are routed through renewed identifications and re-memberings as they actively, even intentionally, contribute to processes of transnationalization of labor and business through re-coded online and offline subjectivities. Verification of specific acknowledged "Indian" cultural literacies are often used in authentication rituals. Thus, byte-sized enactments, representations, and authentications of Indianness travel and flow through digital circuits, circulating and remixing into formations that articulate global identities.

AVATAR/PROFILE/ICON AS (PERFORMATIVE) TECHNOLOGY

On Second Life, the avatars and their profiles become identifiers of particular traveling cultural practices that are simultaneously situated within specific geographical locales as well as within global virtual-real markets. Thus, we view the crafting of avatar selves as situated practice—at radically varying contextual disjunctural and conjunctural online-offline intersections. The avatar is a technological artifact as is the apparel designed for it. Without the avatar, the sari on Second Life cannot exist. However, an avatar also exerts agency. The avatar forms an identity and takes on roles in the communities that it participates in. Without value in Linden dollars or in terms of contributing social and cultural meanings within at least some Second Life communities, the avatar identity will cease to exist.

How are identities expressed and agencies exerted in Second Life communities where sociocultural traditions and digital technologies overlap at the interface? Participating in online communities sometimes requires (re) situating literacies that gain acceptance and inclusion in unfamiliar cultural traditions. Performing identities through digitally created avatars also creates an ambiguous state in which the body at the computer keyboard is invisible and, hence, uncategorizable. In Second Life, an actor's agency depends greatly on technical skill and cultural capital, a situation not altogether different from factors that influence exerting agency offline. Production and consumption of and within online networked communities, of course, are not dependent on physical presence, geographic locations, or time constraints associated with offline environments. When interacting in online spaces, the physical body is neither disembodied nor disembedded from the affective presence at the interface of human and machine. Indeed, a sense of belonging online is derived from identifying with places and groups that "feel" accepting, comfortable, homey, and, at times, familial and nostalgic. But personal affinities for particular people and places associated with past experiences are not the only factors that affect where and how bodies are positioned and identities are performed.

NOSTALGIA REPRODUCED: AUTHENTICATING INDIANNESS

Writings about postcolonial diasporas and imagined community have been filled with discussions of nostalgic connections to the homeland. The notion that a simple linking of nostalgia for a past homeland locates the logic of diasporic emotional yearnings is problematic and nothing new to postcolonial, feminist, and other critical theories of diaspora and transnational travel. For instance, Jigna Desai (2003) has pointed out that formulations about diasporas that see nostalgia as the diasporic emotion that yearns for a past (manifested as a "homeland") ignore the economic and political power relations and implications of diasporas. Further, it is clear from past work on South Asian diasporic identities that the politics of transnational mobility in any moment in history requires us to rescribe our identity in relation to the current political moment in racial politics. Thus, Avtar Brah (1996) notes that the referent "home" in two different questions (posed to her during an interview for a US education scholarship by an all-male US panel of interviewers) had two different meanings. One question invokes "home" in the form of a simultaneously floating and rooted signifier. "It is an invocation of narratives of *the* nation. In racialized or nationalist discourses this signifier can become the basis of claims . . . that a group settled 'in' a place is not necessarily 'of' it." The other question asked of her, she wrote, implied

> an image of "home" as a site of everyday lived experience. It is a discourse of locality, the place where feelings are rooted ensue from the mundane and the unexpected of daily practice. Home here connotes our networks of family, kin, friends, colleagues and various other "significant others." It signifies the social and psychic geography of space that is experienced in terms of a neighborhood or a hometown. That is, a community "imagined" in most part through daily encounter. This "home" is a place with which

we remain intimate even in moments of alienation from it. It is a sense of "feeling at home." (Brah 1996, 215)

In recent decades there has been a shift in how transnational business and media networks play out that highlights for us the fact that diasporas are not (and actually have never been) pulled together merely by a nostalgic pull back to one single "homeland." The articulations of a nostalgia for such a "return" to a homeland miss the productive and re-membering nature of how nostalgia and the politics of affect play into emerging futures of diasporas. Here we intentionally spell it as "*re*-membering." By doing so, we highlight the psychic acts of remembrance through individual and group memory as well as the social relations produced through the assertion of commonality in specific ways to increase the membership of such groups. This implies then that the re-membering of such diasporic communities happens through choice, selection, and recruitment, signaling active inclusions and exclusions in social relations based on the politics of what counts as correct emotion and nostalgia. Particularly, we focus on the emerging futures of diasporas that travel transnationally, carrying packaged and byte-sized "homes" as they re-articulate their sense of self and place themselves—and are in turn placed by others—as South Asians or Indians in diaspora. Avtar Brah asks, "What is the relationship between *affect, psychic modalities, social relations,* and *politics?*" (Brah 1996, 245; original emphasis). In this essay we signal toward such relationships in Indian digital diasporas.

In an interrogation of the Indian films in English that came out in late 1990s, such as *Hyderabad Blues*[1] and *Bombay Boys*[2], Jigna Desai has argued that the notion that "diasporas are 'hailed by' the narratives of the homeland nation-state that activate sentiments of nostalgia and belonging" is limiting (Desai 2003, 1). Pointing to the strong impact that South Asian diasporic populations have had on South Asian nation-states, she writes that "focusing only on the homeland nation as origin of culture, tradition, and values and the state as authority and granter of citizenship can overshadow an examination of the economic and political power in relations between diasporic communities and nation-states" (Desai 2003, 1). In her unpacking of how diaspora and the nation-state function dialectically to produce a transnational South Asian politics, she does not discount the use and function of emotion and affect in diasporic yearnings for return but instead suggests that the relationship between diasporic populations, the nation-state, and the articulation of "nostalgia" for a homeland is shaped through the politics of transnational capital and labor flows. Thus, she notes "that while diasporas hail the homeland through nostalgia and return, they do so when convenient. The homeland nation's heralding of diaspora has little to do with the everyday lives and interests of the non-elite classes who are clearly critical of and ambivalent in regard to diaspora" (Desai 2003, 11).

Thus, although we cannot totally discount the role that nostalgia plays in how the home nation can mobilize, shape, and invoke the involvement of those in diaspora, we need to observe how the mutual influence functions through production and reproduction of tradition and culture in various contexts and how nostalgia then comes into play in these reproductions. As shown in previous literature on South Asian diasporas online, the "hailing" based in specific selective kinds of caste-based and religion-based nostalgias did produce certain kinds of community that exerted specific types of political influence in the "homeland."[3]

Indian-identified offline bodies are building online socially networked Indian diasporas through such a placement of affect and through communicative labor. Technologically mediated diasporas occur at online/offline intersections. Community formations that emerge through their wired and networked portable digital devices help counter the sense of isolation and alienation faced by today's youth as they continually uproot and replace locations in their mobile work and play lifestyles. In such mobile portable communities, affective links, manifested sometimes as "nostalgia," are produced through re-membered pasts that are articulated through a placement of affect.

Divya Tolia-Kelly (2004, 314) writes about "locating processes of identity" through an examination of how everyday artifacts and individual objects relate to individual biographies but are simultaneously significant in stories of identity on national scales of citizenship and the intimate domestic scene left behind. The new site of home becomes the site of historical identification, and the materials of the domestic sphere are the points of signified enfranchisement with landscapes of belonging, tradition, and self-identity. Such enfranchisement is produced through a reconfiguring of memory and affect in processes of placing and locating people geographically, socially, and culturally through specific practices of authentication based in mediascapes and ethnoscapes that are crafted through seemingly scattered and gathered media in online and mobile transnational environments.

Particular South Asian cultural commonalities have also emerged through mass media and communication technologies since early 1960s in communicative spaces of diaspora. The recognition of these culturally representative images, texts, and sounds serve as remediations of an imagined community. Rituals of authentication emerge through expectations of recognition of these commonalities present in reproduced and remixed digitally mediated images, texts, and sounds within spaces of globalization. The reproduction and remixing occurs through a post-1990s "Bollywoodization" of South Asian–centric digital environments (Rajadhyaksha 2003, 25–39). These cultural formations are increasingly "Indianized" in a continuing synergy with satellite TV (the South Asian package), where themes such as *Yeh Mera India* ("This is My India") are reiterated through a continuum commercialization, Bollywood films, music, TV serials, and Global TV–format-based productions such as Indian Idol, as well as advertisements for New York Life Insurance and so on (Punathambekar 2005, 151–175). Communities of online and offline bodies form around digitally mediated communicative practices often centered around the sharing of Bollywoodized media. They thus build pockets and enclaves of networked affect. The emergence of these seemingly disconnected yet representative cultural symbols in these spaces function to re-articulate emotional histories through replacement of affect in transitional place. Thus, these online networks transform from contact zones, where people from diverse backgrounds encounter each other, to transitional zones, where people build virtual commonalities and practices as they place themselves and enhance their skills in global work and play environments.

In the recent past, transnational traveling and diasporic South Asians have placed and transmitted affect audio-visually and sensually through radio, cinema, television, cassettes, video, and letters (and continue to do so). These traveling signifiers combine with physical objects—such as artifacts for living rooms, spices for "authentic" home food, fabric, and incense—carried along in suitcases and scattered memories to allow the South Asian diasporic to feel "at home" in various nooks and crannies of the globe. In the digital web 2.0 age, this packaging has come online in the form of hybrid "desi" popular cultures that leave behind spatiotemporally layered stains and traces of material artifacts in digital space. These are virtual objects that have been placed there by South Asians and those linked to South Asian culture and experience in some form. Such artifacts acquire multiple meanings through symbols and associations journeying through various networks. Thus, the use of remixed Bollywood tunes and digitally ethnic avatars mark South Asian digital diasporic place in virtual worlds such as, for instance, Second Life and Sims 2. Facebook and iPhone "apps" (applications) also code nostalgia and affect through circulating image and sound. Zynga, the makers of Farmville, reputedly the most widely played Facebook game in 2009, was compelled by Facebook-based "activism" (e.g., the campaigning of Indian-identified Farmville players through a Facebook group) to include the Indian flag as one the artifacts/objects to use in building one's farm, and they also recently launched visual artifacts such as auto-rickshaws, monkeys, and elephants to signal the opening of a branch of Zynga in India.

Identities produced within digital contexts enabled by computer software and hardware are made possible through the coproduction of sociocultural digital place and global networks involving time-space compression. These sociocultural contexts are coproduced by inhabitants who access these contexts. The sociocultural literacies of these inhabitants determine the kinds of free labor they contribute toward the building of these spaces (Terranova 2000, 33–58). The continued inhabiting of these spaces leads to a reorganization of social space and everyday practice similar to that experience by call-center workers from India who are oriented to time zones and cultural

Radhika Gajjala
then which is the enactment and which the representation?

Radhika Gajjala
working on producing an "authentic" offline maami self for presentation...

FIGURE 6.2

practices in the Western worlds as described by Ananda Mitra (2008) in his work on outsourced call-center workers. Therefore, they experience a social, affective transformation that orients them toward life in global multicultural communities similar to those encountered by those in diaspora. But it must be noted that this social, affective transformation in and of itself does not automatically transform these sorts of digitally mobile travelers into members of the "diaspora." The use of the term "digital diaspora" is not meant to imply that these people are part of the South Asian / Indian diaspora. The problematic and tricky nature of this usage itself signals the split of identity, performativity, and enactment in global environments of labor and leisure in today's world.

The term "digital diaspora" is easily used to talk about how diasporic populations the world over use the Internet to connect to each other. Scholars such as Anna Everett and Jennifer Brinkerhoff (2009) have used the phrase in relation to specific situated histories of forced migrations (e.g., African American histories of slavery) and transnational travel, respectively. However, the link to labor flows and hierarchies of colonialisms and digital globalization is not always clear in the way this term is mobilized in general usage. In most general usage of the phrase "digital diaspora," it is used to describe migrant populations without attention to the specific conditions of subjectivity that produce diasporas. Further, international NGOs (specifically, the United Nations) and transnational corporations as well as national businesses have mobilized the notion of digital diaspora in "reverse brain-drain" efforts where successful transnationals and migrants with money to invest actually get to return home (Gajjala, Rybas, and Altman 2008).[4]

The global/local binary that is used in conjunction with such uses of the notion of digital diaspora positions specific placed "locals" outside of a repeatedly unnamed global. However, as cultural geographers have pointed out, the separation of global and local into mutually discrete concepts is problematic. In this articulation and coupling of digital diaspora and global/local, it appears as though digital diasporas are what make us global, whereas the local is somewhere out there in "subaltern" space. This sort of articulation is not only "a denial of a fundamental ontological fact of our time: namely, that the global is in the local," but it also ignores the fact that the global is made up of multiple locals (Castree 2004, 135).

So what is at stake in conceptualizing the users of online communication tools from various offline locations as "digital diasporas"? Various scholars have examined how terms such as "diaspora," "postcolonial," and "multiculturalism" tend to get deployed academically at a time when free-market ideologies need nations to open up to transnational flows of capital, consumer goods, and labor.

BOLLYWOODIZATION OF SOUTH ASIAN DIGITAL DIASPORAS

In mapping affective South Asian / Indian social networks online that emerge from the placement of affect as (im)material artifacts are produced in digital space, we suggest that memory, nostalgia, and affect simultaneously work to place and locate South Asian / Indian identifiers online. In doing so, we focus mainly on the circulation and proliferation of "Bollywood" media (whether as clips of music, video, image icons, or Second Life and Sims avatars), as well as on specific symbols and artifacts such as the sari. Many of these signifiers work in sync with a post-1990s opening of the Indian markets to transnational labor and trade as they reconfigure and "remix" older images and sounds for the techno-mediated "desi" global workforces that increasingly live in "digital diaspora" spaces and global-local offline hubs such as dance clubs and coffee houses as well as multinational corporate environments as they work and play. Thus, these groups of young men and women live in remixed and cross-routed communicative spaces of diaspora living partially in nostalgias from previous generations as they carve out futures containing a medley of sound-bites, icons, and visual loops that produce meaning and community identifications in nodal points and momentary (re)placements of skilling, re-skilling, and laboring.

The role of Bollywood-based music in these online and offline settings provides a link through the scattered visual signifiers as bodies and avatars sway in motion to sound clips coded digitally through online portals, offline loudspeakers, or iPods and smartphones. Nilanjana Bhattacharjya (2009) notes the shift in how Bollywood films are now funded since the economic liberalization of the Indian economy in the 1990s. She describes how the Indian government's increased encouragement of privatization and international investment led to the Indian film industry increasingly being funded through contributions by non-resident Indian investors. This, in turn, led to a shift in the orientation of the films produced. More and more films were produced for the South Asian diasporic audiences. Ashish Rajadhyaksha (2003) refers to this process as the "Bollywoodization" of Indian cinema. On the other hand, Gregory Booth (2008) refers to this period as "New Bollywood" and notes the shift in the production technologies and processes for film and music in the Indian film industry shifted to privilege digital formats: "When younger, more technically sophisticated filmmakers and technicians finally introduced digital sound and filmmaking techniques and computers became widely available, a new era began that I call 'New Bollywood'" (Booth 2008, 85). It is this transition in Indian Film—whether we call it a "Bollywoodization" or a transition to the "New Bollywood"—that allows the byte-sized packaging of images and sounds from the Indian film industry into South Asian digital diasporic spaces.

DESI YOUTH HANGING OUT IN DIGITAL DIASPORA

There are several transnational venues in the digital diaspora that are inhabited by iPod-carrying, smartphone using young men and women with their casual dress code and urban manners. Some of these spaces are less US-centric than the previous Internet-based South Asian generations. Social network systems and blogs (masked in semi-anonymity) blur notions of transnational sexuality as they hide behind Bollywood, Manga, and other pop icons and game-based avatars. There is a continuing play on gender and identity as the Bollywood icons produced in such communities are subjected to a gaze that blurs the boundary between heteronormative idolization of Bollywood stars and queer pleasure, also producing uncertainty about geographic location as they appear to multitask between work, fun, and offline/online formations of friends.

For this generation, being online is no more unusual than being on the phone, and individuals incessantly text message, tweet, and "FB" every mundane moment and download and exchange ringtones, pix, and flix. This group of young South Asians/Indians in digital diaspora are multiply literate and socioculturally flexible and mobile as they "hang out" in online communities of open-source developers, fan groups, and so on. This Indian digital diaspora is producing new layers of hierarchies and skills. Even as some of these youngsters seem just to be "hanging out" they are re-skilling themselves quite desperately in an attempt to outsmart the job market. At the same time, some other youngsters from more materially privileged backgrounds are indeed "hanging out" for leisure. The everyday practices of mobile generations in digital diasporas involve and invoke new and different kinds of problem-solving spaces from those inhabited by the materially underprivileged of the world.

In her article on "Henna and Hip Hop," Sunaina Maira writes:

> The youth subculture created by South Asian American youth in New York City is based on remix music that was first created by British-born Asian youth in the 1980s and that layers the beats of bhangra . . . It mixes a particular reconstruction of South Asian music with American youth popular culture, allowing ideologies of cultural nostalgia to be expressed through the rituals of clubbing and dance music . . . This remix subculture includes participants whose families originate from other countries of the sub-continent, such as Bangladesh and Pakistan, yet these events are often coded by insiders as the "Indian party scene" or "desi scene," where the word "desi" signifies a pan–South Asian rubric that is increasingly emphasized in the second generation, and which literally means "of South Asia," especially in the context of the diaspora. (Maira 2000, 240)

DESIS ON SECOND LIFE: DEEP HANGING OUT WITH RADHIKA

On Second Life are several dance clubs, where young men and women of South Asian descent and their non–South Asian friends "hang out." At least, so it appears to the Second Life avatars who visit these clubs. Here Radhika's descriptions and observations are based mostly on her experiences during the years 2007, 2008, and 2009.

I must make clear that my understanding of these encounters comes from a "deep hanging out" in various dancing clubs on Second Life to understand some apparently socio-technically scripted codes for behavior in such environments. Thus, I have visited dancing clubs that self-describe as Hispanic, Middle Eastern, Reggae, Jazz, "desi," Bollywood focused, and so on.

I describe these environments based on specific visits that I made to a few Indian- and South Asian–themed dance clubs. In Second Life, no "place" stays static for long. Groups and individuals are continually rebuilding and relocating; therefore, the dance club experiences I discuss here can only be located in my affective experience and memory of the events and on snapshots and various YouTube videos taken by Second Life residents as they visit these clubs. (See the website http://www.youtube.com/watch?v=y2w2p3v7WSE& feature=related to see how this scene looks.) However, merely viewing the video does not give us a sense of how it actually feels when immersed in the environment. Thus, my own readings of performative cues are what I rely on as I describe these clusters of activities.

All these dancing clubs have basic scripted objects—a dancing ball or a floor with dance scripts—to animate the avatars.[5] They all have streaming media set up where the songs are streamed from a server (such as SHOUTcast or something else) onto the Second Life location. Most of them have tip balls or some form of money-collecting object and some also have exploding objects that are scripted to allow visitors to enter into a competition to win the jackpot by making a money contributions. Some clubs have themed dances and competitions for dancers to enter (this is also done through scripted objects), and fellow dancers can vote for the "best dressed female in pink" or another theme decided by the club owners.

In dance clubs focused on Indian interests, there is often a stock set of Bollywood remix music (and sometimes even video) streaming in. The Second Life avatars in these clubs are dressed in a variety of clothes but more and more of them (since 2007) are dressing in ethnic garb mostly modeled on Bollywood characters' dresses.

In the dancing clubs with Bollywood music, Indianness is established mainly through familiarity with the music played and a basic minimum knowledge of Hindi, which is demonstrated in conversation among avatars in the club as they dance. "Where are you from?" is a question often asked of newcomers in an attempt to connect to a South Asian origin story. Bollywood is invoked as representative of India in such mediated environments but also serves as an apolitical and safe common language.

IS SHE "MORE" REAL BECAUSE I "KNOW" HER ON ORKUT?

In 2007, I met a young lady (or so the avatar said she was) who told me she was on Second Life because she had heard of the available jobs there after seeing an advertisement in a regional vernacular newspaper in India. She started to type to me in a roman-script version of my mother tongue, saying she felt more "at home" on Second Life now that she had found someone who understood the same vernacular Indian language as the one she spoke everyday offline. When she told me where she was logging on, I was more than mildly surprised. The region was not remote or rural, but it was not one of the high-tech cities like Bangalore and Hyderabad or the more elite cosmopolitan cities like Mumbai, Delhi, Kolkatta, and Chennai. She had found a job on Second Life that would pay her the equivalent of about a dollar a week. She said that she was annoyed at all the male-type avatars that kept asking her for sex, which she considered silly and ridiculous. She wanted to learn all there was to learn about scripting and building in Second Life, and along the way she was making some interesting friends. She has visited many India-centric places and confessed to feeling uncomfortable in the dance clubs. She did not clearly say why. Certainly—if we are to believe the avatar's story—this person behind the avatar was clearly in diasporic space through Second Life and not because she has physically traveled outside her home region. She was encountering versions of "America," "China," "the Netherlands," and even "Australia" as she interviewed for jobs.

Some of these interviews were done through the voice feature on Second Life. The accents of the people behind the avatars came through to her, and that was her way of identifying where they were from, based on her knowledge of the geographic location of the accent (gleaned from exposure to other media such as television and film). Do I believe the story about this young lady I met on Second Life? And what are the truths I believe about her and why? Does the fact that she linked to my profile on orkut, where she has several friends from the region she claims to hail from and they all seem to think she is a young woman mean that she is real? What is "real" in this instance?

My experience and her experience are certainly real. That I chatted with someone who understands my mother tongue is real. That there was an advertisement in the regional paper the avatar mentioned is real. (I found a copy of the newspaper on the Internet, so it must be real.) The fact that she is working for Linden dollars in Second Life, building a shop, and designing saris and jewelry is real. So why should her stories about her offline life not be real? But that does not matter to the present articles and our understanding of digital diasporas in this framework. That the avatar has certain specialized knowledge of a specific geographic context and has language skills specific to a region attest to a certain kind of authenticity. S/he is a real Indian. Does it matter if she may be a he or that she may be someone who has recently traveled physically away from the region she claims to be from? Not for the understanding of digital diasporas within my framework for writing. But certainly it is of great importance that she is authentic in terms of Indian origin and that she is looking to make Linden-dollar money on Second Life. And it is also important and relevant that she has told me that Second Life is being advertised in various media in India, because this information can be verified.

What these truths about this Indian woman's presence on Second Life point to is the economic pull of Second Life for young IT people living in India. This makes sense in relation to all the talk about crowdsourcing and outsourcing via Second Life. Businesses such as Wipro and IBM India have moved into Second Life to recruit and train. A visit to these areas reveals that they are fairly deserted at the moment, but the fact that these big companies have announced their presence on Second Life draws more young job-seeking Indians and other Asians into Second Life, thus changing the cultural, visual, and interactive climate within this three-dimensional reality.

As digital diasporas from these regions increase in size, the demographics and practices in Second Life will shift. Identifying, and identifying with, particular cultures or locations can be tricky in online spaces where anonymity is desired and identity deplored. For example, claiming an "authentic" identity online runs contrary to collective non-identities sought by the online hacker group Anonymous. Michael Wesch, in his contribution to this collection, explores how this seemingly faceless group conceptualizes identity as a "superficial struggle" that inevitably brings rejection, constraints, and exclusion from others based on set standards of naming oneself (in)correctly. Rather than viewing the self through nostalgic identity narratives, Anonymous offers freedom through a lack of identity, an uncertainty and ambiguity that opposes individualism and socially normed categories. Unlike other online communities where participants are perhaps curious and/or concerned with "true" identity, Anonymous abhors labels or markers that construct social hierarchies. The idea of obliterating identities in exchange for absolute anonymity reflects the multiple alternative choices for (non)identity play in online spaces. By recognizing the fluidity of identity and rejecting the notion of a fixed identity, we come to realize that "it is only through address that the body is brought into existence"; therefore, by refusing to address oneself as this or that, we are creating a "body impossible to interpellate" (Sunden 2003, 164) and thus impossible to appropriate. Reconceptualizing identity as an ongoing process that defies fixed categories and destabilizes traditional ways of identifying self and others provides an opportunity to explore various ways of becoming (in)visible in a variety of socially networked spaces. This is evidenced in Second Life, where people make visual contact with a representative avatar at the intersection of "real" and "virtual."

In the online virtual world of Second Life, one of the ways in which participants attempt to identify themselves is in regard to location, yet their online presence indicates that they are "here" and "there," simultaneously blurring "virtual" and "real" spaces. With the advent of audio capabilities, dialects are indicators of identity, but if a participant knows how to "speak" a particular vernacular, we still don't *really* know, do we? Unlike Facebook, Twitter, and e-mail, which require identities to be "verified," virtual worlds such as Second Life encourage playful exploration of identities by performing "self" through the participant's representative avatar. Identifying someone's status in this online space is generally evidenced as they negotiate new ways of performing through a digital device with particular codes required to navigate as well as interact socially through text and voice. Those more familiar with/in Second Life are recognizable by their more "polished" performances in regard to mobility and avatar appearances.

INTERLUDE

Radhika (age 50):

In the mid-1980s, when small businesses that previously offered typewriter tutorials began to provide computer training, I was compelled to sign up. As a housewife, freelance writer/amateur poet, and mother of a toddler who was fascinated with his mother's typewriting, I sought to improve myself by going to computer tutorials. I learned early programs such as Word, BASIC, COBOL, and a smattering of Fortran. I have read books about artificial intelligence and "Eliza" (http://www.knowledgerush.com/kr/encyclopedia/ELIZA/) and hoped to have the computer spit out poetry for me as well. As I learned more about computers, the punch cards that I had often stumbled across in my brother's strewed belongings when he came home for vacation from his IIT campus began acquiring historical significance to me. Later these punch cards acquired even more significance as I realized their similarity to the cards on the Jacquard loom as I began examining offline and online technologies in global/local contexts. Little did I know that in my search for magic and in my laziness, I was to stumble upon complex, nuanced intersections of science, technology, text, image, subjectivity, and gendered spaces of technocultures. I did not know it then, but the business that offered these tutorials was training the future offshore labor forces for transnational businesses.

Globalization in digital formats had arrived in my backyard in Bhopal, India, in the mid-1980s. Thinking historically, it is no surprise that the infamous Bhopal gas tragedy (in December 1984), resulting from manufacturing industries offshoring outmoded technologies to third-world urban spaces, signaled a transition into a different phase in globalization. The resulting globalization appeared more sanitized and benevolent, even as more manufacturing jobs and computer hardware factories continued to be moved into borderlands (maquiladoras) and other third-world regions, because this move was virtually invisible in the clamor of the digital. Thus, as audiences the world over watched the broadcast of this disaster and made meaning, protesting the transfer of outmoded technologies, the focus of communication scholars conveniently shifted to examining empowerment through information technology (IT).

Aditi (age 24):

Way back in the sixth grade, I was introduced to the world on the Internet by my sister. I used to frequent rediff.com chat rooms and used to select rooms like 'teen love' and 'Calcutta cafe' in the hope of meeting someone similar to me who would have compatible 'a/s/l's [age/sex/location]. I remember having multiple e-mail IDs and chat IDs through which I used to play pretend. Some chat rooms were eighteen and above and I used to pretend to be a college girl with a different location from mine. I was role playing, a different alternative identity. This went on till the tenth grade, and after that my sister again introduced me to orkut.com, a weird sort of website where I had to connect to people I already knew in real life; really, I thought to myself, nothing could be dumber that this concept, friending friends you are already friends with! But who knew? Orkut was getting me prepped and sensitized toward and for a bigger and better place: Facebook!

Script 1

Older Generation: Youngsters these days are always on Facebook. They need to get a real life.

Younger Gen: I know she really went to Club Soho's VIP lounge! She just put a picture right now on Facebook! Its really happening!

Chorus: What is real? Why is this real? What does this really mean?

Script 2

Younger Gen: My mother is so embarrassing, she put up pictures of the Winter vacations and put it on "Public" View.

Older Gen: Isnt it wonderful that I can share my pictures with all the extended family members through Facebook?

Chorus: What is real? Why is this real? What does this really mean?

Script 3

Younger Gen: My boyfriend proposed to me a week back, but his relationship status is still "single."

Older Gen: I've closed off my FB account with my real name, I now have an alternate identity. My children and my spouse are not my friends.

Chorus: What is real? Why is this real? What does this really mean?

Final Script

Younger Gen: So I decided to unfriend my mother today, but I couldn't find her account anymore!

(*She doesn't find her mother's Facebook identity anymore . . .*)

Chorus: *What is real? Why is this real? What does this really mean? Can we locate our social networks?*

CONCLUSION

What are the identities we acquire and what are the identities we lose, and why? Digital diasporas, as we see from the stories and examples described in this chapter, contribute to a transnational labor and management force necessary for the functioning of digital global economies. The functioning of such global economies rests on the coded interface that structures the practices in specific ways. Liberal discourse points to the rampant "multiculturalism" online as evidence of progress and democracy, but in coded fact this multiculturalism is almost accidental, shaped by a labor force that is based in a tiered hierarchy of layered literacies and material access.

Identity production and technocultural agencies and subjectivities are shaped through the interplay of multiple offline and online contexts, histories, and literacies. Thus, as Mark Andrejevic (2009) notes, even the interactive interface provided by digital media reconstitutes public space in a manner that scatters the collective into individual scattered spaces. Networks, in fact, keep us away from each other as we work alone toward similar goals, so that we cannot physically be digging at the same path. But we do share a feel-good virtuality that makes us seem connected. The binary that then emerges begs the question, are you in my networks or are you in my everyday life; not, are you real or are you virtual. According to Hayles (1999, 156), "[t]his construction necessarily makes the subject into a cyborg, for the enacted and represented bodies are brought into conjunction through the technology that connects them." What might this mean for continuing processes of globalization and the transnationalization of labor forces? Such questions need to engage the historical formations of transnational ("local" and "global") communities of production in relation to specific contexts of technological design and use. Therefore, sociocultural descriptions of technological environments as well as their political and economic situatedness are essential to the study of transnational technological and digitally diasporic environments.

NOTES

1. *Hyderabad Blues*, directed by Nagesh Kukunoor (1998; Stevenson Ranch, CA: Tapeworm, 2001), DVD.

2. *Bombay Boys*, directed by Kaizad Gustad (1998; Mumbai, India: Eros, 1998), NTSC.

3. See Deepika Bahri, "The Digital Diaspora: South Asians in the New Pax Electronica," in *Diaspora: Theories, Histories, Texts,* ed. Makarand Paranjape (New Delhi:

Indialog, 2001), 222–32; Amit S. Rai, "India On-line: Electronic Bulletin Boards and the Construction of a Diasporic Hindu Identity," *Diaspora* 4, no.1 (1995): 31–57.

4. This situation is also problematic, but we will explore the details of mapping digital diaspora in this chapter. See work by scholars such as Lily Cho (2008) and Ella Shohat (2006) to understand some of the nuances of the concept "diaspora" in current times.

5. Kelly's world blog (http://www.kgadams.net/2006/06/11/my-second-life-deflowering) describes scripted objects as follows: "Objects a user creates can have scripted behaviors—a table could have a fold out extension, or those ears I mentioned could wiggle. Even more intriguing, an object's behavior could be based on something outside the game: virtual weather in an area could be based on real-world weather reports, for example—or a soccer ball could move based on telemetry from a real-world soccer ball."

REFERENCES

Anderson, B. 2006. *Imagined Communities: Reflections on the Origin and Spread of Nationalism.* London: Verso.

Andrejevic, M. 2009. "Critical Media Studies 2.0: An Interactive Upgrade." *Interactions: Studies in Communication and Culture* 1 (1): 35–51. http://dx.doi.org/10.1386/iscc.1.1.35_1.

Bhattacharjya, N. 2009. "Popular Hindi Film Song Sequences Set in the Indian Diaspora and the Negotiating of Indian Identity." *Asian Music* 40 (1): 53–82. http://dx.doi.org/10.1353/amu.0.0012.

Booth, G. 2008. *Behind the Curtain: Making Music in Mumbai's Film Studios.* New York: Oxford University Press.

Brah, A. 1996. *Cartographies of Diaspora: Contesting Identities.* London: Routledge.

Bratich, J.Z. 2008. "From Embedded to Machinic Intellectuals: Communication Studies and General Intellect." *Communication and Critical Studies* 5 (5): 24–45. http://dx.doi.org/10.1080/14791420701839163.

Castree, N. 2004. "Differential Geographies: Place, Indigenous Rights and 'Local' Resources." *Political Geography* 23 (2): 133–67. http://dx.doi.org/10.1016/j.polgeo.2003.09.010.

Cho, L. 2008. "Asian Canadian Futures, Diasporic Passages, and the Routes of Indenture." *Canadian Literature* 199:181–201.

Desai, J. 2003. "Bombay Boys and Girls: The Gender and Sexual Politics and Transnationality in the New Indian Cinema in English." *Journal of South Asian Popular Culture* 1 (1): 45–61. http://dx.doi.org/10.1080/1474668032000077113.

Everett, Anna, and Jennifer Brinkerhoff. 2009. *Digital Diaspora: A Race for Cyberspace.* Albany: State University of New York Press.

Gajjala, R., N. Rybas, and M. Altman. 2008. "Racing and Queering the Interface: Producing Global/Local Cyberselves." *Qualitative Inquiry* 14 (7): 1110–33. http://dx.doi.org/10.1177/1077800408321723.

Gajjala, V. 2006. "The Role of Information and Communication Technologies in Enhancing Processes of Entrepreneurship and Globalization in Indian Software Companies." *Electronic Journal of Information Systems in Developing Countries* 26 (1): 1–20.

Hall, Stuart. 1993. "Culture, Community, Nation." *Cultural Studies* 7 (3): 349–63. http://dx.doi.org/10.1080/09502389300490251.

Hayles, K. 1999. *How We Became Posthuman: Virtual Bodies in Cybernetics, Literature, and Informatics.* Chicago: University of Chicago Press.

Hayles, K. 2006. "Unfinished Work: From Cyborg to Cognisphere." *Theory, Culture & Society* 23 (7): 7–8. http://dx.doi.org/10.1177/0263276406069229.

Law, J. 2004. *After Method: Mess in Social Science Research.* London: Taylor & Francis. Kindle edition.

Maira, Sunaina. 2000. "Henna and Hip Hop: The Politics of Cultural Production and the Work of Cultural Studies." *Journal of Asian American Studies* 3 (3): 329–69. http://dx.doi.org/10.1353/jaas.2000.0038.

Mallapragada, M. 2000. "The Indian Diaspora in the USA and around the Web." In *Web Studies*, ed. D. Gauntlett, 179–85. London: Arnold.

Mitra, A. 2008. "Working in Cybernetic Space: Diasporic Indian Call Center Workers in the Outsourced World." In *South Asian Technospaces*, ed. Radhika Gajjala and Venkataramana Gajjala. New York: Peter Lang.

Naficy, H. 2001. *An Accented Cinema: Exilic and Diasporic Filmmaking.* Princeton, NJ: Princeton University Press.

Narayan, U. 1990. "The Project of Feminist Epistemology: Perspectives from a Non-western Feminist." In *Gender/Body/Knowledge*, eds. A. M. Jaggar and Susan R. Bordo, 256–269. New Brunswick, NJ: Rutgers University Press.

Punathambekar, A. 2005. "Bollywood in the Indian-American Diaspora: Mediating a Transitive Logic of Cultural Citizenship." *International Journal of Cultural Studies* 8 (2): 151–75. http://dx.doi.org/10.1177/1367877905052415.

Rajadhyaksha, A. 2003. "The 'Bollywoodization' of the Indian Cinema: Cultural Nation-alism in a Global Arena." *Inter-Asia Cultural Studies* 4 (1): 25–39. http://dx.doi.org/10.1080/1464937032000060195.

Rajagopal, A. 2001. *Politics after Television: Hindu Nationalism and the Reshaping of the Public in India.* Cambridge: Cambridge University Press.. http://dx.doi.org/10.1017/CBO9780511489051

Sassen, S. 2004. "Local Actors in Global Politics." *Current Sociology* 52 (4): 649–70. http://dx.doi.org/10.1177/0011392104043495.

Schiller, D. 2000. *Digital Capitalism: Networking the Global Market System.* Cambridge: MIT Press.

Shohat, E. 2006. "Travelling 'Postcolonial' Allegories of Zion, Palestine, and Exile." *Third Text* 20 (3–4): 287–91.

Sunden, J. 2003. *Material Virtualities: Approaching Online Textual Embodiment.* New York: Peter Lang.

Terranova, T. 2000. "Free Labor: Producing Culture for the Digital Economy." *Social Text* 18 (2): 33–58. http://dx.doi.org/10.1215/01642472-18-2_63-33.

Terranova, T. 2004. *Network Culture: Politics for the Information Age.* London: Pluto Press.

Tolia-Kelly, D. 2004. "Locating Processes of Identification: Studying the Precipitates of Re-Memory through Artefacts in the British Asian Home." *Transactions of the Institute of British Geographers* 29 (3): 314–29. http://dx.doi.org/10.1111/j.0020-2754.2004.00303.x.

7

Avatar

A Posthuman Perspective on Virtual Worlds

Gray Graffam

When paraplegic Jake Sully takes virtual form in the film *Avatar*, he enters the world of the Na'vi, where he assumes the fully functional physical form of an alien humanoid species and falls in love with the young, attractive, and highly spirited Ney'tiri. At the end of the film, struggling and dying, he succeeds in transferring his life essence into his avatar form and completes his transformation to a living being in an alien world.

For those who have played Second Life or World of Warcraft, the film *Avatar* is a powerful allegory for life experience in an online virtual world (Graffam 2011). For some, the idea of being an avatar on a regular and continual basis is a powerful attraction for entering such online worlds. Taking the form of an avatar represents—however fleeting—a means of seemingly overcoming a number of inadequacies in real life. For some, it embraces love, passion, and an overwhelming sense of heartfelt emotion, filling a void of loneliness and longing. For others, it represents a wholeness of being, allowing a sense of movement, re-creation, and fulfillment and a release from pain and suffering and, at times, physical disability. Still for others, it represents a

DOI: 10.5876/9781607321705.c07

131

form of entertainment and social interaction, at times embracing the exotic and experimental and relieving a sense of loneliness and boredom. It can also be a means of staying in touch and maintaining real-life friendships and family relationships at a distance. In essence, taking the form of an avatar allows people to interact in new and novel ways that push the boundaries they encounter in real life and to derive a sense of enjoyment and fulfillment in ways that may be denied them in the real world.

Of course, all of this begs the question of whether we, as a species, are quite ready to embrace the virtual. The growing body of posthuman research and theory suggests that perhaps we are not, at least not completely and not without serious consideration of how virtuality can alter our sense of family, sociality, and psychological well-being. But research also reveals that people are indeed experiencing the virtual more and more and that some are spending inordinate amounts of time in such worlds, so much in fact that a virtual world can form a primary means of communication and social interaction.

The research foundation for my work comes from having spent more than 2,000 hours in Second Life and World of Warcraft over the past two years, plus a number of hours on Skype, Ventrilo, Facebook, YouTube, Yahoo Messenger, and texting platforms of various sorts. I have interacted via computer, cell phone, and tablet, and I have been fully immersed (some might prefer to say addicted), interacting with hundreds of people and, in the case of World of Warcraft, also joining one of the oldest guilds in the game and attaining a level 85 ranking (currently the highest in the game).

Can views on the posthuman help us to understand the cultures and people who "live" within such worlds? I believe so, in particular because such views allow us to frame our research in ways that acknowledge how fiction, illusion, and reality can blend together in ways that fashion computer-mediated experience and craft online performance. They provide a perspective on virtuality and materiality within which to reflect and interpret actions and behaviors in modern context. They allow us to address such topics as imagination, disembodiment and re-embodiment, courtship and romance, identity and social identity, gender and sexuality, sociality, materiality, performance, and performative mastery, among a great many others. Moreover, such views force us to look at the intricacies of human behavior and the dynamics of culture as they are shaped and heavily influenced by virtuality. As mentioned by Whitehead at the outset of this volume, such views force us continually to ask how the "human subject" is best viewed when it comes to online agency.

By "posthuman," I am referring to that growing body of literature and theory that deals with computer-mediated human interaction, where imagination and sensation extend beyond the reach of the human body. Along with others (see Whitehead 2009, this volume; Cool, this volume; Hayles 1999), I argue that the term serves as a useful concept for reflection on those aspects of humanity that concern us here, particularly in terms of computer-mediated space. I disagree with those who deny its utility or seem to lack an understanding of its theoretical underpinnings, breadth, and scope (Boellstorff 2008, 29). But to return to the central question, is humankind ready to embrace virtuality? Are we prepared for what virtuality on a regular, routine, and immersive basis means to us? As will be shown below, some appear to be achieving just that end within Second Life, and surviving quite well, but others are less successful.

THE INCREASING POPULARITY OF VIRTUAL WORLDS

What constitutes a virtual world? One definition that seems workable from an anthropological perspective is an environment that enables people to interact in virtual form as avatars as part of a computer-mediated environment, such as an MMO (massively multiplayer online) or MMORPG (massively multiplayer online role-playing game). For the most part, all virtual worlds have the same basic components: (1) the capacity to adopt avatar form, that is, to represent oneself in a digitized human, humanoid, animal, or other shape that is graphically represented to others; (2) the capacity to communicate through various forms of synchronous and asynchronous communication, that is, to send messages via e-mail clients, to text via chat utilities, to talk via VoIP applications, and to make visual gestures; (3) some form of virtual map in which localities and geography are represented and some means by which teleportation may occur; (4) some way in which an avatar may interact with world objects, that is, to pick up or animate various represented forms such as horses, winged mythical beings, or various bits of clothing and equipment, to name just a few; and (5) the virtual world continues to exist whether the individual avatar is logged in or not. As such, virtual worlds differ from computer-mediated space, such as Facebook, YouTube, and eHarmony, which may be regarded as communities in their own right but differ considerably in how they represent and facilitate human behaviors and interactions.

As of this writing, World of Warcraft and Second Life are two of the most popular virtual worlds accessed on the Internet today. There are upward of 12 million active players of World of Warcraft worldwide, roughly equal to the current population of Greece, and there are approximately 800,000 active players of Second Life, roughly today's population of Cyprus. Together they represent a combined annual revenue of more than $300 million, or just over 1.2 percent of the total annual US video game spending of $27.4 billion (Newzoo, cited by Gamasutra, December 20, 2010). Considering that neither of these virtual worlds existed until recently—World of Warcraft launched in 2001 and Second Life in 2003—it seems that 3-D fantasy worlds have sparked imaginations the world over and also dramatically changed what might be called "playscape" in a rapid explosion of the posthuman (Graffam 2010).

There is little sign that the popularity of such worlds is abating. World of Warcraft continues to release its updates to its virtual world, and its number of players has steadily increased over the years. Furthermore, Second Life continues to hover at 800,000 players and just recently announced the highest earning quarter in the company's history (Linden Labs 2011). These two worlds have continued to thrive in a context in which there has been growing interest in virtual worlds (Table 7.1).

Table 7.1. A list of virtual worlds and their release dates

Virtual World	Launch Date	Virtual World	Launch Date
Active Worlds	1997	Papermint	2010
Cybertown	1995	Second Life	2003
Disney's Toontown	2003	The Sims Online	2002
Dreamville	2004	There	2003
Kaneva	2004	Virtual Ibiza	2002
Lord of the Rings	2007	Virtual Magic Kingdom	2005
Muse	2002	World of Warcraft	2001

Over the past decade, the number of adult players online has increased substantially. According to Park Associates (Shack News 2007), the percentage of adult US Internet users who play online video games on a weekly basis was 34 percent in 2007. Others, such as the NPD Group (Shack News 2008), have estimated a similar percentage. And that percentage more than doubles for the population ages six to forty-five. In that year, the rate of online gaming adoption actually exceeded that of social networking. Furthermore, Comscore estimated the total number of online gamers worldwide at 217 million in 2007 (Comscore 2007). Various sources indicate that online gaming is one of the most rapidly growing areas of interest among adults, and that the percentages of men and women games are roughly 60 and 40, respectively (Flew and Humphreys 2005; Plunkett Research 2010; Entertainment Software Association 2011).

Of course, these statistics are somewhat difficult to compile and may be subject to disagreement and some degree of fluctuation. The point remains, however, that it is reasonable to conclude that online gaming's popularity is not diminishing and appears to have growing adult interest and participation. Thus, there is a growing need for anthropologists and other social scientists to engage in the study of online gaming activity.

PERSONHOOD AND IDENTITY

Personhood and identity are two major themes that emerge from the study of virtual worlds. Both Boellstorff (2008, 118–150) and Nardi (2010, 158–

166) discuss the importance of taking avatar form, as do a number of others (Bessière, Seay, and Kiesler 2007; Huh and Williams 2010). From my experience in both World of Warcraft and Second Life, the idea of virtual personhood varies substantially among different virtual worlds. For example, many men currently play female characters in World of Warcraft and Second Life. Indeed, my character in World of Warcraft is a female Draenai shaman, which as of this writing is at level 85, that is, an avatar that has just reached the current top level in the game. I also play a female avatar in Second Life, although she is not my main one. I use her to test just how difficult it is to be an attractive female form in Second Life. In neither instance did I engage in voice with my female avatar but relied on texting only. From my research and experience, the nature of engagement is strikingly different between these worlds and their associated behaviors.

In World of Warcraft (WoW), being identified as a woman often carries a negative association, which is drawn from a male misconception that "women can't play WoW." In fact, some women prefer to keep their gender when playing "publicly," in random dungeons, or elsewhere without their guildmates. For example, Nikita (a pseudonym) relates her experience when she was "outed" as a female player playing a female avatar. She saved the dialogue (now several years old) and shared it with me:

[Meg]: Are you telling people that you're a girl, btw?

[Nikita]: Well, it's kind of obvious that I'm Mick's gf, and they'll hear me eventually so . . .

[Meg]: It's not obvious yet!

[Meg]: Kind of unavoidable

[Meg, switches to guild chat to announce to the group.]

[Meg]: Guys, just FYI

[Meg]: Nikita has a uterus

[Meg]: Just wanted to make sure you all knew

[Quin]: Kill it with fire!

[Troy]: Is there anything inside?

[Camp]: That's awesome!

[Meg]: There, now it's out there

[Troy]: I thought Mick had the uterus

When asked about her concerns at the time, Nikita related that she had been fairly nervous about being revealed to be a woman in Warcraft, as her previous guild had engaged in a great deal of female bashing that annoyed her. She stated that it is often worse to be identified as a real-life woman in Warcraft. Men may be teased about playing a girl, but they are usually taken seriously in terms of play if they are good. Women, however, may find that being identified as a woman in real life means that other players will not listen to your suggestions or follow your lead, even if you are more experienced and a better player than many others. I did play with Nikita to gain some insight on how well she played Warcraft and found that she was indeed one of the most knowledgeable and skilled players I had encountered. Hence, it seems fair to interpret her conclusion as being fairly accurate. If once she was identified as a woman in the game she was ignored and her ideas not listened to, it is fair to consider this an example of gender bias in game play. Men, on the other hand, when identified as playing a female avatar are often simply teased about the choice.

[Agile]: Why do you play a female char, if you're a guy?

[Gray]: Oh, I started as a male, but I had a sex change . . . lol

[Agile]: Hehe. Really?

[Gray]: Well, the male Draenai is kinda ugly and all, and I just couldn't stand looking at him

[Gray]: So I changed.

[Agile]: ROFL

[Agile]: Well, enjoy watching the wiggle

[Agile]: LOL

The above exchange follows closely what Nardi (2010, 159) has also observed about men playing female characters. It reflects more what men prefer to watch on-screen while playing the game than some deep-seated aspect of sexuality. In my case, being identified as a man playing a female character had no consequence in my game play. In fact, people were much more concerned about my ability to undertake a given task, and appreciative when I could achieve it. When leveling with Agile, he never once was concerned about my sexuality, nor was I for that matter, and he was simply happy when I was able to save him from one catastrophe or another. Indeed, the subject was never mentioned again.

Gender switching in Second Life, however, is a different experience. There is a tendency, as noted by Boellstorff (2008, 141), for people to experiment with gender roles, cross-dressing, and other aspects of sexuality and gender. This experimentation is highly meaningful given some of the main motivations and drivers for playing Second Life, namely dating, romantic relationships, companionship, and cybersex. Playing the other sex in Second Life greatly affects game play, dramatically changing the context and the potential meaning behind gender play. Boellstorff (2008, 142) discusses these matters and states that taking avatar form provides the opportunity for sexual exploration and transmutability of gender. It is a key aspect of this virtual world. Gender play in Second Life, however, is not limited to playing the other sex in avatar form. Experimentation with, for example, gay genders, transvestism, and cross-dressing takes place in this virtual world. Comments from those who frequent gay and transgendered space in Second Life often reflect how it lets them relax and feel comfortable among those "who accept them for who they are, and do not judge." In this instance, Second Life is like the Lesbian Café bulletin board written over a decade ago (Correll 1995). A space in which people interact takes on a special attachment that facilitates symbolic meaning. It fires the imagination and creates a context for role play, and in so doing transcends the fictional and embraces the real.

For the most part, my experience in Second Life has been as a male avatar, and what I have witnessed and experienced in terms of identity pertained primarily to group culture. This is by far one of the key differences between Second Life and World of Warcraft. In Second Life, appearance is much more malleable, both in terms of physical characteristics, such as shape, skin, and hairstyle and color, and also in terms of clothing, such as biker gear, flowing ball gowns, or punk wear. Although fictive races also present in Second Life, such as Night Elves, Werewolves, and Vampires, most avatars are presented as human. The ability to alter fine details of facial appearance, the height and musculature of the body, or the details of one's clothing, all far exceed the ability to modify appearance in World of Warcraft or other programs. Moreover, the ability to alter one's appearance for purposes of affecting social identity is very high in Second Life. You can easily appear as a lover of country and western music and horse rancher wearing western boots and a cowboy hat or as an urban youth, a Goth, a BDSM slave, a biker, a martial arts Ninja, or any other number of social identities that define group culture. Thus, identity is exceedingly personal in Second Life and much less so in World of Warcraft. Not only does this affect role play and point to differences between these two worlds, but it also shapes the very basis of social interaction in these two worlds. In Second Life, you craft and adapt your appearance to fit into the group culture that you wish to join; in World of Warcraft, you accept more limitations. Symbolic representation is much more active in Second Life primarily because symbols are easily adopted and worn, such as a Hell's Angels "support crew" jacket that marks you as part of the biker world or the "ownership" collar that represents an association with the dominant-submissive culture of BDSM clubs.

FORMING AND MAINTAINING RELATIONSHIPS IN VIRTUAL WORLDS

Virtual worlds are considered by many to be first and foremost a form of entertainment. People play and interact in them primarily to have fun. Within World of Warcraft and Second Life, various relationships are created and maintained. For the most part, such relationships can be classified as forms of friendship. Between World of Warcraft and Second Life, the nature of these friendships varies considerably. The former are primarily based around teasing and joking camaraderie focused on game play (Chen 2008; Williams et al. 2006). The latter are mostly centered on social relationships, dating, and courtship with rules that are defined by the role-play of the participants (Boellstorff 2008). Immersion in virtual worlds governs reality in the sense that virtual environments often guide interaction, discussion, and the general sense of virtual being.

In both World of Warcraft and Second Life, and for that matter undoubtedly all virtual worlds, players engage the world using their imaginations. Here, one's ability to visualize and project oneself provides a foundation in terms of disembodiment and re-embodiment—two key aspects of virtuality. All virtual worlds contain aspects of movement and fantasy that are decidedly unreal and fictive, for example, flying on creatures' backs, engaging in mock battles, and shape-shifting into other forms. Most players suspend disbelief when they enter these worlds, much like they do when reading a novel, watching a play, or going to a movie. In so doing, they allow their imaginations to flow freely and they engage in aspects of fantasy and role-play as they interact with others. Although they are actively engaged in a fictive sense, they undertake virtual actions and activities from which real emotions and a sense of emotional satisfaction (or dissatisfaction) is drawn.

The more time they spend in virtual form, the more emotionally attached they become to their avatar, as well as to the creation and sharing of memories and a recollection of a mutual past with others. Space, place, and virtual actions are recognized as having "happened," and imagination and projection, which triggered the setting in the first place, allow players to draw emotions from such virtual occurrences. Of course, for this to happen, there is also a large amount of "in-filling" that happens, as all virtual worlds tend to diminish some senses and heighten others. For example, vision (as illusion) is embraced, as is hearing, whereas touch (other than the illusion of touch), smell, and taste are all lacking. But the suspension of disbelief tends to overcome this, which is at times reflected in texting, for example, when someone mentions the smell or someone's hair or the taste of a certain food. At some level, therefore, all virtual worlds share a means of facilitating posthuman experience, whereby imagination facilitates experience that enables real emotions, feelings, and passions (Figure 7.1).

The main drivers that motivate people to enter a virtual world seem to be somewhat world-specific, and there is a striking difference between Second Life and World of Warcraft. Many who choose to enter Second Life are searching for a relationship of friendship, love, romance, virtual sex, or some combination thereof, perhaps accompanied by a sense of sexual exploration, for example, BDSM. Many who play World of Warcraft, however, are

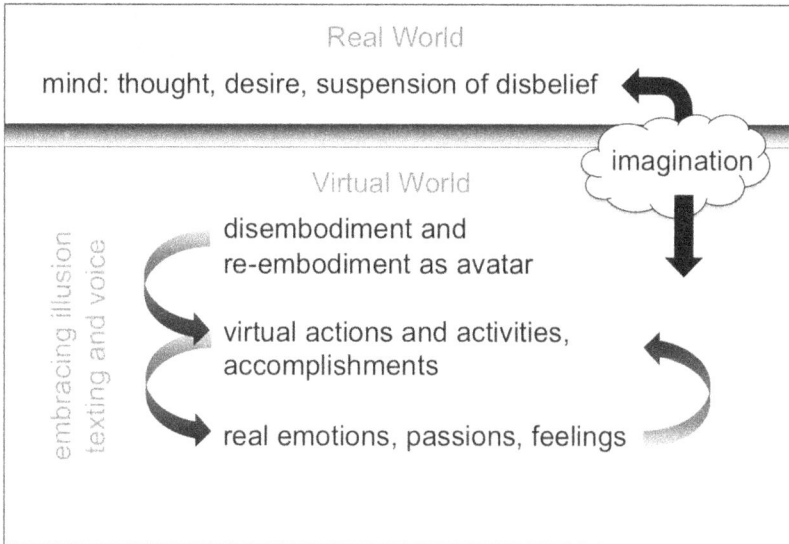

FIGURE 7.1.
Modeling virtuality of the posthuman

searching for a sense of accomplishment and a relief from boredom. How satisfied someone is in real-life relationships seems to be a vital factor for many in Second Life, but it is much less of a concern with those playing World of Warcraft.

I encountered many people in Second Life who had experienced one or more failed romantic relationships in the virtual world, but I encountered few in World of Warcraft. The main drivers and desires that lead a person to engage in one type of virtuality over another seem to be based on their needs, hopes, and wants in real life. Of course, these worlds overlap, particularly where friendship and interaction are the desired goals. The difficulty seems to concern expectations. In Second Life, relationships often evolve along romantic and sexual lines. This is usually not the case in World of Warcraft, because most WoW players are not playing the game to facilitate romantic and sexual relationships. Even when couples play WoW together, the game is not a vehicle for exploring love, passion, or sex. Second Life with its dance animations, portrayal of sex acts, and emphasis on romance is decidedly different.

From my own experience, fantasy is a powerful force driving immersion in virtual worlds and has the potential for dramatic real-life consequences. In World of Warcraft, leveling my character and developing a top-level ranking in several professions took approximately 800 hours of play time, and along the way I was fortunate to join one of the oldest and longest-lasting WoW guilds. Doing this in a matter of months meant that I spent a lot of time in this virtual world—and not participating in real life. At around level 50 in World of Warcraft, my wife began to comment on my daily absences. A daily commitment of three to four hours of gaming is noticeable, and your partner needs to be a gamer, very tolerant, or both. Around level 70, my teenage son said to me, "Dad, you're playing computer games too much," and at level 80 my family celebrated my top ranking (only later did Cataclysm "up" the top level to 85), hoping that now I would finally stop playing WoW. However, as anyone playing the game knows, "life begins at 80" means that only at that level do you have access to a number of dungeons, can participate in raids, and acquire the highest performance gear. When the game opens up at this level, play changes from leveling up to facing some of the game's greatest challenges with others in your guild. For me, attaining level 80 was my first opportunity to really play with some of my guildmates, who had attained that ranking years ago.

When Cataclysm was released in 2010, there was a resurgence of interest in leveling to the highest level in the game, and in beating the game itself— the ultimate task, which frustrates many players and guilds, because beating the game requires the coordinated efforts of many. The desire to support the group and not let them down in reaching a goal, and eventually beating the game, is a powerful driver governing play. It led to my full immersion in WoW, which came at the expense of engaging in real-life activities. The sense of responsibility and moral obligation to those you are playing with online conflicts with real-life duties and responsibilities. The potential consequence, of course, is that immersion in this world causes you to disconnect from reality, potentially harming relationships with friends and family.

When asked if it was important that a partner also play World of Warcraft, Rich (a pseudonym) responded: "We have a lot of friends that have wives now that don't play games . . . They'll pop on to play for a little, and then all of a sudden they're like, we can't play this, we don't have the time, so they'll cancel their accounts. Since me and Sarah are married, of course, and we both like gaming, it's definite . . . we both play games constantly, whether it's WoW or something else." And according to Steve (also a pseudonym), "It only works cause my wife plays." Indeed, she is member of the same guild. The investment of time in World of Warcraft—over the long term—is often a barrier to play when a significant other appears on the scene, unless that person also enjoys online gaming.

The commitment to spending time in a virtual world is also shared in Second Life. In this world, although it is less structured and the rules of play are defined by those in world, people want to spend time together and to stay "up" with occurrences and friends. Indeed, some activities in Second Life demand the same kind of attention as real-life activities. For example, raising horses involves feeding and breeding them on a daily basis, which can easily take an hour, depending on the size of the virtual herd. But even when role-play is more flexible, many spend hours immersed in this virtual world on a daily basis. This is not dissimilar from visiting friends in real life, and it stems from the true desire to spend time with friends.

From my research, relationships appear to be governed primarily by sub-culture and group culture. Particularly significant is the way that support and governance are crafted and how they define groups and behavior. Few people actively engage in Second Life alone. They form groups of friends, sometimes share residences, and role-play as "family" to one another (fictive kin relations), where a player will ask another to play the role of, for example, sister, mother, daughter, or brother. By defining relationships in these ways, the players impose expectations of behavior. In Second Life, one's "family" acts as a form of governance and provides support and guidance, particularly during times of emotional need, whether in the virtual world or out. Moreover, it serves to define the nature of group culture and subculture in terms of beliefs, values, and interests.

In both World of Warcraft and Second Life, one can easily find people who have fallen in love in the virtual world and who have then subsequently formed a long-lasting relationship in real life as well. Being immersed in the same virtual world appears to be important for the long-term success of a real-life relationship. What surprised me most in World of Warcraft was the number of couples in my guild, that is, the number of players who have a significant relationship in real life with another player in the guild. Of the guild's thirty-five players, there were at least four couples, meaning that almost a quarter of the guild was romantically involved. This seems high for guild statistics and may be a result of the age—and the long-term stability—of this particular guild. With the exception of one, all women in the guild were attached to another player. Of course, falling in love and maintaining romantic relationships seem more common in Second Life than in any other virtual world, primarily because romantic activity is fostered through dance, gesture, and avatar animation. For many, maintaining a relationship is why they play Second Life, and they engage in hours of online interaction daily as a form of sharing, building, and maintaining their relationships.

But maintaining such virtual relationships, whether in World of Warcraft or Second Life, is not easily done through the virtual world alone. Difficulties are encountered, particularly because virtuality lacks key senses, as mentioned above. As a result, many use Skype or a similar program to video chat, share photos, or also interact as friends on Facebook. Some get together in real life to establish meaningfulness in a relationship that they then carry back into the virtual world, as they rely on personal intimacy to help maintain the virtual. In this way, memory of the real is drawn into the virtual, where it helps to overcome the sensory deprivation of the virtual environment.

OVERCOMING DISABILITY

People in virtual worlds occasionally engage in represented actions they can no longer do in real life, given personal disabilities, age, illness, and so forth, drawing a sense of renewal and emotional happiness from these actions. For some, this ability forms the primary motivator for their immersion in virtual environments. In my experience in both worlds, I encountered a number of people who stated they were suffering in real life, from people who were terminally ill to those who were bedridden or confined to a wheelchair. There is no doubt that people who are experiencing pain in real life are engaged in virtual worlds for reasons that go beyond entertainment or relief from boredom. These players often spend an inordinate amount of time in the virtual world, where they are able to escape the pain of real life.

In my experience, there is a difference between Second Life and World of Warcraft with regard to these players. Some in Second Life talk openly about their pain and disabilities, and they may also take up specific actions to provide an experience that they miss in real life. For example, a woman who loves to dance but can longer do so in real life enjoys the experience through virtual representation, and the disabled male athlete, who can no longer walk, virtually re-creates the sense of taking part in the sport he loves. In World of Warcraft, this manner of virtuality is not as individually tailored, but even there it seems to relate strongly to the sense of a personal past and a desire for rejoicing virtual performance.

DISCUSSION

How can views on the posthuman help us to understand virtual worlds and the cultures and people that occupy them? According to Hayles (1999, 3), "the posthuman subject is an amalgam, a collection of heterogeneous components, a material-informational entity whose boundaries undergo continuous construction and reconstruction." Moreover, Cool (this volume) discusses the posthuman in terms of "digital intermediation" that serves to "reconfigure experiences and imaginaries of place, identity, and embodiment without dematerializing these as sites of subjectivity or rendering them obsolete as sources of anthropological insight." In this discussion of World of Warcraft and Second Life, we see that, indeed, there is a multifaceted blend of real and virtual, fueled by genuine desires, transformed by the imagination into virtual forms that interact with others in virtual space, and experienced in terms of real emotions, passions, and feelings that are reinterpreted as actual experience. It is not surprising, given this sense of posthuman transformation and interaction, that those who spend an inordinate amount of time in a virtual world experience something akin to culture shock when they leave that world.

The power of such fantasy is at times overwhelming, decidedly disorienting, and often completely thought absorbing.

Such virtual worlds clearly embrace the posthuman. The World of Warcraft and Second Life are two excellent examples of this kind of virtual environment and of the activities that typify online behaviors. Avatars engage in a wide range of activities in virtual space, occupy fictive landscapes, and actively employ the imagination in the creation and celebration of virtuality. From killing fictive beasts in World of Warcraft to engaging in BDSM sexual role-play in Second Life, the range of possible experiences substantiate that many people enjoy a rich posthuman fantasy life. But how much is fantasy and how much is real? Where is the dividing line between what is objectively human and what is decidedly computer-mediated illusion? It seems that the line is most clearly defined on an individual basis. Some people maintain a clear sense of being when in avatar form and resist the temptation to enter a fictive world. Others easily become "lost in the moment" and find that the line between fictive and real can be elusive.

Are we ready as a species for posthuman virtuality? Perhaps we are, but if this is the case, we need to understand that virtuality is not as simple as being online and texting the voice of an avatar body; it goes well beyond such a literal understanding of representation. In many ways, posthuman virtuality embraces the work of Butler (1993) and others (Fausto-Sterling 1997; Martin 1997) on a theoretical level, where scripting on to the body enables both representation and the filter through which our interpretation of actions and consequence takes place.

In this chapter, the topics of identity and personhood, forming and maintain relationships, and overcoming disability have all touched on the posthuman. These themes reveal that there is much more to understanding virtual environments than many recent scholarly works have touched on (Ducheneaut and Moore 2005; Ducheneaut et al. 2006a, 2006b, 2007; Malaby 2007; Golub 2010; Pace, Bardzell, and Bardzell 2010; Bainbridge 2010; Chen and Duh 2007; Castronova 2002; Ito 1997; Moore, Ducheneaut, and Nickell 2007). I have tried to demonstrate that an anthropological study of the World of Warcraft and Second Life requires a researcher to invest a great deal of time in virtual environments to develop performative mastery or to engage with others in understanding the nature of virtuality and experience as part of building an overarching ethnographic perspective. This necessity, of course, condemns those disciplines that do not embrace an ethnography (e.g. psychology), making their research in this arena dubious at best (Bessière, Seay, and Kiesler 2007; Levene and Dickins 2008; Longman et al. 2009). You cannot study World of Warcraft or Second Life from the sidelines anymore than you can understand the Cuckoo Nest through Nurse Ratched's eyes; better that you become the inmate if you want to truly understand virtual behavior. It is imperative to become fully immersed in these fictive worlds to study them.

Researchers need to develop a fully competent understanding of what virtuality and materiality mean to fully understand these worlds. As Whitehead (this volume) states, such concerns over human behavior pose a major challenge for anthropology today and a need for us to reflect on how we are, in fact, posthuman.

Do people online in virtual environments emulate the world of Jake Sully in *Avatar*, spending inordinate amounts of time online in the pursuit of virtual existence, happiness, and fulfillment? The answer for some is yes; indeed, this is the world they have embraced and the kind of posthuman experience that typifies their daily world. Desires fuel motivations for entering virtual environments like World of Warcraft and Second Life, and imagination, aided by computer-mediated technology, transforms the body through disembodiment and re-embodiment into avatar form. All of this is not fictive, however, or even fictional fantasy, because the emotions, passions, and feelings that result from the interaction with others in virtual worlds while undertaking virtual activities are drawn back into real-life awareness, enjoyment, and perception.

REFERENCES

Bainbridge, W. S. 2010. *Online Worlds: Convergence of the Real and the Virtual.* London: Springer-Verlag.

Bessière, Katherine, A. Fleming Seay, and Sara Kiesler. August 2007. "The Ideal Elf: Identity Exploration in World of Warcraft." *Cyberpsychology & Behavior: The Impact of the Internet, Multimedia, and Virtual Reality on Behavior and Society* 10 (4): 530–5. http://dx.doi.org/10.1089/cpb.2007.9994. Medline:17711361.

Boellstorff, Thomas. 2008. *Coming of Age in Second Life: An Anthropologist Explores the Virtually Human.* Princeton, NJ: Princeton University Press.

Butler, Judith. 1993. *Bodies that Matter: On the Discursive Limits of "Sex."* New York: Routledge.

Castronova, Edward. 2002. "On Virtual Economies." *CESifo Working Paper No. 752*, July 2002.

Chen, Mark G. 2008. "Communication, Coordination, and Camaraderie in World of Warcraft." *Games and Culture* 4 (1): 47–73. http://dx.doi.org/10.1177/155541 2008325478.

Chen, Vivian Hsueh-hua, and Henry Been-Lim Duh. 2007. "Understanding Social Interaction in World of Warcraft." *Proceedings of the International Conference on Advances in Computer Entertainment Technology* 203: 21–24. ACM International Conference Proceedings Series.

Comscore. 2007. "Worldwide Online Gaming Community Reaches 217 Million People," last modified July 10, 2007. Accessed June 16, 2011. http://www.comscore.com/Press_Events/Press_Releases/2007/07/Worldwide_Online_Gaming_Grows.

Correll, Shelley J. 1995. "An Ethnography of an Electronic Bar: The Lesbian Café." *Journal of Contemporary Ethnography* 24 (3): 270–98. http://dx.doi.org/10.1177/089124195024003002.

Ducheneaut, Nicolas, and Robert J. Moore. 2005. "More Than Just 'XP': Learning Social Skills in Massively Multiplayer Online Games." *Interactive Technology and Smart Education* 2 (2): 89–100. http://dx.doi.org/10.1108/17415650580000035.

Ducheneaut, Nicolas, Nick Yee, Erik Nickell, and Robert J. Moore. 2006a. "'Alone Together?' Exploring the Social Dynamics of Massively Multiplayer Online Games." *Proceedings of CHI 2006*, 407–416. ACM.

Ducheneaut, Nicolas, Nick Yee, Erik Nickell, and Robert J. Moore. 2006b. "Building an MMO with Mass Appeal: A Look at Gameplay in World of Warcraft." *Games and Culture* 1 (4): 281–317. http://dx.doi.org/10.1177/1555412006292613.

Ducheneaut, Nicolas, Nick Yee, Erik Nickell, and Robert J. Moore. 2007. "The Life and Death of Online Gaming Communities: A Look at Guilds in the World of Warcraft." *Conference on Human Factors in Computing Sciences, Proceedings of the SIGCHI Conference on Human Factors in Computing Systems*, 839–848.

Entertainment Software Association. 2011. "Game Player Data," last modified in 2011. Accessed June 16, 2011. http://www.theesa.com/facts/gameplayer.asp.

Fausto-Sterling, Anne. 1997. "How to Build a Man." In *The Gender Sexuality Reader*, ed. Roger N. Lancaster and Micaela di Leonardo, 244–248. New York: Routledge.

Flew, Terry, and Sal Humphreys. 2005. *Games, Technology, Industry, Culture*. South Melbourne: Oxford University Press.

Gamasutra. "Report: Total U.S. Game Spend to Hit $24.7B in 2010." Last modified December 20, 2010. Accessed June 16, 2011. http://www.gamasutra.com/view/news/32120/Report_Total_US_Game_Spend_To_Hit_247B_In_2010.php.

Golub, Alex. 2010. "Being in the World (of Warcraft): Raiding, Realism, and Knowledge Production in a Massively Multiplayer Online Game." *Anthropological Quarterly* 83 (1): 17–45. http://dx.doi.org/10.1353/anq.0.0110.

Graffam, Gray. 2010. "Representation, Participation, and Virtual Ethnography." Paper presented at the annual meetings of the Canadian Anthropological Society, Montreal.

Graffam, Gray. 2011. "Posthuman Anthropology and Immersive Participation in Virtual Worlds." Paper presented at the annual meetings of the Canadian Anthropological Society, Fredericton, NB.

Hayles, N. Katherine. 1999. *How We Became Posthuman: Virtual Bodies in Cybernetics, Literature, and Informatics*. Chicago: University of Chicago Press.

Huh, Searle, and Dmitri Williams. 2010. "Dude Looks Like a Lady: Gender Swapping in an Online Game." *Online Worlds: Convergence of the Real and the Virtual*, ed. W. S. Bainbridge, 161–174. London: Springer-Verlag. http://dx.doi.org/10.1007/978-1-84882-825-4_13.

Ito, Mizuko. 1997. "Virtually Embodied: The Reality of Fantasy in a Multi-User Dungeon." In *Internet Culture*, ed. David Porter, 87–110. New York: Routledge.

Labs, Linden. 2011. "Q1 2011 Linden Dollar Economy Metrics Up, Users and Usage Unchanged." Last modified on May 6, 2011. Accessed June 16, 2011. http://community.secondlife.com/t5/Featured-News/Q1-2011-Linden-Dollar-Economy-Metrics-Up-Users-and-Usage/ba-p/856693.

Levene, Rebecca, and Thomas Dickins. 2008. "Sex-Related Invariance across Cultures in Online Role-Playing Game." *Journal of Evolutionary Psychology (Budapest)* 6 (2): 141–8. http://dx.doi.org/10.1556/JEP.2008.1010.

Longman, Huon, Erin O'Connor, and Patricia Obst. 2009. "The Effect of Social Support Derived from World of Warcraft on Negative Psychological Symptoms." *Cyberpsychology and Behavior: The Impact of the Internet, Multimedia, and Virtual Reality on Behavior and Society* 12, no. 5 (October): 563–6. http://dx.doi.org/10.1089/cpb.2009.0001. Medline:19817567.

Malaby, Thomas M. 2007. "Beyond Play: A New Approach to Games." *Games and Culture* 2 (2): 95–113. http://dx.doi.org/10.1177/1555412007299434.

Martin, Emily. 1997. "The End of the Body." In *The Gender Sexuality Reader*, ed. Roger N. Lancaster and Micaela di Leonardo, 543–58. New York: Routledge.

Moore, Robert J., Nicholas Ducheneaut, and Erick Nickell. 2007. "Doing Virtually Nothing: Awareness and Accountability in Massively Multiplayer Online Worlds." *Computer Supported Cooperative Work* 16 (3): 265–305. http://dx.doi.org/10.1007/s10606-006-9021-4.

Nardi, Bonnie. 2010. *My Life as a Night Elf Priest: An Anthropological Account of World of Warcraft.* Ann Arbor: University of Michigan Press.

Pace, Tyler, Shaowen Bardzell, and Jeffrey Bardzell. 2010. "The Rogue in the Lovely Black Dress: Intimacy in World of Warcraft." *Proceedings of the 28th International Conference on Human Factors in Computing Systems, Games and Players*, 233–242. ACM.

Plunkett Research. 2010. "Entertainment & Media Industry Overview." Accessed June 16, 2011. http://www.plunkettresearch.com/Entertainment%20media%20publishing%20market%20research/industry%20statistics.

Shack News. 2007. "Gaming Still America's Favorite (Online) Pastime. Last modified August 17, 2007. Accessed June 16, 2011. http://www.shacknews.com/article/48521/gaming-still-americas-favorite-online.

Shack News. 2008. "NPD: 72% of U.S. Population Played Games in 2007; PC Named Driving Force in Gaming." Last modified April 02, 2008. Accessed June 16, 2011. http://www.shacknews.com/article/52025/npd-72-of-us-population.

Whitehead, Neil. 2009. "Post-Human Anthropology." *Identities (Yverdon)* 16 (1): 1–32. http://dx.doi.org/10.1080/10702890802605596.

Williams, Dmitri, Nicolas Ducheneaut, Li Xiong, Yuanyuan Zhang, Nick Lee, and Eric Nickell. 2006. "From Tree House to Barracks: The Social Life of Guilds in World of Warcraft." *Games and Culture* 1 (4): 338–61. http://dx.doi.org/10.1177/1555412006292616.

8

Technology, Representation, and the "E-thropologist"

The Shape-Shifting Field among Native Amazonians

Stephanie W. Alemán

This chapter centers on both the familiar and the arrestingly new. On the one hand it is about my long-term relationship with the Waiwai (Carib-speaking Amazonians in Guyana and Brazil) as collaborators and friends, familiar territory for me. In fact, this territory is not only familiar but rather comforting to me.

On the other hand, this chapter is also about following them as they venture into cyberspace and online worlds—places with which they are relatively unfamiliar, but also places in which I am not a familiar participant. This aspect of emergence that is ongoing and shifting makes following ethnographic subjects into new spaces speculative. Their Internet forays make my ethnographic situations arrestingly new because in addition to the nuances that our mutual lifeworlds-in-progress may reveal in other spaces are the very real and increasingly relevant opportunities for pause and reflection, including the opportunity to deepen the significance of the reflexive exercise as method and to contemplate the utility of such reflexivity toward an emergent understanding of the shifting nature of the fieldwork process itself. Thrusting

DOI: 10.5876/9781607321705.c08

the ethnographer into a new, interactive venue for participation with the members of a community with whom they have lived and worked in close somatic proximity brings to light the personal relationship the ethnographer has with this interactive venue. Following the Waiwai into online worlds is like traveling with them in other contexts—along rainforest trails, on winding rivers, or even, ultimately, into "hidden" cosmic and spiritual worlds—and yet these "new" Internet spaces are places I come to with some inherent bias based on my own experience.

But anthropology has been here before, even if I and my collaborators have only recently ventured together into "Cyberia" (Escobar 1994), and there are many things to consider and many trajectories to take. As Wilson and Peterson asserted in 2002, the transformations and changes that the Internet might bring about "have been less dramatic and more embedded in existing practices and power relations of everyday life" (Wilson and Peterson 2002, vii), and this is certainly the case among the Waiwai. On the other hand, it is also important to consider questions such as, is the concept of community itself misleading? and will an anthropological approach to these phenomena necessarily differ from other types of anthropological investigation? (ibid., viii). On the positive side for the e-thropologist, anthropology seems "uniquely suited for the study of socioculturally situated online communication within a rapidly changing context," and it is an opportunity for the discipline to explore and theorize communicative technologies and cyber-created discourses and relationships (ibid.).

The creation of a virtual ethnographic paradigm is still and will remain "in progress." While we grapple with ideas of the Internet as place or the Internet as cultural artifact, or both, ethnographic subjects interact with the Internet in exponential ways that are difficult to capture. Authenticity and identity become more nuanced and face-to-face ethnographic techniques are no longer possible (Hine 2000).

In a more localized sense, this chapter examines the collision of what is characterized as *modern* with what is desired to be *traditional*—that is, the imposition of Western, or perhaps better, the *technologized*, aspects of the human cultural experience on what is to some the iconized, unmodernized, unglobalized refuge of desire, the comparatively remote-dwelling indigenous Amazonian Indian or Amerindian. In this respect, interpretations of this collision resemble the denial of native agency in the face of overwhelming directed change, such as when Amerindians discard their feathers for trousers and dress shirts or take up shotguns over long bows, motorized cassava graters over handmade stone-encrusted grater boards, metal axes and adzes over stone implements, or even boomboxes for bamboo and bone flutes. These changes are viewed as forms of postcolonial victimization rather than conscious choices. We can comprehend the desire to be like the "unfettered" native Amazonian (the fetters in this case being the complexity of urban life, the obligation to technology, and perhaps a sense of dehumanization), but we may not consider that they may actually want to be like us. This is especially true if this emulation involves aspects of what we consider our less-desirable selves, the part that is jaded and anxious and needs sleep aids, antidepressants, stimulants, and lattes to function.

In this context, indigenous forays into these other worlds are not met with the same acknowledgment or even praise that our own progressive directive often evokes. In other words, modernities, technologies, and virtual worlds are for other humans, not those that inhabit the forests of our Amazonian imaginations. Thus, the crossover can be quite jarring.

If we consider the construction and representation of Amazonians in terms of their cultural transformations over the past few decades, we recognize the emergence of an increasing number of images that juxtapose the native with the trappings and gadgets of modernity. In pictures that use seemingly incongruous juxtapositions, Yanomamo and Kayapo, in full feathers and beads, sport cameras, and a native Andean woman uses a cell phone. In the popular media *The Far Side* cartoon implies that "natives" hide their technology from anthropologists, and that "natives" want to use explorers' laptops to check their hotmail accounts.

Yet these images now seem to infringe on certain realities that take away from the humorous and the ironical, robbing them of their once humorous and ironical punch. Today a new set of similar, but different, images has emerged that represents something else. The feathered native with the flat screen and hands poised over a keyboard is no longer amazing but increasingly common, and the native in the trappings of Western conservationism as a GPS-wielding forest ranger does not provoke the same startled response.

In fact, the image of the native asking to use technology probably should be replaced by an image of the non-native interloper borrowing a native's computer to access a now distant world, and the same caption now describes a new possibility. The use of technologies introduced from outside sources and their integration with internal worldviews are not new courses of inquiry in Amazonian anthropology. Terence Turner's long-time study of the Kayapo's use of media technologies for their own uses is seminal and inspiring and has given special attention to the phenomena of indigenous media (Turner 1992). Before him, Faye Ginsburg ventured into issues of online worlds and the use of technologies by indigenous persons, asserting that a study of these habits has the potential to reveal transformations in cultural identities and innovate different perspectives on social process. Indeed, Ginsburg found that they use new forms of communication for internal and external communications, for self-determination, and for resistance to outside cultural domination (Ginsburg 1991). Later, Beth Conklin showed that the use of these same Internet and communication technologies has transformative effects on Amazonian interethnic politics and self-representation and reveals some contradictions and potential liabilities (Conklin 1997). In these good works addressing indigenous Amazonians' use of new technologies, the issues of fieldwork and ethnography loom in the background. Thus, the project of confronting change and humanness among indigenous Amazonians also becomes a project about the continued relevance and shifting nature of fieldwork.

Elsewhere I have presented another aspect of cultural change for the Waiwai related to musicality and the construction of identity and personhood: a generational shift from the use of the flute to the use of the boombox as a communicative device (Hill and Chaumeil 2011). Here I underscore the uneasiness with which such shifts are perceived by Others.

Over two years ago I fulfilled a request by a young Waiwai man for a laptop computer. I was not the first one to introduce the Waiwai to computers; their ongoing engagement with the Conservation International (CI) agenda had already provided computer technology to their southern Guyanese village. But this previous computer experience had not included Internet access. I suppose such access was considered impossible given the location, logistics and cost. But once CI installed a satellite dish and paid for their $250 a month Internet service, things were different. After the computer from myself and two others were being used in the village, I saw firsthand how technology engenders certain forms of outrage among others when juxtaposed to native Amazonians and how this is usually masked as some hope or desire to leave them untouched and untrammeled by the rolling juggernaut of global engagement. I received a semi-anonymous e-mail from "Hawkfeather" regarding my part in the corruption of Amerindian society. "Why don't you just leave those poor people alone?" Hawkfeather wrote. "You won't be happy until they are all running around with cell phones sticking out of their ears and are just as depraved as we are." These are not the simple (or cognitively dissonant) accusations of persons not engaged or unfamiliar with online worlds and Internet access. From across disciplines, ideas about the ultimate utility and suitability of online communities and interactive discourse through cyberspace have begun to emerge. Against a backdrop of "Western concern" over the erosion of our intellects (Carr 2010), the Amazonian people I know have embraced cyberconnectivity in a way that has to be examined. As we worry over the "technopoly" emerging to potentially overtake our lives, other peoples in other cultural contexts are less concerned (Postman 1993). Musings of an almost self-help nature have emerged to confront "Western" discomfort with screens (on computers and the like), incessant self-reverence, and philosophical views on connectedness and the nature and meaning of solitary pursuits as well as the "inwardness of technologies"(Powers 2010). Amid these views, however, actual communities of persons from across indigenous Amazonia continue to appear online and to develop online identities, spending time in these places in larger measures and participating with the rest of the connected world from within their rainforest homes. No one has yet had to tell them, "You are not a gadget" (Lanier 2010).

For over a decade I have witnessed Waiwai persons presenting and projecting themselves into a larger world and engaging in an ongoing discourse with globalization. Rather than passively observing the world, they repeatedly engage, preparing and delivering a version of Waiwainess that reflects these interactions and further underscores their own knowledge of the intersubjectivity of persons and the necessity of Others in the creation and maintenance of the self. Young men, just as with the boombox, are replicating Waiwainess with reference to both the past and the present in terms of power and prowess. The black-painted hunter is at the same time the keyboard-tapping e-mailer. But even as I make the attempt to follow the paths of their self-representation, I am met with more questions than answers.

The advent of cyberlife among the Waiwai follows a certain discernable pathway. The first use of this technology was by the gendered age grade of *karipamsham*, or newly adult young men, who now have introduced a familiar aspect of competition among computer users. A working knowledge of Internet "places" has come to be a key aspect in Waiwai young male personhood, just as prowess in hunting and having traveled to faraway places represented, and still represent, this same personhood. Within the last few months, older men—especially those in positions of leadership—have made a concerted effort to master the Internet. In addition, an absolutely new development—the entrance of Waiwai young women into these cyberworlds—has forced a consideration of the shifting expression and representation of gender among the Waiwai and what this shift may entail.

To show how the Waiwai have accessed other social worlds through the use of the Internet, we will consider one of the young Waiwai men. The images on his Facebook page show the young man in a variety of roles. For example, one image shows him in a Taekwondo uniform and pose, and another, in a gangsta pose with a knit hat, with dark glasses and headphones and making hand signs. Yet another shows him covered in soap while bathing in a creek, and another, with a laptop and clipboard, doing forest ranger work.

I have known this Waiwai man since he was a small boy. I saw him excel in the small village school and pass the national exams that allowed him the chance, and the hardship, of attending secondary school far from his village. He left the village at age twelve and returned at age seventeen, fully intent on marrying a Waiwai girl (which he did) and remaining not only a village member but a Waiwai man (which he has certainly become).

His foray into Facebook has some interesting aspects. He was introduced to it by the computer tech for Conservation International and quickly found that his old school friends had already discovered Facebook; thus, he joined to be able to interact with them. Without too much explication, one can see the emergence of an online identity through the images he has chosen to represent himself. Here is his online profile:

CURRENT PROFILE STATEMENT = Rum 'til I die!!; Sex: Male; Birthday: November 20; Hometown: Brazil, Lethem, Guyana; Relationship Status: In an Open Relationship; Interested In: Women; Looking For: Friendship, A Relationship, Networking; Political Views: not interested; Religious Views: which ever; Mobile Number: +592-69****; Skype name: *******; Yahoo ID: *******; Education and Work, High School: Aishalton secondary school '05.

But this Waiwai young man is also experiencing the development of a multifaceted identity, in which he is at the same time this person we see here and other "persons" that are situationally performed. As I explore his Facebook persona, I can't help but ask myself why does he not include other images that show him doing more "native activities"? I have many images of him in full black paint, shooting at targets with a bow and arrow, pounding fish poison in a rhythmic group on a large rock in the river, coming into the village with other hunters after a week or ten days with large baskets of smoked and fresh meat for village feasting, and dancing in the Umana Yana communal house at Kresmus.

It is at this point that I find myself questioning my ability to represent this person and this culture that I have known for so long. Do I know how this process is being enacted? Can I understand this construction of self that not only this young man, but other Waiwai men and women are engaged with in terms of some reflection of Waiwainess? And, if so, what will I ultimately want to say on their behalf?

How will I be able to address his and other Waiwais' multiple and complex entailments with the regional and global networks that they now not only have access to but actively seek to engage? And, perhaps even more challenging, how will I facilitate access to and potentially help to construct the emergent narratives of Waiwainess that their experiences create?

For now, a focus on the young male Internet users is also a focus on the next generation of Waiwai leadership. But it is not as if this generation is the first to move both figuratively and actually "out of the forest"; the preceding generation, of men now in their late forties, also struggles with technology and change, but they have used once-new technologies such as the radio, solar and limited electrical current, gas-powered generators, outboard motors, and small engines for years. In addition, it is not merely computers and the Internet that have come to the Waiwai village but also cell phones, MP3 players, and DVD players.

Although each of these changes seems to pose particular challenges to representation, one theme has remained consistently clear: that rather than becoming us through the use of our technologies, the Waiwai are using these technologies to represent and maintain their own culture, as well as to fulfill their very real desire to project themselves through the space-time continuum.

This leads me to my first tentative conclusion: that is, the Waiwai, both young and old, have come to see the Internet, along with the computer that allows access to it, as the shamanic device of the young. Just as the shaman can access hidden worlds, find hidden individuals and entities, and communicate with beings and persons that others cannot, the Internet opens a cyberspace that is comparable to the shaman's space containing the places and worlds to which shamans have access and to which they routinely travel.

Because of my understanding of Waiwai production and projection of identity, it was less surprising to me to see them in a twelve-month period embrace e-mail and Internet technology as a form of communicative expression, injecting Waiwai patterns of representation, syntax, communication, and discursive relationships into the media they use to form and maintain relationships.

I cannot help but think, however, that it is perhaps more important at this point to focus on the nature of identity and the form of experience. As Neil Whitehead discusses in his article on "posthuman anthropology," Amazonian persons conceive of themselves and others as divisible and possessing an unstable materiality, meaning that they are material beings whose identities are not fixed but highly dependent on social context (Whitehead 2009). Although the concept of the instability of the human category is certainly not limited in space or time to Amazonia, the shamanic tradition in Amazonia nevertheless suggests that among other knowledges, shamans know the cosmological rules for the transformation of beings between ontological states. In other words, they are familiar with both the shifting, fluid concept of the person and the presence of the person.

The Internet and its ability to make present those who are physically absent or to "be" in terms of an intellectual or mindful presence in a place that one is not physically present seem shamanic. This immateriality of cyberspace, which might intimidate those grounded in a imperative of physicality, does not confound them; in their thinking, one is never really sure of the reality of any living being, because every being may in fact be wearing the disguise of another. Therefore, accessing and entering virtual worlds created by the "communicative programming" the Waiwai mainly explore and employ are comparatively easy for them. Because creating identities in a different space is a recognized activity, the possibility of existing in a space without a body is completely real for them in ways that it is not necessarily for someone like you or me.

For them, humans may not be totally human and may be composed, and probably are composed, of inhuman elements—hence the idea that an animal encounter is really an encounter with *toto*, or "someone," or that a person is capable of manipulating energies against or within another person without being physically present. They have been sending such virtual messages and causations long before the advent of e-mail. Thus, they have little anxiety about the concept of constructing formless presence, especially in online situations and spaces. In this sense, they are not re-creating humanness but are perhaps engaging in a form and comprehension of humanness that has long existed in their own ontologies.

So again the question becomes not so much how the Waiwai and others might be doing this, although this process is certainly worth exploring, but how the anthropologist might attempt to share this disembodied, subjective experience. And perhaps for the Amazonianist, this entails a major shift in sharing "the field" with our ethnographic subjects. The somatic endurance requirements disappear only to be replaced by other requirements. In these subjective engagements, the field begins to shape-shift.

As the Waiwai experience change, new domains open for an anthropological praxis that responds to changing human experience more generally. Within these new domains, it seems relevant to remember what Neil Whitehead has also iterated, that ethnographers must further engage with their own reflexivity and that "such inadequate coverings as the fig leaf of scientific observation will now not be enough to hide the bulge of anthropological desire" (2009, 27). New methods of discussing the mutual construction of experience between ethnographers and their "subjects" will have to be created, and we will need to recognize that entering into certain forms of experience—sharing online space, for example—is actually another form of ethnographic performance.

In considering how to approach the phenomenon of Internet usage and "virtual" identity construction among the Waiwai, we might do well to consider the inversion of the formula of participant observation to that of an *observant participation*, which allows us to see ourselves as we work. This method suggests that concepts such as reflexivity are not merely a cue to be confessional but opportunities to create a purposeful research design that acknowledges the ethnographer as person-acting-in-the-world, especially when that world is a virtual one.

The repositioned ethnographer is then better able to contemplate such issues as change, humanness, and the relevance of fieldwork, or even the field itself. This does not necessarily mean replacing one field with another but— even more challenging—attempting to balance the multi-sited ethnographic project that shifts even as it is described.

For my own work, it means venturing into fields such as e-mail, Yahoo Messenger, Skype, each with its own set of peculiarities and each manipulated by the Waiwai to position themselves using these tools of modernity. The challenge for the e-thropologist or netnographer is to provide a context in which both online and offline worlds can exist as the actually do—simultaneously.

The phenomenon of online Waiwai is new and somewhat unstable. There is no guarantee that they will be able to maintain their online presence in the face of having to pay for the satellite service that makes it possible, and there is little information to predict the direction they will go within their cyberworlds, nor the space here to discuss all the cyber places they go and what they do when they get there.

Now, and I mean that literally, the Waiwai continue to hone their communicative skills using the Internet. But even as they do this, I have not seen the emergence of a "virtual community" among them. At present, they only interact with persons they already know from face-to-face contexts and who they anticipate to have face-to-face interaction with in the future. They also exist in a textual world rather than an oral/aural world when they e-mail, chat, and instant message. For all their ability to comprehend the disembodied person, they still rely on contextual face-to-face cues in their discourse; they have a strong concept of the *eye soul*, for example, and an equally strong concept of the necessity to develop senses that the Internet does not necessarily require. They do not use the Internet much for information technology, web searching, researching, and knowledge. They instead use it as they do all non-Waiwai things, from Christianity to boomboxes, as a device to project themselves into the consciousness of others, a way of revealing others through conversation, a way of cloaking themselves in possible identities, and, even if it still seems ironic to our jaded sensibilities, a way of remaining distinctly Waiwai.

REFERENCES

Carr, Nicholas. 2010. *The Shallows: What the Internet Is Doing to Our Brains*. New York: W. W. Norton & Co.

Conklin, Beth. 1997. "Body Paint, Feathers and VCRs: Aesthetics and Authenticity in Amazonian Activism." *American Ethnologist* 24 (4): 711–37. http://dx.doi.org/10.1525/ae.1997.24.4.711.

Escobar, Arturo. 1994. "Welcome to Cyberia: Notes on the Anthropology of Cyberculture." *Current Anthropology* 35 (3): 211–31. http://dx.doi.org/10.1086/204266.

Ginsburg, Faye. 1991. "Indigenous Media: Faustian Contract or Global Village?" *Cultural Anthropology* 6 (1): 92–112. http://dx.doi.org/10.1525/can.1991.6.1.02a00040.

Hill, Jonathan D., and Jean-Pierre Chaumeil, eds. 2011. *Burst of Breath: Indigenous Ritual Wind Instruments in Lowland South America*. Lincoln: University of Nebraska Press.

Hine, Christine. 2000. *Virtual Ethnography*. London: SAGE Publications.

Lanier, Jaron. 2010. *You Are Not a Gadget: A Manifesto*. New York: Knopf.

Postman, Neil. 1993. *Technopoly: The Surrender of Culture to Technology*. New York: Vintage.

Powers, William. 2010. *Hamlet's BlackBerry: A Practical Philosophy for Building a Good Life in the Digital Age*. New York: Harper.

Turner, Terence S. 1992. "Defiant Images: The Kayapo Appropriation of Video." *Anthropology Today* 8 (6): 5–16. http://dx.doi.org/10.2307/2783265.

Whitehead, Neil L. 2009. "Post-Human Anthropology." *Identities: Global Studies in Culture and Power* 16 (1): 1–32. http://dx.doi.org/10.1080/10702890802605596.

Wilson, Samuel M., and Leighton C. Peterson. 2002. "The Anthropology of Online Communities." *Annual Review of Anthropology* 31 (1): 449–67. http://dx.doi.org/10.1146/annurev.anthro.31.040402.085436.

9

The Adventures of Mark and Olly

The Pleasures and Horrors of Anthropology on TV

James B. Hoesterey

If images lie, why are they so palpable of the life
between us? I want to look, sometimes sidelong, at
the spaces between the filmmaker and the subject: of
imagery and language, of memory and feeling. These
are spaces charged with ambiguity, but are they not
also the spaces in which consciousness is created?

DAVID MACDOUGALL (1998, 25)

Taking a cue from MacDougall's questions about the spaces between filmmakers and subjects, in this chapter I reflect on my experiences as anthropological advisor for several documentary programs broadcast internationally
on Discovery Channel, National Geographic International, Travel Channel,
and the BBC.[1] In my roles as translator, cultural broker, and "fact-checker," I
learned about how television executives conceive, produce, and market primitivist media in the digital age. This chapter draws from these experiences—the
good, the bad, and the ugly—but I direct most of my analytical gaze toward
Travel Channel's reality TV series *Living with the Mek: The Adventures of*

DOI: 10.5876/9781607321705.c09

Mark and Olly.[2] The production company Cicada Films cast Mark Anstice and Olly Steeds as two swashbuckling British adventurers who meticulously evoke the essential features of classic Malinowskian participant observation. Ex-military officer and survivalist Mark yearns to learn the ancient lore of noble savages who live, supposedly, in ecological equilibrium. Olly, an investigative reporter and "explorer-adventurer," is intent on capturing the final glimpse of disappearing worlds. The "voice-of-God" narration from the series teaser sets the tone of exploration:

> British explorers Mark Anstice and Olly Steeds are extreme travelers with a difference. They're on a unique expedition in one of the most remote places on earth *[shots of Olly and Mark in a London flat, looking at map of their destination, which reads, "Relief Data Incomplete"].* Their goal, to live with the mysterious Mek tribe *[shots of Mek wielding axes, firing arrows],* whose ancient way of life has barely changed for thousands of years . . . and they can only be found deep in the tropical highlands of West Papua. The Mek are hunters and farmers who speak their own language and have a tradition of tribal warfare, ancient rituals, and superstition. In the village of Merengmen, the tribe had never met a Westerner until Mark and Olly's expedition arrived. But can these two adventurers survive Mek life? *[shots of Mark firing arrows].* Mark's a former soldier who travels the world, learning ancient survival techniques. Olly's a different kind of explorer. He's a journalist driven to record the traditions of the world's most remote tribes before they disappear forever *[shots of Mark and Olly wearing penis gourds, carrying bows and arrows].* Now for Mark and Olly it's total immersion in a totally different world *[shots of natives screaming, crying, fighting, and dying].*

In this chapter I examine Mark and Olly as character-subjects whose own desires and fantasies are produced in the editing room and tailored for a television audience. This fantasy of swashbuckling British men who leave the comforts of civilization and travel to distant and foreboding lands has a long history in colonial travelogues and Victorian literature. On Travel Channel's website, the show's fans can read Mark and Olly's journals, ask questions, and swap theories about the program's shocking cliffhangers. Some viewers fantasize online about the sexual allure of these rugged adventurers. With this focus on Mark and Olly as fantasy characters, I join my colleagues in this volume who would like to push the study of subjectivity beyond a Western humanist notion of the embodied *anthropos*. I also turn the ethnographic lens inward, on both myself and our discipline, to reflect on how anthropologists look at Others looking at Others. By examining anthropologists' responses to the celebrated film *Cannibal Tours*, I explore Nicholas Thomas reference to "forms of contemporary colonialism which left-liberal culture in the West is not dissociated from, but deeply implicated in" (1994, 170). I conclude by suggesting that some of our anthropological critiques (and the belief in anthropological exceptionalism on which they rest) display the very colonial proclivities of the primitivist media and pop ethnographers against which we argue.

THE GAZE OF HUMANISM: VISIONS OF ANTHROPOLOGY, VERSIONS OF CULTURAL CRITIQUE

There is no shortage of critiques—from anthropology, art history, cultural studies, and elsewhere—of primitivist art and media that reveal legacies of Western philosophy and colonialism in which the West has placed the savage Other, sometimes literally, into its own diorama of social evolution. Perhaps the best articulation of the academic critique of primitivist media is Catherine Lutz and Jane Collins's pathbreaking book *Reading National Geographic* (1993). Lutz and Collins compellingly illustrate how social evolutionist thought, mixed with a heavy dose of postwar humanism, guides the Western photographer's gaze and structures the aesthetics of the magazine layout. Lutz and Collins also note the market appeal of exotic imagery, distant places, and strange others: "In the marketplace of images, National Geographic relies on two inter-twined strategies . . . offering readers what they already know and believe in new and appealing ways . . . and sales also turn on the classic humanism . . . to portray all humans as basically the same 'under the skin'" (1993, 164). Viewed in this way, the "gaze of Western humanism" is part of a colonial regime of symbolic domination (Faris 2002). As Lutz and Collins contend, "By arguing that people are basically the same under the veneer of 'race,' National Geographic photography both denies fundamental differences and reifies the cultural boundary that it depicts" (1993, 278). Two decades later, these images have moved from the pages of magazines to the screens of cable television—*Tribe* with Bruce Parry, *Man vs. Wild* with Bear Grylls, *Bizarre Foods* with Andrew Zimmern, to name just a few.

National Geographic Channel's *Worlds Apart* is another example of the narrative conventions of televised travel to faraway lands. In this series, middle-class white families from the Midwest were plunked down, helpless, smack dab in the middle of cultural Otherness (Hoesterey 2006). Similar to Mark and Olly's, the family's mission is to immerse itself in native life, especially its horrors and hardships. Can they survive two weeks of living like the natives? Will their children realize that, even though these people must slaughter their own chickens to eat, they are really just like us? The narrative arc typically rises to a climax of cross-cultural conflict that is resolved by the soothing knowledge that, down deep, we are all alike. Lutz and Collins point to the peril of casting encounter in this way: "[T]his humanism cannot find in the third world anything more than a pale reflection of American values . . . differences that could tell us something important about history, differences that could be turned critically on practices in our own society become construed as superficial, even if attractive, flourishes that can be pulled back to reveal confirmation of important Western values" (1993, 277). Despite contrived displays of cross-cultural understanding, most episodes actually reinforce the supposed moral supremacy of Midwest American values. In an interesting narrative twist, episodes of *Worlds Apart* also have a second ending with equally little insight into history and culture. In the final sequence, the American family is back home, waxing nostalgic about their time "slumming" in the third world. Nonetheless, they are ecstatic to be home, once again surrounded by comfortable markers of difference and distinction—running water, Dominos pizza, and white neighbors. These contemporary television tales must be understood within longer histories of colonial travelogues about faraway lands and strange savages.

FIRST CONTACT AS COLONIAL NARRATIVE

In *Living with the Mek* the notion of "first contact" with a primitive Other is arguably the most important fantasy that frames the filmic encounter and structures the narrative arc. Prior to this series, Mark Anstice charted his travels to Papua in his 2004 book *First Contact: A 21st Century Discovery of Cannibals*, in which he reportedly made first contact with a group of Korowai people in the lowland Papuan jungle while traveling with friend and adventurer Bruce Parry (presenter for the BBC/Discovery Channel program *Tribe*).[3] The photo on the book jacket—of Mark Anstice donning a penis gourd adorned by a British flag—provides a sense of first contact as colonial conquest. The following excerpt provides another glimpse into the fantasy of first contact and its impact on narrative convention:

> The excitement was intense. In my wildest dreams I had never thought to experience such a feeling of exploration, such a thrill at the unknown. Every sense I possessed felt as highly-tuned as it could possibly be . . . (93)
>
> We must have appeared like nothing these people had even conceived of before we invaded their clearing. Their universe was the Korowai . . . For hundreds of years their ancestors had remained hidden from the outside world. And now we had turned up, ending their seclusion. (96–97)
>
> . . . We were in the twenty-first century and had made first contact with a new group of human beings! (98–99)

Accounts of first contact in New Guinea are especially prominent in popular media and adventure tourism. Anthropologist Rupert Stasch (2011a, 2011b) critiques the primitivist media that, for over a century, has inspired iconic images of the Korowai as the "tree house people." Stasch describes tourists' deeply felt sentiments about the epic grandeur of adventure tourism to visit the Korowai: "Framed by this cosmology, the act of visiting Korowai has an aura of profound significance. Travelers live out in personal experience a human drama of world-historical proportions. This aura propels mass media interest in Korowai and makes travel narratives marketable. Through forms like *civilization* and *the outside world*, travel writers construe Korowai and themselves as incarnating whole mythic types on a vast spatiotemporal scale" (2011a, 7).

As Stasch (2011b) also notes, imaginations of Papuan natives and images of Korowai tree houses have long histories in popular travelogues and colonial reports. Similarly, colonial expedition reports in Mek territory include fanciful tales of potentially violent first contact in which episodes of danger were reportedly resolved by the colonial officer's adept cross-cultural maneuvering. From 1910 to 1912, Dutch colonial officer A. C. de Kock traveled up one of the southern watersheds of Dutch New Guinea, past the Korowai and Kombai territories on the Eilanden River and eventually up to the highlands, where he reportedly discovered the Mek, whom he called the "Goliath Pygmies."[4] Writing almost a century prior to Mark and Olly's supposed first contact, de Kock employs literary conventions of suspense and conjures the danger of imminent first contact:

> [A] small group of Papuans, whose numbers could not be estimated, indicated with much clamour that the visit was not appreciated at all; they expressed their feelings by throwing large stones and rolling some rocks of considerable size down the slope . . . Was it a matter of chance or had we already been detected by the highlanders and did they find the slope near the beacon a useful point to watch our ways? Anyway, just as we too approached that point, we heard people shouting in confusion . . . The man walked out in front, talking loudly and vigorously, and he did not notice us until he turned around a corner of the trail and suddenly stood there, 5 m from us. He was terrified; he screamed, looked at us with wide anxious eyes, while his mouth closed and opened without being able to make a sound. (De Kock 1912 in Godschalk 1993, 173)

In rather stark contrast to the dangerous thrill of first contact and savage violence, in his later accounts de Kock waxes nostalgic about his friendly relations with the Mek. In a colonial narrative that later became the formula and fodder of reality TV, de Kock seems quite pleased with his ability to establish close bonds with the native (man). Yet, he remains blissfully ignorant of evidence to the contrary, opting to believe in his genuine connection with the Mek:

> Since then [de Kock's "first" contact] I have been in their village another two times and they have come and visited me in the bivouac several times. I never got to see women, however, and I was never allowed to have a look inside the houses, even though we were the best of friends . . .

> Thus, our trips to the inhospitable Goliath, though tiring, have been worthwhile from an anthropological perspective, too. When will this small

group of people, living peacefully there in the mountains, again come in
contact with Western civilization? Perhaps the story of our visit will live on
as a legend among their descendants. (Godschalk 1993, 175–179)

De Kock was certainly not alone among colonial officials who fancied themselves as rugged adventurers capable of taming the untouched savage. Danilyn
Rutherford (2009) examines similar narrative tropes from Dutch colonial travelogues and government reports in Dutch New Guinea during the late 1930s.
As Rutherford details, Dutch colonial officers often read popular academic
and travel narratives prior to assuming their posts in New Guinea. These
travel accounts, such as a popular one by Dr. H.J.T. Bijlmer, recounted fanciful
tales of primordial identification. As Rutherford observes: "Bijlmer himself
accounted for the unexpected affinity he felt for his hosts by classifying the
Papuans as the Caucasians' Stone Age ancestors, 'survivals' descended from a
racial missing link. In Hume's terms, Bijlmer engaged in a fantasy of resemblance in the course of inferring the Papuans' feelings and thoughts, only to
relegate his interlocutors to the past" (2009, 11–12). Building on Ann Stoler's
inquiries into the "habits of the colonial heart" (2009), Rutherford describes
the ways in which some colonial officers were concerned with cultivating
(and writing about) close affective ties with native people near Enaroltali. The
humanist gaze of colonial governance evokes the threat of violent encounter and the ecstasy of primordial identification. Rutherford puts the dynamic
eloquently: "[T]hese agents of empire combined a fantasy of familiarity with
thoughts of the remote—that is, of an era lost in the distant, Neolithic past . . .
the threat of proximity and the dream of the Stone Age went hand in hand"
(2009: 9). Nearly a century after de Kock climbed those very same mountains,
Mark and Olly told similar tales of first contact and cultural intimacy.

COLONIAL HUMANISM: THE FICTIONAL REALITY OF REALITY TV[5]

In *Living with the Mek*, for several days on end Mark and Olly must trek over
steep mountain slopes and through treacherous terrain. Yet these fearless
extreme travelers marched on, trailed by fifty porters. These porters, neighboring Yali people who had already shed their traditional garb for tattered
shorts and shirts, no longer fit Mark and Olly's fantasy of first contact. When
Mark and Olly finally arrive in a Mek village, the threat of a violent encounter is aesthetically "enhanced" by loud shouts, decontextualized shots of Mek
swinging axes, and Mark and Olly's face-to-camera stories of porters who,
scared for their safety, refused to go any further. In this genre of popular travel
and primitivist media, the adventurer must go on.

Similar fantasies of first contact can be found elsewhere in other forms
of media that academics often fancy to be more informed and intellectually
rigorous. In 2005 *The New Yorker*, one of the literary jewels of the liberal left,

could not resist yet another formulaic rendering of first contact ("Strangers in the Forest: A Guided Tour to an Isolated Tribe"). Even though the author, Lawrence Osborne, notes that "romanticization of primitive life is one of the persistent tropes in the history of Western thought" (Osborne 2005, 128), he still seems enraptured by the sublime pleasures of visiting primitive lands. He muses on Malinowski's writings about finding nirvana in the South Pacific and even quotes colonial scientist Carleton Gajdusek (who had a quite different fetish for New Guinea; see Anderson 2009): "It is strange how mediocre all in civilization seems—art, journalism, philosophy, motion pictures, and even music, whenever I leave or 'come out from' the New Guinea bush . . . Perhaps it is their great remoteness from the real nature of man and his natural world environment that makes them appear flat and unreal" (Gajdusek in Osborne 2005, 139).

Osborne, who also authored the travel book *The Naked Tourist*, grasped the idea that first contact is fantasy. Yet he seemed unable to realize that his notion of contact presupposed a (white) Westerner penetrating virgin territory. Osborne had little appreciation for possible ripple effects of contact and colonialism (Whitehead and Ferguson 1992). Osborne quotes from his interview with me, when I explained several layers of globalization and zones of contact in New Guinea: "Chinese bird hunters, Dutch Colonial officials, Indonesian military expeditions, Western tourists, Indian sandalwood traders, and American miners and missionaries" (in Osborne 2005, 129). Yet, he uses my next comment about a critical approach to how we define "first contact" only to set up his own first contact punch line: "But Hoesterey cautioned, 'I wouldn't call such tribes uncontacted. These people are indeed caught up in modernity, even if they haven't actually seen a white tourist before.' Perhaps they had engaged in trade, or seen tire tracks in the mud" (in Osborne 2005, 129).

Contrary to Osborne's understanding, however, globalization as experienced and navigated by Kombai in the Papuan jungles (and Indonesian cityscapes) is not about tracks in the mud. Rather, global connections include long histories of interaction with Papuan peoples, transcontinental chains of contact that brought the sweet potato from South America, and, lest we forget, over a century of colonial and corporate powers making claims on Papuan bodies, lands, and resources. Contemporary stories of first contact, however, ignore these histories, obscure the economic extractions of the filmic/journalistic encounter, and conveniently remain silent about those Papuans who ventured to the "outside world," only to eke out an existence on the social, political, and economic margins of urban Indonesia. Despite evidence to the contrary, the "tracks in the mud" understanding of globalization in Papua endures.

Producers at Cicada Productions, who first pitched the concept to Discovery Channel, also relied on similar understandings of first contact and globalization as something that happens *to* Papuans. I recoiled in horror as I read a preliminary outline that would be included in the formal proposal for the first series, *Living with the Kombai Tribe: The Adventures of Mark and Olly*. The following are excerpts from the original document sent on January 25, 2006 (typographical errors included):

> [**Bullet point #1**]: We meet Mark and Olly as they prepare in London. They tell us why they are passionate about the trip. For Mark, it is clear that he wants to prove that there are still untouched civilisations surviving a remote existence, while Olly comes to the trip from the conservationist point of view—the more understanding and admiration Westerners have for these remote people, the less likely governments will be to destroy their habitat. We also find out how they have been preparing themselves, physically and mentally, for the months ahead.

> [**Bullet point # 5**]: Bob [the Indonesian guide] tells them that they have travelled along the river far enough, and that it is now time to look for a clan. The jungle seems deserted and they seem to wonder whether they will ever see another living soul. The next day, however, they glimpse a tribesman. He sees them and runs back into the bushes. They follow. Are they getting into dangerous territory? Should they carry on? How will they be able to show the tribesmen that they come in peace? They hear screaming in the sky and realise that it is the noise of terrified women in a tree-house observing them from high in a tree house. Some of the men are rocking backwards and forwards tapping their heads. Anthropologist Jim tells them that this means that the clan thinks the sky is falling on their heads, such is their shock and terror at the appearance of strangers. Mark and Olly have to work hard to convince the tribe members that they are not supernatural beings.

Similar to Osborne's "tracks in the mud" understanding of Papuans' place in the world, the "sky is falling" narrative structures the narrative conventions of first contact—shot selections, quick cuts, sound effects, and contrived threats of violent encounter. Importantly, and as we noted in Dutch colonial accounts, the force of the first contact formula is not simply the threat of violence but the capacity for Westerners to tame that violence through transcultural identification or, in the words of the producer at Cicada Productions, to "work hard to convince the tribe members that they are not supernatural beings."

In *Living with the Mek*, the excitement of first contact and the lament of culture change also took on moral tones. Mark and Olly viewed themselves as the Western vanguards of the Mek way of life (at least their version of what Mek *should* be like, timeless and untouched). During pre-production, Mark and Olly explicitly told producers that they did not want to be a corrupting influence or agent of change. In one of the later episodes, Mark and Olly travel to a neighboring village to purchase pigs as expressions of gratitude for their host families. Upon arrival, Mark experiences a profound melancholy because *these* Mek wear tattered secondhand clothes, had converted to Christianity, and had imported corrugated iron roofs. During an interview aside, Mark reflects about his first impression of this neighboring village: "From what I had heard, I was sort of expecting a few clothes here, but not quite as many as this." During the final stage of post-production, editors opted to discard Mark's subsequent musing: "And it seems to be a bit more, I don't know if cosmopolitan is the right word." The visual dissonance of Papuans in clothes weighed heavy on Mark. After Mark and Olly purchased their pigs and were ready to head back, Mark explained his angst in a face-to-camera interview: "I'm actually quite keen to get out of here, now that I've got the pigs, 'cause it, it's just got such a different feel to it, this place. It's, it's not the Merengmen [village] I know and love. And, uh, it's odd. I mean, it's so similar in some ways. And yet, it even looks quite similar, apart from the clothes. But it's just very different." This candid reflection betrays a deeper anxiety about the desire to uphold dichotomies that separate civilized from savage. We can read on Mark's face a sincere feeling of the uncanny, a moment when civilization and Stone Age meet, or rather the moment at which evidence to the contrary threatens to shatter the false dichotomy between the two. Uncomfortable with those Mek who now wear clothes and worship a Christian God, Mark tries to salvage the savage. He glorifies those Mek from his village of Merengmen (that he "knows and loves") who still fit his image of the uncontacted native. To cope with this dissonance, Mark's response is to lament the fate of those seduced by the temptations of modernity and to express his solidarity with those who, like him, want to preserve the "ancient" ways.[6]

In similar fashion, Olly fancies himself a modern-day salvage ethnographer. He wonders whether their host village will begin to wear clothing or remain "traditional." Ever the lay anthropologist, Olly returns to his village to ask locals about change, especially the role of the missionaries who allegedly ordered them to burn all relics related to indigenous religion. In what one observer later told me was a staged scene, a Mek man takes Olly to what is supposed to be the cave where they actually kept sacred stones and ancestral shields hidden from the missionaries. Eerie music dominates the soundtrack as they disappear into the hidden recesses of the jungle. For Olly this event symbolizes the Mek's trust in him as a vanguard of their secrets and customs.

The fantasized intimacy with the Mek—both affective and intellectual—informs Mark and Olly's self-identification as cultural protectors and pop ethnographers. According to the narrative arc, they marched into the heart of darkness and befriended Colonel Kurtz. When the time came for Mark and Olly to go home, the extreme travelers waxed nostalgic about the deep bonds that will remain long after they leave the Mek. Viewers, in turn, are meant to believe that the Mek will forever pine for the rugged explorers. Excerpts from the final episode's teaser shed light on the affective dimension of colonial humanism:

Narrator: The people of Merengmen opened their doors and their hearts to the two explorers. They've laughed together . . .

Cut to Mark: Some of the best moments for me have undoubtedly been those times when the whole village has gone out and there's been an enormous expenditure of energy.

Narrator: They've cried together. They've shared hardship. And they shared triumphs. They've grown to trust each other with their deepest secrets. But in three days time, Mark and Olly will bid farewell to their friends . . .

Cut to Olly: We've got new friends here, and I'm really gonna miss them.

Mek #1: Personally, it will be hard for me to say goodbye to them.

Mek #2 [voiceover; shot of woman wiping her eyes]: It won't be easy to forget them.

Mek #3: When they go, we will have brothers in another land.

[Cut to rainbow over mountain range. Episode title fades in: "Farewell to the Mek."]

During the series finale, Mark and Olly's Mek families throw a farewell pig feast (financed by the film company, of course). Mark and Olly proudly donned penis gourds for the celebration. For Mark and Olly, this sartorial display communicated their cultural intimacy with the Mek. During the ceremony, the village gave Mark and Olly a chicken as a "token of friendship." Mark's adopted father, Markus, supposedly commended both of them for going native: "They were great at the party. They put on penis gourds like us. It's amazing." Later that evening, Mark shared his feelings in a night-vision video diary piece: "At times today I've sort of felt a buzz of 'yes, we're going. We're going tomorrow.' But it's tinged with a lot of sadness, actually. It's been a fantastic stay here and I'm really not looking forward to saying goodbye to them. And it's gonna be a tricky one." The next day Mark continued to reflect: "It didn't matter that Olly and I didn't speak the language. It was just important that we threw ourselves into it with as much enthusiasm as everyone else."

The series ends with a montage tribute to Western humanism. Olly's friend Yonas shared his feelings on camera: "We were lonely in this place, and they came here to cheer us up." It seems as if something was lost in translation here, somewhere in the spaces between local Papuans, Javanese translators, and British producers who control final subtitles. Olly's adopted mother, Yuliana, described Mark and Olly as her sons. Olly then expressed his gratitude for his adoptive family, especially his sister Miriam: "She's intelligent, smart, funny. She radiates a beauty and a smile which fills me with joy every time I see it." Then Markus reminisces: "They have impressed me. And they have become like us." Next, Mark laments having to leave the tranquil simplicity of such an existence: "We in the West would do well to look closely at peoples like this. People living in a place that does support them easily, and yet where they don't have a lot to distract them from living their lives in a fulfilling way." Mark's fantasy of the savage living blissfully in environmental equilibrium, however, obscures recent histories of hunger in the highlands and marginality in the cities. Olly's farewell sequence is equally structured by bittersweet feelings of cross-cultural intimacy. When Olly's adopted mother Yuliana hugs Olly goodbye, she cannot hold back her tears. The sequence then cuts to Olly's video-diary articulation of how it feels to leave the Mek:

> They have been my guides, my teachers, my hosts, and my friends.
> And they have showed me the meaning of community, of kindness, of generosity, of giving. [Cut to shots of women wiping their tears away]. And I'll carry them with me wherever I go. They have become a part of me.

Cut to long shot. Adventurers hike into the horizon. Roll credits. The End. Cut to commercial.

MARKETING THE STONE AGE: REALITY TV AS VISUAL IMPERIALISM

Primitivist media are products of a wider culture of broadcasting (Ginsburg 1975; Hughes-Freeland 1992; Turton 1992). In the current climate of broadcast television—where Mark and Olly compete for market share against Bear Grylls, Bruce Parry, and future young guns of the reality TV industry—producers can be anxious about straying too far from their bread-and-butter formulas. It is not that television producers are unaware that their narratives are formulaic or that alternative narratives exist. Many producers are wary to depart too much from a proven formula. As Kathleen Kuehnast argues, we must understand the political economy of broadcast television: "[T]he visual export is often a constructed commodity of the Other that is then packaged in the form of entertainment or as a ploy in an advertisement . . . it is a complex and interactive market, where the players, the rules, and the stakes are constantly shifting; where, as Althusser argued, economy and ideology are interwoven, they are inseparable" (1992, 186).

During another television project on which I worked, I urged the director to propose a film about a Papuan minister who was leading an effort to build an airstrip in the remote Zombandoga valley (*Planes, Pigs, and the Price of Brides*, for Discovery Channel and Essential TV in 2003). This story would necessarily portray the Migani people in a global context (or so I hoped). Already on location, we read the e-mail reply from the executive producer of the production company: "I don't think our audience is ready for that yet." Aghast at this response, the film crew went over his head to a producer at Discovery Channel. We were pleasantly surprised that she actually liked the concept. And months later, after reviewing the rough cut, she even praised the final program as a departure from the more formulaic films about New Guinea. Even this congratulatory language is informed by a certain market logic, namely the producer's own desire to find new ways to tell old stories.

Despite the prevalence of first contact narratives, many television producers do not actually believe in first contact. They are quite willing, however, to play with the first contact genre to secure contracts and keep clients happy. As one producer once told me, Cicada Productions was simply trying to accommodate the wishes of older male Discovery Channel executives who were heavily invested in the suspense, rising action, and imminent dangers of first contact narratives and traditional clothes. The following are excerpts from an e-mail exchange after I received the proposal for the original Mark and Olly series (dated January 27, 2006):

> **From my e-mail to producer/researcher (not the aforementioned executive producer):** I understand the kinds of projects that get good ratings and why. This being said, my reservations about the outline concept revolve mostly around the framing of explorer Mark going off in search of the last "untouched" people in Papua. In my comments in the attached document, I expand on why anthropologists and historians think this is impossible from a conceptual and historical point of view.

> **From producer/researcher's reply:** All the information I have is from other people's accounts of the trips—some of it is actually from X and Y, but I think what has happened is that I have written an amalgamation of information on lots of different tribes all thrown into one pot. I will change anything that is factually wrong and obviously stop you from committing professional suicide—although I would never tell you to say something you didn't mean, or have anything in that was incorrect. I just had to give Discovery of how we would fill 6 hours.
>
> What I am really worried about is penis gourds. From the start it has been really important to Discovery that we find a tribe who wears them. Personally, I think it infantile that this is a priority, but it has always been part of the proposed programme that the tribe wore them. Do the Kombai at least wear them for festivals?
>
> Re: untouched. Mark thinks the idea of first contact is phony too, and has never wanted to do that. But I think what he was driving at when he said what he said, was that he wanted to meet people who lived a remote existence unaffected by the outside world. But I will change the wording because it has obviously been misunderstood.

In this culture of broadcast, vague ideas about primitivity are much more important than the details of any single Papuan people. I call this the "Mr. Potato Head Effect." Despite the façade of highfalutin academic jargon, this analogy to the affable potato doll—whose wardrobe can be mixed and matched to produce different subjective states such as happiness, sadness, anger, and despair—is perhaps the most apt way of characterizing how the category of the primitive functions in the minds of producers. Ethnographic context is of less concern than whether a production company scout can go ahead of the film crew to find natives who are willing to act in another episode of first contact (for a price, of course).[7]

Mr. Primitive Potato Head's cowry shell nasal implant can readily be replaced by a boar's tusk nose ring, and the penis gourd of a highland film gives way to the penis wraps of lowland Kombai people. Interestingly, the DVD cover art for *Living with the Mek* includes a fine-print disclaimer stating that the natives pictured are not necessarily Mek people. The image was actually a shot of Kombai people from the original series. As long as they *look* native, the ethnographic details are of little concern. What is more important is that the film can include giddy phrases like "penis gourd" and "barebreasted" alongside more solemn disclaimers about indigenous nudity.

In the minds of producers, the perceived market value of such programs depends on these primitivist aesthetics. This means no clothes, no tin roofs, and no television sets (at least not in frame), lest the coevalness of time and Other collapse, thereby shattering the viewer's fantasy. Producers even send scouts on reconnaissance missions specifically to find people who are not wearing Western clothing (or who are willing to shed their clothes and hide any evidence of "civilization"). I once received a distressed phone call from a producer in London who, in turn, had just received a frantic satellite phone call from his scout in the Papuan highlands. Even after a two-day hike from the small mountain airstrip, the scout was apparently still finding candy wrappers on the trail and that the Mek were all in clothes. Emblems of prior contact can be distressing indeed.

The producer wanted to know how much deeper into Mek territory his scout would have to travel. After suggesting they go further east, away from the tourist trail, I reminded the producer about A. C. de Kock's 1912 report about "first contact" with Mek. I hoped this explicit reminder might preclude any claims to first contact. Unfortunately, the allure of the first contact fantasy proved irresistible and the series boldly claims that Mark and Olly were the first Westerners to step foot in this Mek territory. We gain little analytical purchase, however, in simply casting aside claims of first contact narratives as inauthentic. It is precisely the staging of first contact that sheds light on the cultural logics of television production and the narrative conventions of primitivist media. Debunking the fictions of reality TV has become another way for anthropologists to reassert ethnographic authority and to starkly contrast anthropologists from pop ethnographers. Although much of this critique is necessary and welcome, I suggest that the differences between us and them are not always so stark. In the final section I turn my attention to how anthropological critique of primitivist media and pop ethnography betrays deeper disciplinary anxieties about the expertise we presume to wield.

JAMES B. HOESTEREY

THE PLEASURES AND HORRORS OF THE ETHNOGRAPHIC
GAZE: A CULTURAL CRITIQUE OF ANTHROPOLOGY

When many anthropologists view and react to primitivist media and pop ethnographers like Mark and Olly, we often demarcate ourselves, our expertise, and our methods. We try our best to distance ourselves from these characters who simultaneously remind us of our disciplinary past and haunt our digital present. We demarcate *our* expertise in relation to *their* naïveté. We tell ourselves that *we* understand them (the cultural Other). *They* do not. *We* speak the language, *they* do not. *We* can forge intimate ties, yet *their* connections to locals are believed to be mired by mistrust, deception, and economic exchange. When anthropologists look at others looking at others, we conjure yet another Other. Perhaps our (my) abhorrence toward pop-culture icons such as Mark and Olly, Bear Grylls, and Bruce Peary also betrays a deeper anxiety, an uncanny stirring evoked by primitivist media and its lay anthropologists. In this final section, I offer word of caution and argue that self-congratulatory anthropological critiques of pop ethnography can themselves reveal a certain colonial gaze and recast new forms of evolutionism and colonial humanism.

In this final section I reflect on how anthropologists watch, evaluate, and derive particular pleasures from primitivist media and cannibal tourism. Perhaps ours is not the "gaze of Western humanism" (Faris 2002), but I will argue that it is a colonial gaze nonetheless. In colonial fashion we collect Mark and Olly—even try to possess them—as ancient relics, modern-day survivals, Stone Age anthropologists doing salvage ethnography. In doing so, we produce a new version of evolutionism in which contemporary anthropological expertise and social theory—not salvage ethnography or bounded cultures—are presumed to be the most advanced way of knowing. Some of this is warranted and welcome, yet other aspects of this critique reveal certain professional anxieties about the importance of our expertise and the relevance and role of our discipline in the public sphere.

The blend of pleasure and horror with which many anthropologists view primitivist media and pop ethnography requires an understanding of experts and expertise that goes beyond knowledge and rationality. In his vision for an anthropology of expertise, Dominic Boyer calls for anthropologists to study the affective dimensions of experts and expertise, what he refers to as the "irrational halo of expert rationality." Boyer urges anthropologists to take seriously the "place of desire, fantasy, and anxiety in the production of expert knowledge" (2008, 43). In reference to the ways anthropological expertise is being appropriated by military and business, Boyer raises important questions about anthropologists as anxiously knowing subjects: "What are we to make of these monstrous encounters with expert knowledge that is both ours and not ours . . . ? What does it indicate about specificity and validity of our jurisdiction as anthropologists? Are anthropologists threatened with eventual superfluity under these circumstances?" (2008, 42). We might ask these same questions about the appropriation of ethnographic method by reality TV. In the case of Mark and Olly as pop ethnographers, one disciplinary anxiety concerns the presumably unwarranted reappropriation of what we anthropologists believed was *our* knowledge, *our* method. What also emerges is disciplinary frustration and lament that pop pundits are not only using our ideas but getting them wrong (Besteman and Gusterson 2005).

When I screened a video clip of *Living with the Mek* at the 2009 American Anthropological Association meetings, the audience burst into laughter at the assertion of first contact and took great pleasure in performing disgust at the PowerPoint picture of the book jacket image of Mark Anstice donning the British flag on his penis gourd (AAA website has a link to the panel). Silly extreme traveler trying to go native, we giggled. If only *they* knew what current anthropological theory and method has taught *us*, they would be busy deconstructing the gaze of Western humanism rather than making supposedly misguided efforts for transcultural connection. Mark and Olly do what anthropologists used to do decades ago. But *we* moved on. We are so beyond salvage ethnography and Edenic fantasies of untouched tribes. And semiotic approaches? *Sooo* 1970s, we say. It is as if Mark and Olly were stuck in an anthropological Stone Age. Scoffing at their claims to cross-cultural connections, we would remind them that culture goes "all the way down." Or so we think. Some anthropologists, myself included, have tried to reassert ethnographic authority through a refracted ethnographic gaze. With our mocking laughter at "The Mark and Olly Follies" (Sheppard 2011), we transform them into contemptible Malinowskian figurines inside an intellectual-evolutionist diorama of anthropology's past. Mark's fantasies of first contact undoubtedly sound like nails on a chalkboard; yet, we also take particular pleasure in performing our disgust.

To further explore the idea of anthropologists as anxious experts, I now turn to anthropologists' commentaries about Dennis O'Rourke's 1988 film *Cannibal Tours*. This film—about a tourist boat that goes up the Sepik River in New Guinea—provides a fascinating portrait of primitive culture's commodification and the tourist's colonial gaze. In the lore of anthropology's story about itself, this film has served as a badge of honor of sorts that validates anthropological expertise and soothes anxieties about the importance of anthropological expertise and ethnographic method. I should note that the filmmaker Dennis O'Rourke is not an anthropologist and he actually admits ambivalent feelings of affinity and disgust toward the ethnographic enterprise (O'Rourke in Lutkehaus 1989, 432–34). For the present purposes, however, I am more interested in how anthropologists come to identify with and seemingly take pleasure in O'Rourke's filmic contempt for silly tourists in a strange land.

In her introduction to an interview with O'Rourke, anthropologist Nancy Christine Lutkehaus lauds the filmmaker's self-reflexivity, scorns the "rich Western tourists," and proceeds to mock the tourists' lack of meaningful interaction with the locals (Lutkehaus 1989, 423). Anthropologists also derive a peculiar pleasure, albeit laced with abject horror, at watching tourist Others *mis*-understand culture. I venture to guess that most anthropologists at some point have taken pleasure in telling the occasional "stupid tourist" story. The unspoken assumption, of course, is that *we* have meaningful relationships because *we* know how to establish rapport and get to the *real* culture. Lutkehaus describes her connection to the film by recounting her own story about cannibal tourists:

> As an anthropologist who has worked in Papua New Guinea and has had the experience of traveling with a group of tourists on the same boat as the tourists in the film, *Cannibal Tours* has a strong impact on me. O'Rourke's images of the tourists with the villagers provoked in me the unease that I had felt . . . Although the tourists I accompanied were not as ethnocentric, naïve, or paternalistic . . . our encounters with villagers were as superficial, based primarily on bargaining for artifacts and taking pictures. (1989, 427)

We imagine ourselves in their relief. Like the Dutch colonial officers de Kock and de Bruyn, we anxiously assert *our* capacity for intimate identification with the native. *We* are noble moral protagonists; those pesky tourists are cultural antagonists. O'Rourke's reflection on his noble role as filmmaker is especially illuminating: "I am a protagonist in all of my films . . . I'm a strong presence like a good painter is a strong presence in his or her work" (in Lutkehaus 1989, 429). In the context of *Living with the Mek*, we tell ourselves that Olly is the one who looks with the naïve humanist gaze; surely not us. We might also ask ourselves, how meaningful *our* interactions really are to the people whom we observe and interview? To what extent does language fluency and social theory really guarantee accurate and authentic insight? Language proficiency does indeed provide a privileged vantage point through which to understand people in context, but it does not guarantee cultural understanding or meaningful relationships.

Dean MacCannell, in his review of *Cannibal Tours*, takes anthropological exceptionalism a step further when he speaks in terms of the emancipatory potential of anthropology: "One does not find among the tourist any similar lightness of sensibility . . . The film is a reminder that the task of anthropology is far from done—we have yet to explain ourselves" (1988; cited in Lutkehaus 1989, 427). Contrasting hapless tourist sensibilities with shrewd ethnographic method enables us to play out our own fantasy of resemblance and cross-cultural intimacy. Such a critique verges on the language of missionization and evokes an uncanny reminder of the aforementioned Dutch colonial officer de Bruyn. Anthropological nostalgia about ethnographic methods and friendships forged during fieldwork sound strikingly similar to the warm welcome de Bruyn reportedly received in highland New Guinea: "When I asked what was up, Soalekigi, who was moved, answered that he was crying because I was like one from out of his midst . . . I ate sweet potatoes, just like the mountain dwellers, I slept in the mountain dwellers' hut, just like he himself did, and now I was taking part in the [feast] . . . just like a mountain Papuan" (in Rutherford 2009, 18).

In addition to acknowledging our pride in *our* ability to connect with native peoples, deserved or not, anthropologists would also do well to reflect on the colonial gaze with which we watch Others watching Others. In one the most memorable scenes of *Cannibal Tours*, an elderly female tourist, armed with her camera and gazing through horn-rimmed glasses, creeps quietly toward a native New Guinea man in the foreground who stands during an ongoing interview with the filmmaker. (Tourists creep. Anthropologists walk, of course.) O'Rourke recalls his role as filmmaker who watches the tourist watch the native, who is listening to the filmmaker, who informs the native he is being watched by the tourist: "One of my favorite moments in the film is the one where [this] woman comes in from behind and suddenly you have fusion. In this case the woman . . . is not doing it as an act of bravado. To her it's perfectly natural. She's just saying, 'Well I'm here to take photographs of things like this young man with these marks and, no problem, there's just this other camera there, you know. We've got him in our cross-fire.'" (Lutkehaus 1989, 430).

Other than including his own voice in the final cut and tinkering with narrative structures, O'Rourke offers remarkably little reflexivity concerning the gaze of the filmmaker in that scene. How dare she enter *his* frame! O'Rourke does not reflect on his pleasure watching (and editing) that sequence, nor does he fully appreciate the metaphor of violence used to describe the photographic encounter between tourist and native. O'Rourke characterizes the tourist as the predatory and violent voyeur. O'Rourke, however, wishes to consume the tourist savage. As James Faris has also observed with respect to this scene, "Everyone is a victim of the camera, certainly the documentary camera" (1992, 177). Our ethnographic gaze—especially when *we* watch *them* attempting *our* work in the land of the *Other* where only *we* are welcome—is profoundly marked by the uncanny ambivalence of watching tourists fumble when they try to establish rapport. In the case of Mark and Olly, we are especially irked by two self-described "extreme travelers" who dare to wave the wand of Malinowskian participant observation.

To study the ethnographic gaze toward pop ethnographers is an endeavor quite different from the postmodern interrogation of text, truth, and authority. Intellectual remorse about anthropology's complicity in colonialism and the fictional dimensions of ethnographic writing are not the only issues at hand; we must also tend to how our deserving, yet occasionally self-righteous, critiques of pop-culture depictions of anthropology and Others have the capacity to unwittingly extend the contemporary colonial gaze. When we bask in self-congratulatory critique and publicly scold those dim-witted pop-culture icons who seek the untouched savage, we anthropologists are in danger of reproducing a different sort of intellectual evolutionism in which anthropologists once again claim the moral high ground and a monopoly on cultural expertise. By insisting that surely *they* could never identify with *our* natives, we render any possibility of transcultural understanding as some quaint fantasy of Western humanism. The decolonization of anthropology is not some mess cleaned up by the postmodernist turn and absolved with an apologetic gaze to anthropology's past. By tending to anthropologists' pleasures and horrors of watching *The Adventures of Mark and Olly*, we might better understand that colonial proclivities continue to haunt anthropology. *Cannibal Tours Redux.* Coming soon to a field site near you.

NOTES

1. I am grateful to several colleagues who graciously read drafts and provided valuable critique: Marshall Clark, Kenneth George, George Gmelch, Sharon Gmelch, Rupert Stasch, Karen Strassler, Neil Whitehead, Kent Wisniewski, and anonymous reviewers at University Press of Colorado. I also extend warm appreciation to several gracious and engaging audiences of professors and students when I presented this material in classrooms and public forums: California State University–Chico, New College of Florida, Taman Ismail Marzuki Center for Cultural Arts, University of San Francisco, and University of Wisconsin–Madison.

2. Unlike most of my other projects, I did not accompany the film crew for this series. Instead, I provided basic historical and cultural information during pre-production and served as fact-checker during the later stages of post-production. In 2002, however, I accompanied a film crew for the Discovery Channel program *Mek Path to Manhood*. German and Dutch missionaries, anthropologists, and missionary-anthropologists have been working among the Mek for decades, a different story of "tribal" warfare that must wait for another day (see Godschalk 1993).

3. In this series Bruce Parry had to survive "tribal" challenges in remote areas of New Guinea, West Papua, Borneo, Africa, and South America. It was an important precursor whose relative success in the United States led, in part, to the Mark and Olly series. Without the space to discuss it here, producers noted interesting differences between the marketing campaigns in England and America, where it was believed Discovery Channel really amped up the exoticism with promotional sound bites like "Explore your inner native!"

4. I e-mailed a PDF version of this report to the producers in the naïve hope that it would preempt any claims to first contact. Clearly, this (and a well-documented list of protests) did not have the desired effect.

5. I borrow the term "fictional reality" from Aretxaga (2000), who originally used it to characterize how state terror is imagined. Nonetheless, it also offers a way to understand staged and scripted behavior beyond the analytical frame of authenticity.

6. Mark reveals the limits of his love for the village later in the episode. For one who does not want to "change" Papuans, he is especially keen for them to cultivate a Kantian sense of reason and rationality. When Mark's adoptive father falls ill, the village suspects witchcraft, but Mark scoffs at the notion. During a face-to-camera interview, Mark reaches his limits of cultural relativism and, in doing so, reveals the contradictions of his ideal vision for the Mek people to remain untouched while breaking out of their prison of superstitions and also joining the oasis of rational science and medicine—just as long as they do not convert to Christianity, wear clothes, or use Indonesian currency.

7. More recently, Mark Anstice has worked with BBC4 to produce a program that examines "first contact for cash" tourism in West Papua. Despite this angle, the encounter is still premised as a voyage to meet possibly uncontacted people that Papuan gold prospectors supposedly found upriver. Anstice even reasserts his previous claim to first contact and advances the notion that Korowai believe that the sight of a white man is a harbinger for the sky falling down on their heads. He says nostalgically, "By blundering into their world, I had changed their lives forever" (http://www.youtube.com/watch?v=jprJBYYRcqQ; accessed May 17, 2010).

REFERENCES

Anderson, Warwick. 2009. *The Collectors of Lost Souls: Turning Kuru Scientists into Whitemen*. Baltimore: Johns Hopkins University Press.

Anstice, Mark. 2002. *First Contact: A 21st Century Discovery of Cannibals*. London: Eye Books Ltd.

Aretxaga, Begoña. 2000. "A Fictional Reality: Paramilitary Death Squads and the Construction of State Terror in Spain." In *Death Squad: the Anthropology of State Terror*, ed. Jeffrey A. Sluka, 46–69. Philadelphia: University of Pennsylvania Press.

Besteman, Catherine, and Hugh Gusterson, eds. 2005. *Why America's Top Pundits Are Wrong: Anthropologists Talk Back*. Berkeley: University of California Press.

Boyer, Dominic. 2008. "Thinking through the Anthropology of Experts." *Anthropology in Action* 15 (2): 38–46. http://dx.doi.org/10.3167/aia.2008.150204.

De Kock, A. C. 1912. "Einige ethnologische en anthropologische gegevens omtrent een dwergstam in het bergland van Zuid Nieuw-Guinea" ("Some Ethnological and Anthropological Data about a Pygmy Tribe in the Highlands of South New Guinea")." *TKNAG* 29: 154–170. http://dx.doi.org/10.3167/aia.2008.150204

Faris, James C. 1992. "Anthropological Transparency: Film, Representation and Politics." In *Film as Ethnography*, ed. Peter Ian Crawford and David Turton, 171–182. Manchester: Manchester University Press.

Faris, James C. 2002. "The Gaze of Western Humanism." In *The Anthropology of Media: A Reader*, ed. Kelly Askew and Richard R. Wilk, 77–91. Malden, MA: Blackwell.

Ginsburg, Faye. 1975. "Ethnography on the Airwaves: The Presentation of Anthropology on American, British, Belgian, and Japanese Television." In *Principles of Visual Anthropology*, ed. Paul Hockings, 363–398. The Hague: Mouton.

Godschalk, Jan A. 1993. "Sela Valley: An Ethnography of a Mek Society in the Eastern Highlands, Irian Jaya, Indonesia." PhD dissertation. Netherlands: Vrije Universiteit.

Hoesterey, James B. 2006. "Teaching National Geographic." *Anthropology News* 46 (4): 47. http://dx.doi.org/10.1525/an.2005.46.4.47.1.

Hughes-Freeland, Felicia. 1992. "Representation by the Other: Indonesian Cultural Documentation." In *Film as Ethnography*, ed. Peter Ian Crawford and David Turton, 242–256. Manchester: Manchester University Press,

Kuehnast, Kathleen. 1992. "Visual Imperialism and the Export of Prejudice: An Exploration of Ethnographic Film." In *Film as Ethnography*, ed. Peter Ian Crawford and David Turton, 183–95. Manchester: Manchester University Press.

Lutkehaus, Nancy Christine. 1989. "'Excuse Me, Everything is Not Alright': On Ethnography, Film, and Representation: An Interview with Filmmaker Dennis O'Rourke." *Cultural Anthropology* 4 (4): 422–37. http://dx.doi.org/10.1525/can.1989.4.4.02a00060.

Lutz, Catherine A., and Jane L. Collins. 1993. *Reading National Geographic*. Chicago: University of Chicago Press.

MacCannell, Dean. 1988. "Review of *Cannibal Tours*." *Anthropos: International Review of Anthropology and Linguistics* 88: 45.

MacDougall, David. 1998. *Transcultural Cinema*. Princeton, NJ: Princeton University Press.

O'Rourke, Dennis. 1988. *Cannibal Tours*. 72 min. 35 mm.

Osborne, Lawrence. 2005. "Strangers in the Forest: A Guided Tour to an Isolated Tribe." *New Yorker* 18 (April): 124–140.

Rutherford, Danilyn. 2009. "Sympathy, State Building and the Experience of Empire." *Cultural Anthropology* 24 (1): 1–32. http://dx.doi.org/10.1111/j.1548-1360.2009.00025.x.

Sheppard, Glen, Jr. 2011. "The Mark and Olly Follies." *Anthropology News* 52 (5): 18. http://dx.doi.org/10.1111/j.1556-3502.2011.52517_2.x.

Stasch, Rupert. 2011a. "The Camera and the House: The Semiotics of New Guinea 'Treehouses' in Global Visual Culture." *Comparative Studies in Society and History* 53 (1): 75–112. http://dx.doi.org/10.1017/S0010417510000630.

Stasch, Rupert. 2011b. "Textual Iconicity and the Primitivist Cosmos: Chronotopes of Desire in Travel Writing about Korowai of West Papua." *Journal of Linguistic Anthropology* 21 (1): 1–21. http://dx.doi.org/10.1111/j.1548-1395.2011.01080.x.

Stoler, Ann L. 2009. *Along the Archival Grain: Epistemic Anxieties and Colonial Common Sense*. Princeton, NJ: Princeton University Press.

Thomas, Nicholas. 1994. *Colonialism's Culture: Anthropology, Travel, and Government*. Princeton, NJ: Princeton University Press.

Turton, David. 1992. "Anthropology on Television: What's Next?" In *Film as Ethnography*, ed. Peter Ian Crawford and David Turton, 283–99. Manchester: Manchester University Press.

Whitehead, Neil L., and Brian Ferguson, eds. 1992. *War in the Tribal Zone: Expanding States and Indigenous Warfare*. Santa Fe, NM: School of American Research Press.

10

Invisible Caboclos and Vagabond Ethnographers

A Look at Ethnographic Engagement in Twenty-First-Century Amazonia

Kent Wisniewski

INTRODUCTION

I had been awake for a while when I heard my research assistant Dal clapping, then pounding, on the door of our two-room, cinder-block dwelling, yelling, *Accorda! Accorda, aí!* ("Wake-up! Wake-up in there!") It was the wet season and I lingered in bed because it was only in the morning hours that my body heat finally dried out the thin foam mattress and I no longer had the feeling of sleeping on a damp sponge. I was reveling in those precious dry moments and wondering how we would ever find a caboclo community to work in when I heard Dal's shouts.

Dal and his wife Léia are Brazilian hippies or *malucos* (literally, "crazies") and also my unlikely research assistants. The hippy culture in the United States is now a thing of the past, but in Brazil it is still a vibrant, viable way of life. There is a national law in Brazil that allows artisans to sell their wares in any public space. Thus, hippies travel all over the country doing just that. They all have some sort of handicraft specialty and live day to day, selling their goods

DOI: 10.5876/9781607321705.c10

FIGURE 10.1.
Author (center) with Léia, Dal, and Jeosadak

in the public plazas around the country. I met Dal and Léia at the beginning of my journey in Manaus, a city of 1.6 million that sits just above where the inky Rio Negro and the turbulent Rio Solimões combine their forces to form the Amazon mainstream. It did not take long for our lives to become intertwined.

Scholars today recognize that the particular historical contexts of colonization and modernity in various locations around the world have produced different social and political frameworks or "alternative modernities" (Gaonkar 2001, 1). The context created by Brazilian modernity is one of these dynamic structures that creates the space for many kinds of experiences and understandings of the world: what can be recognized as plural ontologies (Whitehead 2009). These varied ontological frameworks give people with different experiences and understandings of Brazilian modernity the agency to adapt and innovate to create meaningful lives and find ways to survive in the face of their changing experiences of the world.

My dissertation fieldwork (2005) took me to Brazil to study the adaptations and ontological orientation of one particular group living at the margins of Brazilian society: that of the mixed-heritage *ribeirinhos*, or caboclos, of the Brazilian Amazon along the middle Rio Negro near Barcelos.[1] However, in the end my research program became a collaborative effort between myself, a caboclo anthropologist, and Dal and Léia (the Brazilian hippy couple), whom I have labeled "vagabond ethnographers" because, in addition to traveling the country selling their wares, they make a living as cultural liaisons for tourists. The choice to live as a hippy in Brazil is another adaptation or innovation within the context of Brazilian modernity. These innovations produced by Brazil's hippy culture revealed yet another ontological orientation, and this experience forced me to try to understand what might be shared in the lived experiences of caboclos and hippies in the modernity shaped by the Brazilian state. In this chapter, I will describe the production of our ethnography and its implications for ethnographic methods.

Anthropology, more than most disciplines, has taken great pains to reflect on its own origins and practices. Although the reflexive process can often be painful, the net result has been fruitful. Through this process of self-reflection anthropologists have learned to be more aware of the importance of history in cross-cultural understandings and, in particular, how the effects of contact and colonization shape the lives of the people we study, as well as how our own cultural backgrounds cannot help but influence our understandings of others.

As scholars of humanity we now regularly seek to include the voices of those seldom or never heard before and agonize over how to properly represent those voices to others. In particular the relationship between the ethnographer and informant has been a point of some interest since the beginnings of the discipline. Kaufmann (2002) provides an excellent review of the many ways in which anthropologists have portrayed informants over time. These include minimizing their presence entirely, showing them as uncooperative or even prone to lying, and, more recently, describing them as victims of the ethnographers. Kaufmann discusses that even when informants are described by ethnographers as victims of invisibility, the same ethnographers have done little to right this perceived injustice. He notes, "Perhaps the most difficult way of coming to terms with informants is an honest reckoning of one's dependence on them" (2002, 233). He goes on to show that although many anthropologists have long recognized their dependence on informants and the important role they play in shaping the ethnographic product, it was not until recently that scholars openly acknowledged that anthropological knowledge is always a coproduction of all the various participants involved in a particular study (such as ethnographers, assistants, research agencies, and informants) (Schumaker 2001). Therefore, Kaufmann's intention is to "elevate the recognition of informants in fieldwork" (2002, 231). He describes his own field situation in Madagascar as one that was governed by informants who he characterizes as "resolute overseers" because they controlled and guided his modes and sites of both participation and observation in the field. My intent here is allied with Kaufmann's as I reveal the roles of my hippy research assistants (who were also my overseers) and my caboclo informants (who also played an overseeing role) in the coproduction of anthropological knowledge. However, I also intend to show that an overt recognition of these kinds of collaborations has implications for anthropological practice.

Many of the chapters in this volume highlight two of the newest frontiers for ethnographic investigation: human engagement with virtual worlds, beings, and things and human sociality mediated by technology. As the editors Wesch and Whitehead have noted, these new frontiers require anthropologists to rethink the ethnographic engagement, begging the question, how do we research in a realm of human experience that we can only truly access through measured participation? In other words, how can we as anthropologists theorize our participation in the "posthuman" world of technologically enhanced and mediated societies (Whitehead 2009)?

Many of the contributors in this volume are blazing the trail in beginning to answer these questions, but I believe it is important to note that this questioning moment has wider implication for ethnographic research in general. Confronted with these new research frontiers, anthropologists have the opportunity to reconsider how to engage ethnographically with a rapidly changing world. Anthropology has come a long way from its myopic focus on small-scale societies that were often described as bounded cultural units existing outside of time. It is time, once again, to expand and refine our approach, this time in the direction of a posthuman anthropological approach (Whitehead 2009), one that not only is equipped to grapple with the relationship between humans and technology but also recognizes humans as part of a much larger system that includes relationships with animals, insects, microorganisms, and spirits, as well as people that are not always considered human by others (Whitehead 2009, forthcoming; Heckenberger, this volume).

This approach must also recognize that in our globalized world, the intersubjective relationships that produce meaning and understanding have changed in form and intensity. By form, I am referring to how intersubjective relationships may be created with or through technologies; with or through political or social structures; with or through animals, insects, or microorganisms; with or through supernatural realms; or, finally, with or through the many categories of people treated as marginal or subhuman in our globalized world (Heckenberger, this volume). In addition to the number of forms, the intensity of these relationships has also increased. In today's world, whether in the urban or rural spaces, one has a much greater chance than in the past of interacting with many people whose ontological frameworks vary widely, whether we are speaking of online or offline realities. Globalization has also created the cultural space in many parts of the world for so-called marginal populations that survive based on their own ethnographic insights, such as Brazilian hippies. They are, in a sense, vagabond ethnographers who collect data on the cultural worlds that they move through and dwell in as a method for survival. It is for these reasons that a posthuman approach to anthropology must further theorize ethnographic participation whether the anthropological subjects are digitally mediated or live at the margins of the dominant society. Theorizing participation will give us a clearer understanding of how ethnographic knowledge is produced, revealing it as a shared product, an intersubjective product, not just of and about humans but of and about human interaction with all categories, in a way that does not privilege or overvalue the role of the anthropologist in its production. It is my hope that the ethnographic reflection that follows will help to illustrate this need or at least help to stimulate thought in this area.

STUDYING CABOCLOS

As a graduate student, I became interested in caboclo societies as the most populous yet understudied groups in Amazonia. Throughout its history, Amazonia has been a region of global interest because of its rich resources. The waxing and waning of extractive industries fueled by colonial and then national and international demand for diverse resources (including slave labor, rubber, lumber, tree oils and fibers, Brazil nuts, animal skins, and even aquarium fish) have set the rhythm of the Amazonian economy through the years. In Brazil, caboclos continue to labor in this system even as boom and bust cycles produce a highly irregular economic base. Historically, people living in caboclo societies have had to constantly adjust between two ways of life: everyday subsistence and engagement in various extractive activities that are not sustainable in the long run. Unfortunately, in spite of caboclos' lead role in the region's economy, scholars of Amazonia largely ignored them until recently in favor of studying the seemingly more authentic indigenous cultures. The scholars who did look at caboclo societies dismissed them as an adaptive response to colonial pressures and even a pathological social form just two steps away from complete assimilation (Wagley 1976 [1953]; Moran 1974; Parker 1985a, 1985b; Ross 1978).[2] It is in this sense that caboclos remain illegible as anthropological subjects. This illegibility has lead to invisibility for the caboclos as well. The Brazilian government often views Amazonia as a natural resource warehouse and rarely includes caboclos in development and conservation plans that continue to complicate their subsistence strategies in the region. Even the label "caboclo" can be marginalizing (Pace 1997; Harris 1998). It is most often pejorative when used by outsiders—almost as a linguistic tool for devaluing others. It is something akin to "redneck" in the United States; it can be used by insiders with pride, but used in the wrong way by an outsider it could be a "fighting word." I retain it here because this is how the people with whom I worked self-identified.

Thus, I set out for a Malinowskian field experience, living with a small-scale society in a remote location, but it was not that straightforward because our world has become quite complicated. While waiting for my visa paperwork to clear in Manaus, I explored the city and met Dal and Léia while they were selling jewelry at the Praça de Polícia (Police Plaza). As I walked by the row of hippy salespeople, most of them paid me little attention but one guy yelled out in heavily accented English: "Hey, friend. Come take a look." He was a crazy-looking character in his early forties. He was balding, but the hair he did have was in long dreadlocks. His arms and shirtless torso were a canvas for a wide assortment of tattoos, and he sported a pair of drugstore reading glasses. He told me his name was Dal, and he was immediately glad to learn that I spoke Portuguese because he had already used up all the English he knew when he called me over. I bought several items from him, and he invited me to sit and talk with him while he customized the pieces I selected. I spent the rest of the afternoon talking with him between customers.

It took three weeks to get my visa issues resolved, and during that time I passed many afternoons sitting on the sidewalk and talking to my new hippy friends Dal, his wife Léia, and their three-year-old son Jeosadak. We got to know each other quite well, and Dal became interested in my research project. Dal is one of the most intriguing people I have ever met. He can talk himself into or out of any situation and really makes his living by talking to people. One of twenty-three children of a now-successful banana planter from the interior of São Paulo state, he has lived his life, as he puts it, *andando* ("walking") since he was thirteen years old. He knows Brazil inside out, or perhaps more accurately, from the bottom up. When I met him, he had already spent three years living in and around the Xingú National Park and another two years farming manioc in the Amazonian state of Acre. He was familiar with rural life in the Amazon and thoroughly enjoyed hunting and fishing.

Léia, Dal's wife, was twenty-four when I met her. She had been on the hippy road for about six years. She grew up in the city of São Paulo, graduated from high school, and started working at restaurant jobs. She said she had always been fascinated by the hippies who sold their crafts in the city plazas. She was quite shy at the time but eventually mustered enough courage to talk to some of the hippies. They encouraged her to hit the road, and finally one day she did with a friend of hers. They traveled for several months, barely making it until they met Dal in Rio de Janeiro just before Carnaval. Dal was in a bad state, drinking a lot and selling *lixo* ("garbage"), as he put it—just rocks, sticks, or other things he found—but because of his gift of gab he was able to make money. This infuriated Léia, who worked hard making her jewelry, but she was too shy to be a good salesperson. Dal said it took him seven days of

Carnaval to finally win over Léia, and they eventually hit the road together. Dal taught her well and no one could accuse Léia of being shy today. She is now a verbal force in her own right. Dal stopped drinking at Léia's request and gave up some of his other wild ways, and soon they had a son together. I was to find out that their lifestyle made both Dal and Léia natural ethnographers and excellent interviewers with a boisterous curiosity.

When I met them, Dal and his family had been in Manaus for almost four months, resting after biking a long segment of the Trans-Amazonian Highway; they were ready for a new adventure. Much of the jewelry Dal and Léia made and sold was fashioned from natural materials from the Amazonian region, such as palm fibers, seeds, fish scales, feathers, and animal teeth. Dal suggested that he and his family come along with me since they had never been up the Rio Negro before and they could collect raw materials they needed as we were visiting different villages. Despite my fondness for all three of them, I thought this was a horrible idea and one that would surely hurt the aims of my research, but at the same time, I did not want to suddenly abandon my new friends. I agonized over how to handle the situation for several days, finally telling Dal that I needed to speak frankly with him. I told him that we could travel up the Rio Negro (to my field site of Barcelos) together, but that I was affiliated with a university and I did not know what people might think if I showed up with a hippy family. Therefore, if things did not go well once we arrived in Barcelos, we would have to go our separate ways. He understood completely and agreed to those terms.

We took the next *recreio* (passenger ferry) to Barcelos and arrived at six in the morning after the second night of travel. The first night I spent in a hotel and Dal and family slept in the Praça de Prefeitura (Mayoral Plaza) of this small Amazonian town. I felt uncomfortable about that arrangement and had already seen on the boat trip how being with the malucos actually made it easier to meet people and start talking with them. It seemed that my original fears were unfounded. In the urban areas of Brazil most people are quite wary of hippies as they represent a marginal and illegible social category. Hippies may be helpful, friendly, and fun, but they can also be dangerous or unpredictable and are often associated with drugs and petty crime.[3] However, in the rural areas, people reacted to the hippies mainly with a great curiosity, increasing my chance of making local contacts. Thus, our second day in town, I told Dal I wanted him to be my official research assistant. He laughed, saying he knew nothing about research, but he would help me as he much as he could. He suggested that we try to rent a house in town for the time being. We went to the local radio station (Dal's idea) and had them announce that we were in the market for a house. Within an hour we had four houses to choose from. We settled on a two-room, government-built dwelling whose owner was a young single mother with two children. That same afternoon, she moved in with her mother and we moved into her house.

FIGURE 10.2.
Dal and Léia

We soon set about the main task of research: trying to find a riverine community whose residents would allow us to live with them for an extended period of time. We tried a number of approaches and day by day got to know more people in town who could give us some leads to the communities in the area. Dal convinced me to buy a seven-meter-long wooden canoe and a five-horsepower motor with a long propeller shaft, known locally as a *rabeta*. We tried to find a guide—someone who knew the area and knew people in the communities—but this proved difficult. Barcelos has grown a great deal in the last forty years because of the *piaba* (aquarium fish) and the *pesca esportiva* (sport-fishing) industries. Both industries are seasonal and can only be performed during the summer, or dry, season. Hence, the winter, or wet, season is a difficult time, especially for people in town, many of whom have little or no income during this time because their jobs are seasonal. The wet season is also a difficult time for some subsistence activities such as fishing because as the river floods, the fish spread out, and it can be difficult to find them day to day.

One would think that the off-season, with so many people unemployed, would be the best time to find a guide and even a cut-rate one, but many things about this area are counter-intuitive. The sport-fishermen who visit the area are relatively wealthy. On average they pay between US$4,000 and US$7,000 for a week of fishing for trophy peacock bass, known locally as *tucunaré* (*Chicla* sp.). Unfortunately, I was put into the same category as the sport-fishing tourists. As one of the town merchants said about me to one of my neighbors from the community on a trip back to town, "That gringo is just full of money. All you need to do is pick him up by the heels and give him a good shake." This attitude was prevalent all over town. We were approached by many men who said they were guides, but none of them would lower their price—not even when we were supplying the canoe and motor. The small research stipend I had would not have lasted long at the price they were asking; throughout this time Dal was invaluable in seeing that I was not swindled. Eventually, we found a local man who was willing to work for the going daily rate for laborers, and with him, we made several short trips to communities with minimal success. Either people did not know what to make of us or hardly anyone was there in the community. It soon became obvious we needed someone to give us an introduction.

Dal turned out to be the best research assistant I could ask for. He did enough worrying for both of us. He wanted to ensure that we found a good site and wanted to make it happen as soon as possible. After several weeks, we were left with two choices of possible field sites. An American missionary in Barcelos traveled to an upriver community called Ponta da Terra every weekend, and he offered to take us there and introduce us to the community. I was a little uncomfortable with this situation because I did not want to be associated with a church for better or worse. Our second option was to go to another community upriver. We met a local guide named Carlos, who was a friend of someone we trusted in town and his uncle was the president of this community. The community voted to let us come and stay, but we were going to be paying Carlos as our guide the whole time we were there. The community also voted to charge us for every photo that we took while there. Neither of these options seemed very promising, but the morning before we were supposed to head upriver with Carlos everything changed.

During our down time in Barcelos, I was teaching Dal and Léia English. They were keen to learn because English would help them sell their wares to *gringos* (foreign tourists), many of whom speak English regardless of their national origin. They were diligent students and each kept their own notebooks with words and phrases they were learning. The morning that we were planning to leave Dal pounded on the door. After rising early, he had taken his notebook with him to the edge of the river to study and to worry about our impending trip. While he sat on the high bank near the riverside gasoline station, a small, partially covered canoe powered by a rabeta pulled up along the bank. Its pilot was a small, weathered old man wearing a black felt hat popular among some of the river folk. Dal helped him land his canoe and immediately struck up a conversation with him. He assisted the old man up the steep, slippery bank of clay with his gas can, all the while winning him over with conversation. Dal soon found out that his name was Brasilino and that he was the seventy-nine-year-old founder of a small community five or six hours downriver called Lago Grande. Dal explained to Brasilino who he was, that he was working with me, and that we were trying to find a community where we could stay for a while. He then invited Brasilino to come to our house for breakfast and coffee. Brasilino accepted and soon Dal was at the door pounding and shouting to wake Léia and me.

By the time I crawled out from under my mosquito net and stepped into the main room, Léia had already let in the two men. It was then that I first met Brasilino Anício da Silva. As we shared coffee and biscuits with butter, I explained to Brasilino that my project was about people, people like himself, and that I wanted to understand what life was like in the rural communities and how they think about the past. He thought this was a great idea. I could learn about them and they could learn about me. Brasilino is a thinker and philosopher of sorts, exactly the type of person every ethnographer is looking for as an informant. He has an innate curiosity about other people and other places and spent his whole life traveling the Rio Negro and its tributaries. As Brasilino told me, "In each locality I go, I go observing. I am an observant fellow. What happens in the corner, I'm recording in my brain" (*Em cada localidade eu ando, eu ando observando, eu sou sujeito observante. O que acontece num canto eu tô gravando na minha mente*) (Wisniewski 2009, 74). Brasilino was aware of the many researchers who come to Amazonia but said they were always studying nature: plants, fish, animals, or birds. Not one of them ever

FIGURE 10.3.
Brasilino

wanted to know about the people. In this sense I see Brasilino as an amateur anthropologist. Brasilino immediately recognized that we would be involved in a multi-directional cultural exchange in which we would learn about each other. He saw our work as his work and saw our presence as having great value for his community. Brasilino encouraged all residents of his community to participate in our project, and after our first few interview sessions together, he began to set the research agenda, announcing to me the topics that he wished to talk about and also what he wanted to learn about my life. This was the beginning of our adventure into Brasilino's changing world.

In many ways, hippies share caboclos' illegibility and in some sense their invisibility. They are a part of the urban streetscape of most Brazilian cities, such as São Paulo, where they sell their wares in the city plazas during the day and often pass their nights on the city streets as one of several groups that are seen as marginal or even subhuman to members of the dominant society (see Heckenberger, this volume). Hippies reject work-a-day lives, forging their own anarchic way of life in the interstitial spaces. They are an illegible social category to much of the rest of society and are feared by many because of their liminal status. This liminality allows hippies to move freely between different segments of society and enhances their invisibility. For example, in the cities, the hippies are able to go into the *favelas*, or shanty towns, where the drug trade is centered and make their purchases fairly easily without being threatened by the drug traffickers or the police, who know they are not worth hassling because they have no money. Thus, obtaining drugs is a service they often perform for tourists in exchange for money or drugs.

Much like caboclos, they have also been ignored by academics. To date (and perhaps to their advantage), no one has made them legible to others. Both hippy and caboclo lives are paradoxes of modernity. They are produced in part by the structure of the dominant society, but they are not fully integrated in it. They survive at the margins of society by "creative adaptation" (Gaonkar 2001, 18) and "audacious innovation" (Gow 1991, 298), and in this way they find protection in their invisibility and illegibility because to become visible and legible to others is to lose some of their autonomy (see Wesch, this volume).

Not long into my association with Dal and Léia it became clear that they survive less from their skill at handicrafts and more from their deep understanding of the various cultural worlds of Brazil and human behavior more generally. They seemed to easily adjust to any social situation and were incredibly respectful when the circumstances called for it. I am not the first anthropologist to recognize that Brazilian hippies make a living through their understanding of human behavior. In the only academic reference I have found on Brazilian hippies, Conrad Kottak (2005) reflects on how the hippy community near Arembepe, Bahia (a small fishing village on Brazil's Atlantic coast), was a new development that he encountered on his second field trip to the area in the 1970s. Kottak admits that he chose not to engage the hippies at that time because he saw them as rival anthropologists.

> Anthropologists are widely thought of as unorthodox investigators
> of strange and mysterious people, willing to forgo the comforts of
> civilization for the romance of distant simplicity. Ethnographers are like
> professional hippies; the hippies were like amateur anthropologists. I
> wanted the amateur anthropologists to leave Arembepe. I wanted "my
> village" preserved for the real anthropologists—myself and my field team
> colleagues. However, realizing that I couldn't have my wish, I avoided the
> hippies and tried to discount their impact on village life. (2005, 27–28)

In my case, I engaged the hippies, and after some handwringing, I collaborated with them.

COLLABORATION

The community received us well and Dal, Léia, Jeosadak, and I entered the community as a family unit, sharing a small house that Brasilino arranged for us to live in. We settled into our new dwelling and began to fit ourselves into the rhythm of the community's daily life. Carlos, our next-door neighbor and current president of the community, called a meeting to introduce us to everyone and for us to state our intentions. To open the meeting, Brasilino gave a beautiful speech about how we are all from the same world and that we need to accept and understand each other because we are all human beings. He also said that he was the one who invited us, and although we were the first researchers to come to the community, we probably would not be the last and all should be accepted as human beings and be given a chance. Dal gave a speech and I gave a speech, saying I only wanted to learn about their lives and they did not have to participate if they did not want to. Overall, we were received very well by the community as a whole, which I took as a good sign. A number of men approached me after the meeting and said they would be willing to give an interview whenever I wanted. I was encouraged and ready to learn about the caboclo way of life on the middle Rio Negro.

Once in the community, Dal and Léia facilitated interviews, took photographs, and shared their insights and experiences with me on a daily basis. Dal was good at engaging members of the community both young and old, male or female, but he was particularly good at drawing men into conversation about a range of topics. His skill as an interviewer certainly played a part, but he also drew from his experiences in other parts of Brazilian Amazonia. Dal's stories about hunting, fishing, and spirits of the forest and river from other places were always met with questions and other stories from the men and women of Lago Grande and soon everyone was talking with us. Our house was always the last to go to sleep because of all the social activity. People were also curious about the hippy lifestyle, and Dal and Léia were happy to oblige them with stories.

While in the village we were Brasilino's guests, but I wanted to give back to the community in ways that were equitable and reasonable based on my budgetary constraints. This issue was important to Dal and he helped me negotiate the difficult situation of who to help, when, and how much. He was certainly my overseer in this regard and he more than once threatened to leave if I did not follow his advice. Fortunately, his instincts in this area were expert, and I left feeling as if we had been as equitable and reasonable as possible, something I know I could not have achieved alone. Dal also helped me negotiate my purchases in town. We met a Spaniard who was married to a local girl and told us that some of the local merchants still try to swindle him because he is an outsider. Dal's vigilance ensured this did not happen to us.

Although Dal was in some ways the leader of our research team (Léia took to calling him General Dal), Léia's contributions were also invaluable. Léia ran our household, cooking, cleaning, and keeping general order. In the course of these activities, Léia spent the majority of her days socializing and working with the women from the village. Thus, she became my access point to the community's world of women, which would have been otherwise extremely difficult for me to know much about. In addition, I should not leave out the role of Jeosadak. Jeosadak and the toys he brought were popular among the kids of the village and another reason why our house was always the center of activity day or night. In general, entering the community as a family unit made it easier to integrate ourselves into the daily routines of the village life. Finally, Dal and Léia supported me with their friendship and genuine care about my physical and mental well-being. They made it much easier to be in an alien environment thousands of miles from home for a long period of time.

One of the most valuable aspects of our collaboration was Dal and Léia's ability to contextualize the cultural information we were gathering. Because of their ethnographic experience in other parts of the Amazon and the rest of Brazil, they were able to help me sort out the many cultural connections that caboclos share with other Brazilians in a way that would have been difficult to do on my own. They were both fonts of knowledge about Brazilian national and regional culture. In addition, Dal could tell me about the caboclo societies he encountered in Acre and Mato Grosso and how their traditions and beliefs were both similar and different. Throughout the history of Brazilian Amazonian, waves of immigrants have left the drought-plagued Brazilian Northeast. These immigrants arrived with their own cultural traditions that have meshed with local belief systems. Dal and Léia have both spent a significant amount of time in the northeast and could recognize many of the traditions we encountered in the community that had roots in the northeast. For example, when a woman who was possessed by a *bôto* spirit (an enchanted pink river dolphin) was brought from a neighboring community to ours to be seen by the local healer, Dal and Léia had much commentary on spirit possession and the many forms it takes in other regions of Brazil such as the northeast.

Although almost everyone in the community contributed to our research project, it was our collaboration with Brasilino that was the key. After all, he was the one who invited us into his community, his world. Brasilino saw us as a positive force in his community and thought the longer we stayed the better. Once we were settled in the community, he went fishing for several weeks and then returned to check on how the research was progressing. He continued this pattern several times until it seemed that he was certain we were comfortable there and were not going to leave anytime soon. After those first few months, Brasilino began to set the research agenda, telling me each day what we were going to discuss and what other topics he thought we should cover in the near future. My point is that what I learned from Brasilino was what he wanted to tell me. He asserted his agency by overtly directing our collaboration, sending his own story into the world although through my filter and interpretation. Among other materials, Brasilino provided his own folk history of the economic cycles of Amazonas (the state in which he resides) covering span of 150 years, which provides a framework for understanding the caboclo experience of the boom and bust cycles of the extractive economy in the middle Rio Negro. Truly, this material is not mine and it is no longer just Brasilino's, but it is a product of our intellectual engagement and interaction, of our intersubjectivity.

CABOCLOS AND HIPPIES IN THE SAME FRAME

My experience working with Brasilino and Dal and Léia helped me put caboclos and hippies together in the frame of Brazilian modernity by showing the commonalities between these two seemingly different ways of life on the margins of Brazilian society. Caboclo societies were historically constituted, in part a product of the forces of colonization and later globalization. The hippy way of life is a choice; one is not often born into it. But caboclo identity is quite fluid and many caboclos often move from life on the edge of the river, to the city (where they become just another of the urban poor), and then back to the edge of the river. Thus, one could say that on some level they both are chosen lifestyles.

According to Dal and Léia, the hippy movement in Brazil began in the late 1960s and was a product of American influence in Brazil. The Bahian musician Raul Seixas is credited with popularizing the movement. In the early 1970s, during the military dictatorship, he spent time in exile in the United States, where his wife was from. The hippy movement attracted many urban youths from São Paulo and Rio de Janeiro, including many from wealthy families. However, today it appears to attract Brazilians from many different areas and social classes, and Brazil is a destination for hippies from other parts of South America as well.

A brief look at Dal's life story is instructive here. Dal grew up in the interior of São Paulo state, one of twenty-three children. When he was growing up, his family was quite poor, but his father was industrious and built a banana plantation from the ground up. Dal's father was a stern disciplinarian, but Dal credits his father with teaching him many hard lessons that continue to serve him well. When Dal was thirteen, he had the opportunity to try out for one of São Paulo's famous soccer schools. He was accepted as a student there, but Dal's father would not allow it. This is when Dal decided to hit the road (in 1975). He said it was rough at first, but he learned the hard way how to survive on the street. He returned home for a short period when he was sixteen but eventually left for good. Although he knows that his father's banana plantation became successful, he has never returned home again. Dal continues to travel all over Brazil and he also has spent time in Bolivia and Paraguay. In his hippy life, he has worked as a *garimpeiro* (gold miner) during the gold rush of the 1980s, bandit, and drug smuggler and spent four years in prison. These days he makes a living through his ability to understand and talk to anyone. He is the ultimate guide for the tours that are not in any tourist literature and a well-known character in the hippy world.[4]

For Dal, as for most Brazilian hippies, this lifestyle is a rejection of main-stream society. Many hippies refuse to vote, and thus they have no access to government social programs as voting is compulsory in Brazil. Dal is proud that he has never voted and that the Brazilian identification card that he possesses *foi comprado* ("was purchased").[5] Although there are some permanent hippy communities in different parts of Brazil, most hippies live highly mobile lifestyles, traveling from place to place and supporting themselves by selling their handicrafts in the public plazas of cities and towns they travel through. In many cities are relatively large transient communities of hippies. Some of them are resident hippies who live the lifestyle but do not travel. The majority, however, travel from place to place, spending a few weeks, several months, or even years in a place they find to their liking.[6] Hippies in each location help orient the newcomers, providing information such as the best places to sleep and work, as well as where to get free or cheap food and whether the police are hassling them. New arrivals share the news they have of other places and other hippies, a system referred to as *rádio ipi* ("hippy radio"). Thus, a sense of community and camaraderie forms among the hippies in each location.

What hippies and caboclos share is not only the way they have embraced a life on the margins of society but also an orientation to the present. One common theme in much of caboclo oral tradition is that of constantly changing circumstances in caboclo worlds (Lima and Alencar 2001; Harris 2009; Wisniewski 2009). Many narrative genres in caboclo oral tradition reflect this theme. One such genre I call "histories of goods." Brasilino and his contemporaries told me histories of various manufactured goods they had received over the years and how these goods had changed over time, such as the various light sources they used for spearfishing. Brasilino noted that when he first began to spearfish, they used an *iparonga*, which is a homemade diesel lantern made from a tin can and fashioned with a tin reflector behind the flame to direct the light source. He said that it worked just fine. Then came the first flashlight, one called Ray-O-Vac, which he said was of high quality. After Ray-O-Vac were several other brands; today the most common flashlights are of poor quality and come from China. However, most caboclos now employ a motorcycle headlamp powered by a car or motorcycle battery that can be recharged in town. Brasilino said that as the light sources improved in quality, the fish learned to adjust. When the iparonga was in use, the fish would rest close to the surface, but now that the motorcycle headlamp is common, the fisherman have to use longer spears because the fish rest much deeper in the water. This is just one example of the stories that emphasize the changing circumstances of the caboclos' world. Here we see that even the fish adapt to the changing technologies, just as caboclos must do to survive.

The hippy philosophy is revealed in a number of phrases that Dal often used. As I fretted about various aspects of fieldwork and my personal life, Dal was always there with his counsel. Two of his favorite phrases are *tudo é passageiro* ("everything is a passenger") and *tudo passa* ("everything passes"). Before we found Brasilino and moved to Lago Grande, Dal would reassure me that all of the hardships would be worth it, that before I knew it, I would be home thinking about all that had happened. Dal and Léia really seem to live life in this way. Much like caboclos, they do not dwell on the past but just keep moving forward. Two other phrases that Dal favored are also instructive. The first, *a vida é assim mesmo* ("life is really like that") is an expression used to remark on any possible situation that happens in life—good or bad. It is a commentary on life; life is sometimes great and sometimes extremely difficult. It is unpredictable and anything may happen; that is what lived experience reveals. The second, more colorful sentiment is *a vida é uma merda* ("life is a pile of shit"). This expression underscores the disappointments and difficulties of daily life in the modern world. Life is a pile of shit; thus, all one can do is make the best of it and always try to have a good time. These expressions serve as reminders that whatever happens, there is no point in dwelling on it. One has to keep living. Although these expressions differ from the historical tales that keep caboclos oriented in the present, they appear to serve the same purpose for hippies.

Scholars have begun to recognize how adaptable caboclo societies have had to be to survive the rapid change in the boom and bust extractive economy in the region (Adams et al. 2009; Harris 2009). In a manner analogous to caboclos, hippies are extremely adaptable and even seek out change and new experiences. Both hippies and caboclos live subsistence lifestyles; each day they wake up and find a way to get food and other items they need for survival. The difference is in the way they go about their subsistence. In the city, hippies are extracting their resources from tourists by selling their handicrafts or assisting them in other ways, perhaps as guides, or by begging or stealing if necessary. The recent arrival of tourism in the Rio Negro means that caboclos can now "extract" a resource that is the staple of the hippy economy.

In fact, Dal, Léia, and Brasilino regarded me as a tourist and a resource. For Dal and Léia I was the ultimate tourist to assist, because my visit was of long duration, but tourists have long been their business. Brasilino has been watching the slow trickle of tourists in the middle Rio Negro over the last fifteen years, and although he is well aware of their potential as a resource, I was the first one with whom he had a personal relationship. Some of the families living at Lago Grande have a number of children working in the tourist industry as sport-fishing guides, but these are only seasonal jobs for relatively few people. Thus, the caboclos have a lot of ambivalence about this form of tourism. Some of the young men dream of turning their community into a tourist camp and thought I might be their connection to a steady stream of foreign tourists. Even though the community was aware of tourism when we arrived, I am certain that through interactions with Dal and Léia, the community members realized what a useful resource tourists could be.

Brasilino is suspicious of tourists' motives, thinking they are looking for some valuable resource such as gold or minerals of which he and others are not aware.[7] However, he also sees their value as an extractive resource and knows well that there are both "good" and "bad" tourists. His sentiments are reflected in the following passage: "[T]he tourist, he has a lot of money. He has a lot of money. When he dedicates himself to be a tourist, it is because he has money given to him by the government, given by those that he helps, to the point that he can throw it away [laughing]. A tourist for example, let's see . . . they aren't of one type. There are many tourists that, let's say, are swindlers. Yes, there are and there are another type, there are good tourists" (Wisniewski 2009, 177). Brasilino adds that they come to the region looking for things or just on a trip to see what is here, often under the guise of *pesquisa* ("research"), but they always come with money to spend. That is Brasilino's definition of a tourist, and in this sense I was included in this category. Brasilino knows that some tourists spend a great deal of money to go on the sport-fishing trips, but he has no desire to do that kind of work. All of his life Brasilino has always preferred to work alone, and that is the way he wants to work with the tourist. He wants to tap into this resource in his own way. He realizes that he may not be able to recognize the gold or other minerals they may be looking for; thus, he does not want to prevent the tourists from meeting their goals. But as he told me, he does want to "participate a little bit." And he feels like the residents of the area deserve this. He is willing to do whatever is necessary to keep the tourists' secrets as long as they can help him and help his community. In a way, he is looking for a new patron. Brasilino told me that the caboclos in the area need some help, someone needs to "open their hands" for them, whether it is the government, the indigenous association, or, in this case, the tourist. Caboclos know how to work hard, but they need work to do, and here we can see that at age seventy-nine, Brasilino still has his eyes on any and all possibilities.

CONCLUSIONS

My experiences with caboclos and hippies made it clear to me that the processes of globalization and the technologies driving it have made it difficult to keep up the Malinowskian myth of anthropology, in which participant-observation is rendered as an objective enterprise and the professional anthropologist is a scientist collecting data. In our collaboration, Dal, Léia, Brasilino, and I had different motives, but our individual desires and proclivities brought us together in a shared experience that is the source of any ethnography produced by my hand (Whitehead 2009). All of us contributed our own cultural perspectives and brought unique ethnographic skills to bear in a cooperative effort. This cooperative effort reveals anthropological investigation as a product of our intersubjectivity and a facilitation of cultural exchange rather than a product of scientific investigation.

All anthropologists going into the field have to consider how they enter the society they wish to study and how they will position themselves within it in conventional ethnographic style. However, although I think most of us think a great deal about this before we get there, once we have the contacts and have some way of securing a field site we are content for the moment and do not always revisit this issue when we are examining our data back home. I realize that during the postmodern time in anthropology many of these issues were raised, but the emphasis then was on the question of how anthropologists should place themselves in their work. In my case, participation with the hippies as my research assistants shaped the way I accessed and interacted with the people from Lago Grande. In Kaufmann's terms, they played the role of my "overseers," but their influence went far beyond this to the point of true collaboration (2002, 231). This brings me to what Kaufmann calls the "what if" implication (2002, 251). What if I had not collaborated with Dal and Léia to find a field site? I may have gone to the local church, the American missionary, or through a contact with the government-run aquarium-fish bureau. No matter what the scenario, the experience (and the resulting ethnographic product) would have been quite different. I did not theorize my participation before it occurred. Nor can I propose some grand theory of it here, but upon reflection it becomes useful to think about how my association with the hippies influenced my positioning and perspective.

As we were to find out after living in Lago Grande for some time, it is one of the poorest communities in the area with the fewest resources. It is also very low on the local government's list of squeaky wheels. If I had sought the help of anyone of social standing in town, I would have never been positioned in Brasilino's community. Being with the marginal hippies led me to one of the marginal caboclo communities inhabited by exceptional people, who helped me create a picture of a society seldom seen. Studying with a more marginal community also gave me a better sense of the range of caboclo experience in this region. The collaboration with the hippies led me to a better understanding of the dynamics of Brazilian modernity by demonstrating what caboclos and hippies have in common as modern Brazilians. The time with the hippies also gave me a richer context for understanding what I experienced in Lago Grande.

As those engaging in the ethnography of digital worlds and virtual experiences are grappling with how to theorize their own participation, it seems useful for all anthropologists to take a moment to consider the same in their own work. We must not to be afraid of ethnographic engagement and collaboration with all kinds of subjects, whether digital or marginal, and we should learn how to understand our own involvement in the intersubjective production of ethnographic knowledge (Whitehead 2009). First, necessarily, comes an awareness of our modes of participation and possibilities for observations. Rather than fear the hippies as marginal others or feel threatened by them as rival anthropologists, I chose to engage them as equals, and our collaboration with Brasilino (another ethnographer) produced a much richer ethnographic portrait than otherwise possible. This kind of collaboration is something anthropologists should embrace and celebrate. There are many kinds of collaborators and we should not ignore them, especially as we try to understand the many aspects of posthuman existence (Whitehead 2009). These collaborators may include marginal, vagabond, or amateur ethnographers such as Dal, Léia, and Brasilino, or when focusing on virtual worlds, they may be commentators from other disciplines with different kinds of experience, such as communications and media studies. It should be the strength of anthropologists to synthesize the data produced by different viewpoints; thus, we should not shy away from engaging them in the field or in academe. As many other academic disciplines are beginning to incorporate ethnography as a method, anthropologists need to lead the way not only in highlighting the collaborative, coproductive nature of ethnographic data but also in theorizing the kinds of participation that are most fruitful. I believe that these insights signal not the end of anthropology but a realization that the effects of globalization and the transition to a posthuman perspective demand that anthropologists work in a different paradigm. This paradigm must be rooted in the recognition that the human experience consists of more than just anthropology's traditional subjects and must also foster new ways of understanding human interaction in all its novel forms within an economically globalized but culturally fragmented and discontinuous world.

NOTES

1. The caboclos are a historical peasantry that emerged as the labor force for the extractive economy in the Brazilian Amazon beginning in the mid-eighteenth century, when Portuguese colonial policies encouraged miscegenation. Today, the label *caboclo* describes generally mixed-heritage Amazonians in Brazil who practice manioc-based horticulture, hunt, fish, gather, and supplement their subsistence activities with extractive activities that vary significantly by river system. Along the Rio Negro these activities include rubber tapping, logging, mining, live capture of aquarium fish, and collecting Brazil nuts, tree oils, or palm fibers.

2. See Nugent (1993) for an early critique of this approach to understanding caboclo lives.

3. During the course of my fieldwork, a national news story broke attributing a run of serial killings to a male hippy, adding to the hippies' reputations as unpredictable and dangerous characters.

4. After we left Lago Grande and the Rio Negro, I traveled with Dal and Léia (and Jeosadak) to Santarém, Pará, and we spent a day at Alter do Chão, a beautiful resort village on the Rio Tapajós. There was a small community of young hippies living there

on an island in the river. It was then that I realized that Dal is a hippy legend. The young hippies were awestruck when they found out who he was. They all had heard many stories about him and could hardly believe he was standing there in the flesh.

5. One needs an identity card for many things, including for taking interurban or interstate buses. Thus, it is practical even for hippies to get one, but they prefer to do so in a rebellious way.

6. For example, when I met them, Dal and Léia had been in Manaus for about three months, selling handicrafts on the Praça da Polícia (Police Plaza). They arrived in Manaus after spending four months bicycling part of the Trans-Amazonian Highway (known as BR). Before their bicycle trip, they were in the state of Bahia for the beach season, and before that they spent over a year farming manioc in a small town in the state of Acre. When we parted at the end of my field stay, they returned to Manaus to meet two Italian men they had guided the previous season in Bahia.

7. Brasilino told many stories about mysterious tourists who use the locals to take them into remote areas of the forest and go off alone for unknown purposes. He also reported that a group of Americans built a good school in one of the upstream villages as a front for a mining operation, smuggling out gold in hollow logs.

REFERENCES

Adams, Christina, Rui Murrieta, Walter Neves, and Mark Harris, eds. 2009. *Amazon Peasant Societies in a Changing Environment: Political Ecology, Invisibility and Modernity in the Rainforest*. London: Springer.

Gaonkar, Dilip Parameshwar. 2001. "Introduction." In *Alternative Modernities (A Public Culture Book)*, ed. Dilip Parameshwar Gaonkar, 1–23. Durham, NC: Duke University Press.

Gow, Peter. 1991. *Of Mixed Blood: Kinship and History in the Peruvian Amazon*. Oxford: Clarendon Press.

Harris, Mark. 1998. "What It Means to Be Caboclo: Some Critical Notes on the Construction of Amazonian Caboclo Society as an Anthropological Object." *Critique of Anthropology* 18 (1): 83–95. http://dx.doi.org/10.1177/0308275X9801800104.

Harris, Mark. 2009. "'Sempre Ajeitando' (Always Adjusting): An Amazonian Way of Being in Time." In *Amazon Peasant Societies in a Changing Environment: Political Ecology, Invisibility and Modernity in the Rainforest*, ed. Christina Adams, Rui Murrieta, Walter Neves, and Mark Harris, 69–71. London: Springer.

Kaufmann, Jeffery. 2002. "The Informant as Resolute Overseer." *History in Africa* 29: 231–55. http://dx.doi.org/10.2307/3172162.

Kottak, Conrad Phillip. 2005. *Assault on Paradise: The Globalization of a Little Community in Brazil*. New York: McGraw Hill.

Lima, Deborah de Magalhães Ayres, and Edna Ferreira Alencar. 2001. "A Lembrança da História: Memória Social, Ambiente e Identidade na Várzea do Médio Solimões." *Lusotopie* 2001: 27–48.

Moran, Emilio. 1974. "The Adaptive System of the Amazonian Caboclo." In *Man in the Amazon*, ed. Charles Wagley, 135–159. New York: Columbia University Press.

Nugent, Stephen. 1993. *Amazonian Caboclo Society: An Essay on Invisibility and Peasant Economy*. Oxford: Berg.

Pace, Richard. 1997. "The Amazon Caboclo: What's in a Name?" *Luso-Brazilian Review* 34 (2): 81–9.

Parker, Eugene, ed. 1985a. *The Amazon Caboclo: Historical and Contemporary Perspectives.* Theme issue, *Studies in Third World Societies* 32.

Parker, Eugene. 1985b. "Caboclization: The Transformation of the Amerindian in Amazonia 1615–1800." In *The Amazon Caboclo: Historical and Contemporary Perspectives,* ed. Eugene Parker. Theme issue, *Studies in Third World Societies* 32.

Ross, Eric. 1978. "The Evolution of the Amazon Peasantry." *Journal of Latin American Studies* 10 (2): 193–218. http://dx.doi.org/10.1017/S0022216X00021222.

Schumaker, Lyn. 2001. *Africanizing Anthropology: Fieldwork, Networks, and the Making of Cultural Knowledge in Central Africa.* Durham, NC: Duke University Press.

Wagley, Charles. 1976 [1953]. *Amazon Town: A Study of Man in the Tropics.* New York: Macmillan.

Whitehead, Neil L. 2009. "Post-Human Anthropology." *Identities: Global Studies in Culture and Power* 16: 1–32.

Whitehead, Neil L. Forthcoming. "Loving, Being, Killing Animals." Afterword in *Centering Animals,* ed. Martha Few and Zeb Tortorici. Durham, NC: Duke University Press. wisc.academia.edu/NeilWhitehead/Papers.

Wisniewski, Kent W. 2009. "Brasilino's Changing World: An Ethnography of a Caboclo Community along the Middle Rio Negro in Barcelos, Amazonas, Brazil." PhD thesis, Department of Anthropology, University of Wisconsin, Madison.

11

Marginal Bodies, Altered States, and Subhumans

(Dis)Articulations between Physical and Virtual Realities in Centro, São Paulo

Michael Heckenberger

The very idea of a non-repressive civilization,
conceived as a real possibility of the established civilization at the present stage, appears frivolous. Even if
one admits this possibility on theoretical grounds, as
an extension of the achievements of science and technology, one must be aware of the fact that these same
achievements are being used to the contrary, namely,
to serve the interests of continued domination.

HERBERT MARCUSE (1962, VII)

*A schizophrenic out for a walk is a better model
than a neurotic lying on a couch.*

G. DELEUZE AND F. GUATTARI (1983, 2)

This chapter considers articulations, points of contact, and disarticulations,
distortions, and other "disconnects" between virtual realities both of urban
planning and mass media and on-the-ground or "lived" realities of human

DOI: 10.5876/9781607321705.c11

subjects whose identities and subjectivities are constructed in place, in this case, in Centro, São Paulo. It stems from a long-time interest in urban landscapes in Brazilian cities, developed while living in them for over five years, including São Paulo, Rio, Brasília, Belém, Manaus, and Porto Alegre, among others. This interest was at first a casual sideline to my primary research with Brazilian indigenous groups but grew into a kind of archaeology of urban palimpsests as I watched people's movements and actions in diverse public and private settings and, particularly, how these movements and actions were constrained by and became sedimented in public space. In Centro this was always tightly tied to the urban homeless, sex workers, and drug users and traffic. The subject found me, so to speak, in the sense that it emerged organically, after wandering and dwelling in these places and getting to know some of its people, rather than by research design, and I must disavow any specialized training in the anthropology of urban poverty. However, what began as occasional visits over twenty years developed over the past several years into a more in-depth engagement in the downtown cityscapes, including "immersion" in many of the marginal spaces of the city center, which happened to coincide with an ambitious program of urban renewal or "gentrification" in Centro (see Frúgoli and Sklair 2008).

"Subjectivities," digital and otherwise, are often taken to mean the personal feelings and responses, self-conscious identities, and direct face-to-face (or screen-to-screen) interaction of individual humans agents, as opposed to objective contexts. As a social construction, subjectivity can be defined more broadly as "the dynamic and unresolved tension between bodily, self and social/political processes" (Biehl, Good, and Kleinman 2007, 15).[1] This chapter focuses on the bodily and sociopolitical aspects of subjectivity, as reflected in the actions and discourses that produce individuals and social groups, in particular in representations in electronic media and digitally based urban planning. I reflect upon the long-noted distinction between two urban realities: the virtual realities of urban design and planning and mass media, the bird's eye view, and the street-level realities or experiences of urban dwellers, in this case, Centro's homeless residents (Benjamin 2002; De Certeau 2002).[2] This highlights the dual nature of inner-city urban spaces as hyperdesigned, rigid, and formal settings of social interaction and cultural life and, at the same time, dynamic, flexible, and contested areas reflecting emergent qualities of urban life. The historical cityscape of Centro was constructed as a landscape of grandeur a century or so ago, and monumental architecture and major public spaces are critical features of cultural memory, the historical subjectivity of the city center. The built environment—today in-filled with high-rise apartment and commercial buildings; interlaced by sidewalks, thoroughfares, and overpasses; and, in several edge areas, marked by small, "flat," and, in some cases, dilapidated neighborhoods—provides the general stage and index points for social traffic, which, following Butler's (1993) notion of performative "citationality," in which past practices and discourse orient the movements, actions, and experiences of the human bodies that inhabit these spaces. This citationality of spaces and practices, critical for the construction of the subjectivities of local residents and the flow of human bodies, equally applies to "marginal" and vulnerable social agents, such as the "homeless," who are tied to both public and, notably, interstitial spaces. These other bodies and interactions that lie outside mainstream urban life, like a resilient second skin over the urban landscape, are notable because of their lack of fixity, which undulates throughout the day, during the week, and even across seasons within a nexus of homelessness and criminality fairly ubiquitous in urban settings across the globe.

It is this mobility, or corporeal deixis, that not only defines the daily lives of inner-city poor but makes them particularly vulnerable within historical regimes of structural and symbolic violence. Powerholders, politicians, police, public health workers, and businesses, and other residents attempt to control or curtail this flow of marginal bodies. Today they are aided by the digital subjectivities constructed by urban planners and regulators and in cyberworld representations, notably public propaganda calling for eradication or rehabilitation of marginal groups and cyber-voyeurism. Virtual realities, commonly framed in terms of rationality or "normalcy," flatten, exclude, and erase the alternative realities and histories of people who live and work on the streets, often portrayed as subnormal, subversive, and irrational, most recently in the burgeoning culture industries of digital media. Digital media provides new opportunities for social interaction, including the incorporation of marginal or "muted" groups, as described in this volume, for instance, in the social context of indigenous and traditional peoples, often portrayed as "primitive" or "backward" (Alemán, this volume; Hoesterey, this volume; Wisniewski, this volume). In the present case, the opposite extreme can be noted, relating to how marginal groups are further marginalized by modern media technologies (see Gajjala and McComas, this volume), among marginalized groups in the most technologically advanced "core" areas, commonly portrayed as unrefined, uncivilized, somewhat less than fully human (cultured), or even, as I have heard, "subhuman" and served up as caricatures for public consumption.

SÃO PAULO'S CITY CENTER: A BRIEF HISTORY

Founded in 1554, São Paulo was a small city until the mid-1800s, when coffee and immigration, particularly following the abolition of slavery (1888), transformed it into an economic and political powerhouse.[3] From the 1870s to 1900 the city grew from tens of thousands to nearly a quarter-million, when the historic center of São Paulo entered a period of cultural fluorescence, a "belle epoch" (Needell 1987). During this period, the city's first major intervention of urban planning, the center shifted slightly from old Centro (Sé) to a new, hyper-designed new Centro (República), marked by the construction of major architecture and public spaces, including the central Praça de República (1889), Viaduto de Cha and Parque Ahangabaú (1892), Igrega da Consolação (1907), the Teatro Municipal (1911), and Luz train station and associated Praça or Jardin da Luz (1895–1900), among other constructions.[4]

During the twentieth century, the city grew precipitously to rank among the world's largest cities, with a metropolitan area estimated at nearly 20 million.[5] Like many cities in the developing world, much urban growth has been relatively unplanned, notably in peri-urban "slum" neighborhoods, or *favelas*, often physically and socially juxtaposed to planned middle- and even upper-class neighborhoods. In recent decades, favelas have received considerable attention from social scientists and public media because of the urban "war on drugs" and "militarization of marginality" in these "subnormal agglomerations," as they are characterized in census reports (Holston 2009; Perlman 2007; Wacquant 2008).

Less attention has been paid to urban poor in city centers (see Frúgoli 2000; Frúgoli and Sklair 2008), in part because of the lack of social or spatial fixity—housing and community structure—within the hyper-designed city centers, which are marked by monumental architecture, landmarks, public plazas, and bustling commercial street life.[6] Paradoxically, inner-city poor are characterized by structural overdetermination, living in the interstitial spaces of the city center and driven by the forces of social control, and also hyper-individualism, rampant free will, and lack of social or historical bonds. In public discourse, inner-city poor—street people, prostitutes, drug users, and other urban outcasts of Centro's monumental landscapes—are seen as invaders of the city's inner sanctum, the "other within," who threaten the normal and rational.

This view reflects the legacy of Centro's slave market economy and post-abolition efforts to draw immigrants to the area to curb black social dominance (Fausto 2001 [1984], 217; Müller 1958). In *Crime e Cotidiano: A Criminalidade em São Paulo 1870–1924*, Fausto (2001 [1984]) provides a critical perspective on this period, from 1870, when the city was roughly 35,000 inhabitants, to 1924, when the population was more than 600,000. He bridges the period before and after the abolition of slavery (1888) and emergence of the powerful coffee economy, which transformed São Paulo into a world city, particularly in terms of the social and political structures or "structural violence" that conditioned not only crime but everyday life in the interpenetrating spaces of slavery, prostitution, and criminality in both Old Centro and the new monumental landscape of Novo Centro in Republica.

Since the late nineteenth century, Centro has been characterized as a "transition zone," referring to high racial and ethnic diversity, social mobility, and the high incidence of crime and illicit activities. By the 1920s, the emergent identity of Centro, as an inner-city borderlands with a propensity to innovation and loose taboos and (hetero-normative) moral codes, was well established. These dramatic changes in the city center during the Old Republic (1889–1930) were built upon the remnants of the informal economies that centered on the nineteenth-century slave economy and immigration in the downtown area. Lucia Hermann (1944) summarized this life in the mid-1930s, along the Avenida São João, which bisects Centro:

> It is an area of great material mobility, movement, changes in residency
> . . . Only the prostitutes, we can say, find affinity and professional center
> there. But they do not have the freedom to choose as do other social
> groups because they are constantly controlled by the polícia de costumes
> [vice squads] and are frequently forced by the authorities to move to
> other zones. [The people living in this area] don't have social ties (family,
> relatives, social relations, a sense of neighborliness, human respect,
> associations, etc.); and, therefore, they feel more independent to move
> around. (Cited and translated in Green 1999, 95)

In the 1930s, the authoritarian "Novo Estado" (New State) tried to control the emergent economy of marginality, restricting female prostitution to one neighborhood (Bom Retiro), where "150 brothels and 1,400 women were crowded in a small section of that neighborhood" (Green 1999, 164).[7] Bom Retiro was also one of the city's primary entrance point of immigrants, who came through the nearby Luz train station. Throughout the twentieth century the neighborhoods around this area have provided a central space for marginal social groups and, as discussed below, is currently the core area of the downtown sex and drug trade and homelessness. After the "New State" rule ended in 1945, the area of sex trade once again expanded across much of the original area of Centro. The scope of street life and marginalized persons and behaviors was again restricted during the repressive military dictatorship in the mid-1960s to early 1970s. These restrictions were aided by notions promoted by major industrialists and the political right in São Paulo that the working class was morally defective and that civil unrest should be stemmed at all costs (Weinstein 1996). These attempts at urban renewal succeeded in reformulating the contexts of Centro's "red-light" character but had little success in extinguishing this vital urban life force.

By the mid-1970s and 1980s, this ecology of bodies had returned full force, reinforced by a notable increase in the homosexual sex trade (Perlongher 1987). By the 1990s, in turn, the emergent drug economy became an indelible part of the landscape of inner-city poverty and the sexualized culture of prostitution, cheap motels, flophouses, porn cinemas, and street cruising. At the same time, the dramatic increase in homelessness, corresponding to rapid growth in peri-urban *favelas* and migration to urban centers, became a more permanent feature of public inner-city spaces, including expedient structures in some areas and more ephemeral social groups in parks, traffic networks, and diurnal uses of sidewalk areas. After 2005, the municipal government again mounted a strident campaign, initially called Operation Cleansing, to control "subversive" or "subnormal" elements of the downtown urban public spaces, namely the diverse populations living on the streets or in irregular housing.

ON THE PRACA

The Centro cityscape has changed dramatically over the years, fluctuating with the ebb and flow of more or less restrictive state regimes, but the resilience of homeless groups and the continuity of street life are remarkable. The emergent novelty of Centro's landscapes was not the grandeur of its monumental public spaces, which in fact were hyper-planned architectural afterthoughts of pre-made, virtual models, but instead the way street life, nightlife, and public spaces mapped so smoothly over the building fabric, like a second skin. Indeed, in some respects the street life comprises one of the most enduring features of the downtown historical subjectivity.

Centro's urban spaces are dedicated by day to the practice and perfection of consumer and cultural life, but night street life in these same spaces opens new stages of urban interaction. This is a world filled with "marginal" bodies and behaviors; the life force of sex and drug traffic, informal economy, and pavement dwellers; and cultures typically absent or occluded in studies of urban space focused on daytime observations. When I first visited São Paulo in 1991 for a several days, I stayed in a cheap hotel in the Luz district, arriving straight from Rio, guidebook in hand. Fairly sedate at noontime, I was unaware that after dark the neighborhood would come alive with "streetwalkers," hard to miss (or be missed) as a gringo. Like many visitors, I was initially surprised to find not just monuments and majestic trees in the city's historic center but also these unexpected people and traffic (a point today noted in the Internet reviews of the many downtown hotels). As Barbosa da Silva noted in the 1950s, "During the day, this area was the center of São Paulo's commercial and business district, but in the evening it became home to a bustling nightlife . . . This entire pleasure zone . . . comes alive at sundown and finds greatest movement on Saturday nights and the eve of holidays" (cited and translated in Green 1999, 166; see also Barbosa da Silva 1959).

The contextual or deictic qualities of inner-city urban space, shifting from night to day and from weekday to weekend, are critically important in the lives of those who work and live on the streets (Carvalho and Schicchi 2007). The variable uses of space by different social groups is well described in Low's seminal *On the Plaza* (2001), about public space in downtown San José, Costa Rica; however, as is often true of urban studies, including ethnographies, the scholarly gaze is generally restricted to daytime activities, from about 6:00 AM to 6:00 PM. In Centro, the time from 6:00 PM to 6:00 AM is equally dynamic and filled with bodies and movement, only these bodies and traffic are quite different than those experienced during normal "business hours," reflecting distinctive but no less vital subjectivities and interactions. During the day, traffic in the downtown "pleasure zone" orbits around two poles: female prostitution in the Jardin da Luz, adjacent the Luz train station, and male prostitution in the Praça da República. By night, sex traffic shifts from public parks to the streets but remains spatially segregated into nodes of female, male, and transvestite sex workers.

This diurnal quality of Centro highlights the dual character of these public spaces as places for both casual social interaction and quiet contemplation and also the pervasive informal economy of prostitution and homeless "pavement dwellers," particularly notable in the Praça de República, the centerpiece in Centro's monumental landscape. The "praça," like other parks and major avenues in Centro, has been an important locus of these intersecting economies of marginality throughout the twentieth century because of its central location in the historic city center. It is centrally situated in São Paulo's diffuse "red-light" area, which includes numerous bars, nightclubs, restaurants, and cinemas, providing diverse settings where people from different social classes can mingle (Green 1999, 169; Rosa et al. 2008).[8]

Throughout the downtown area, full-time "pavement dwellers" are distributed across the entire landscape of urban public spaces. During the night, they sleep along the sidewalks, stoops, and interstitial spaces of the traffic network, including under road overpasses, along the commercial avenues, and in public parks, which by day become primary areas to congregate. Like many major urban centers, the informal economy, the sex and drug trade, and homelessness are inextricably linked. Any visitor to Centro easily notes the seamless interpenetration on the streets of "normal" business, consumerism, and cultural life with inner-city poverty, including the diverse groups who live and work on the streets. It is impossible to separate these diverse groups, which form interpenetrating communities of practice against the backdrop of the highly mobile, transient, and deictic qualities of the use of space.

The city center's century-old tradition of great social diversity and "rapid acceptance of innovation and a minimum fixation on taboos, conventions, and common moral codes" (Hermann 1944, 30) made it easy for the drug trade to find inroads and take over the deep historical economies of violence, sexuality, and irrationality. In the 1990s and 2000s, changes to the downtown were accompanied by change in the relationship(s) between the sex and drug trades, which exploded in the 1990s with the expansion of cocaine markets. In the downtown area the drug trade was centered on the Luz neighborhood, situated between the Praça de República and the Luz train station. This area, referred to as the "boca de lixo," a name derived from the entry points into major peri-urban *favelas*, became widely known in public discourse as "Cracolândia" and emerged as a result of the meteoric rise of crack cocaine by the 1990s.

In recent years, the downtown area, most notably the Luz district, has been seen by city planners and commentators, folks who live outside the region, as a public health hazard. The "HazMat" team mobilized after 2005 came in the form of another urban renewal project: Nova Luz, or "new light," referring to the gentrification of the Luz district and the utilitarian vision of São Paulo's city center. The planners had little interest in the actual bodies that peopled this landscape, the street people, including those that slept on the streets and others tied to the pervasive sex and drug trade, who worked the streets and moved between hourly motels, flophouses, cheap apartments, and the street.

URBAN OPERATIONS

The Nova Luz project, widely publicized and propagandized in print, TV, and digital media, seeks to replace marginal groups and businesses with new technology and commercial industries and residential buildings spurred by rich government incentives. It is the centerpiece of the city government's campaign to revitalize the downtown area (see centrosp.prefeitura.sp.gov.br). The project is aimed at curbing rampant drug use and traffic in this downtown distribution center, particularly street-level consumption by so-called *nóias* (crack addicts), a term derived from the "paranoia" attributed to street addicts.

Frúgoli and Sklair (2008), in a brief but incisive essay on the Luz district, describe the "conflicting interests of historical preservation, cultural consumption, and working-class uses of public space," which include neoliberal initiatives to privatize and commercialize large areas of the inner-city neighborhood. Since 2007, the Nova Luz project has involved repressive police interventions and the demolition of diverse "substandard" structures, including tenements or *cortiços* and abandoned buildings "invaded" by homeless residents. The neoliberal agenda, promoted by the city's conservative government, aims to transform the meaning and practices of public space but, like many urban renewal projects, strips the homeless of any right to the city (Mitchell and Staeheli 2006).[9] The project mentions provisions for "low-income" housing, but these provisions are ill-defined and do not deal with the most vulnerable segments of the working class, the people who live and work on the streets.

The Nova Luz project claims to have effectively displaced both sex and drugs by curtailing the supply in this "war on drugs," but the demand remains. Therefore, bodies have simply dressed up and rapidly turned to other spaces in the downtown area. This process draws our attention to a critical feature of Centro's historical landscapes, the fallacy of dividing landscapes to excise a social cancer, but in reality affecting virtually no change in the lives of the habitants. They are simply forced to move, in this case to areas closer to or, more recently, on the other side of the Praça de República.[10] Other aspects of urban renewal in Centro focus on recuperation of historic patrimony and "cleanup" operations in parks and sidewalk areas, the only places the homeless can work and live. This cleanup is framed as refurbishing sites of cultural memory and vitalizing the region's history as a locus of social interaction and cultural production.

As described on São Paulo's city government website CentroSP, "The Praça da República, one of the most noble green spaces . . . is being reformed . . . to be very similar to its original plan. It will return to being a locale for social conviviality and open to rest and relaxation for the community . . . [and neighboring areas] will undergo a process of visual dis-pollution." But, like the Luz district, the people that these projects will expel from the region—pavement dwellers, homosexuals, prostitutes, and other subnormals—were part and parcel of the emergent novelty of these landscapes from the start. And it almost goes without saying that no provisions are made for these people. Where will they go?

This "quiet war" on urban outcasts in the parks and streets has recently reared its head in another urban operation known as Cata-bagulho, or "Collect Trash." In the name of public sanitation and basic functioning of streets, notably in terms of the rainwater runoff associated with major storms (*enchentes*), this project aims to remove major street trash. Like lush, clean parks, trash removal can hardly be seen as a bad thing by the "taxpaying" public. But the target of this operation is not merely unwanted refuse but the belongings of street people, erasing them from the few spaces available to them by using water trucks to spray down their dwellings and even the people themselves.[11]

The architects of urban renewal during the belle epoch (1880–1910s), the New State era (1930s–1940s), the military dictatorship (mid-1960s–1970s), and current urban operations (2005–2009) and their various projects hope to clean up the marginal spaces and bodies, disposing of the "undesirables." Urban planning as a virtual reality of future development—an archaeology of the future, to borrow Jameson's (2006) provocative phrase—promotes utilitarian if not utopian progress, improvement, at the expense of the bad, dysfunctional, or downright dystrophic. Today, modelers attempt to digitally "grow" a new urban landscape, in SimCity-like simulations, promoting normal functionality, social energies, or values, such as productivity, prosperity, creativity, spirituality, authority, and knowledge. "The specialization of the city," says Stephen Johnson in *Emergence* (2001, 109), "makes it smarter, more useful for its inhabitants." Complexity in cities, he goes on, is not "a matter of sensory overload," experienced by the city dweller, but "a self-organizing system—more Santa Fe Institute than Frankfurt School." But, one might wonder, what is the place of irrationality and "sub-normality" in these self-organizing landscapes or complex adaptive systems, which are factors that loom so large in the lived realities of São Paulo's city center?

The emergent novelty of the hyper-designed landscapes of Centro, viewed across its entire centennial history, is the unplanned, self-organizing quality of what urban planners would call irrationality and subnormality, which is invigorated by other social energies: hybrid sociality, sexuality, experimentation, countercultures and plurality, corporeality, and, like everywhere where poverty is a way of life, criminality. This *is* the historical subjectivity of these landscapes, just as much as the monumental architecture and urban spaced oriented to normative cultural production and commercialism, and it is peopled with schizophrenics, drug users and sellers, sex workers, street people, and other irregulars. It is not easily extinguished, but it is, however, easily dehumanized—even demonized—in public discourse that values certain social histories and chooses to marginalize or forget others.

UNHUMAN SUBJECTS AND DIGITAL SUBJECTIVITIES

In his seminal study of criminality in downtown São Paulo from 1880 to 1924, Boris Fausto (2001 [1984]) examines how political and legal views of the normalization of social orders were situated in deeper social relations of production, such as discrimination because of education, occupation, gender, and, most notably, race as São Paulo's political elite attempted to curb the potential threat of "black power." Dramatic changes in the late twentieth century, such as the rapid, accentuated, and spectacular increase in common crime, especially organized crime (drug trade), and the multiplying forms of violence, including violence against human rights and the "criminality of poverty," remain deeply rooted in discrimination against certain social groups and stands in stark contrast to public discourse on racial and social equality (Guimarães 2002; Sherif 2001). And, as was true of the early days, as described by Fausto (2001 [1984]), racial and other subaltern minorities have scant means to publically defend themselves against repressive actions of state agencies (Caldeira 2000, 148)

Institutionalized violence, as Fausto called it, rests—then as now—on the division of city dwellers into *gente de bom* (good people) and *bandidos* (bandits), also widely characterized as *marginais* (marginals) and *malandros* (rogues) (DaMatta 1991; Fausto 2001 [1984]). Over the years, I have heard worse from people on both sides of the divide: *cachorro* (dog), *macaco* (monkey), *lixo* (trash), *descartável* (disposable), and even *sub-humano* (subhuman). As well described for *favela* communities, the popular myths of marginality are not only misleading but have invidious implications when used to justify the eradication of marginalized groups (Perlman 2007). These myths and misconceptions equally apply to the pavement dwellers, those who find short-term shelter in flophouses and motels, and the street people who live in invaded buildings, deteriorated tenements, or *cortiços*, or small groups of temporary makeshift structures (Caldeira 2000).

The latest crackdown aimed at improving social security, preserving heritage, promoting cultural production, and increasing market value is accompanied by a new "poetics" of violence and danger—that is, the anticipation of violence, notably promulgated by mass media. As in many urban settings, minority groups are widely characterized as menacing in public discourse and associated with a variety of substandard social attributes, including cultural deprivation, criminal threat, intellectual deficiency, economic parasitism, welfare dependency, hyper-sexuality, and social and reproductive irresponsibility. This perceived association, in turn, reinforces structural violence, such as forced exclusion, stigmatized labor, and other types of dehumanization (Gilroy 1987; Harrison 1998, 612–613). And public discourse of public health and security, promoting images of violence, danger, pollution, and a generalized "fear of the other" (Low, Taplin, and Scheld 2005, 1–2), has entered a brave new era: the digital age.

Most recently, the *nóia* (addict) has taken center stage as the persona of the irrational and subnormal in public discourse about Centro and are often referred to as "*zumbis*" (zombies), inhabiting a space between life and death. The public is bombarded with images of *nóias* in the streets of the Luz district, and they have become iconic of inner-city violence, danger, and pollution. Reporters trawl the streets of Luz, like common voyeurs armed with cell-cams, setting up surveillance in apartments and other hideouts to capture footage on the shadow spaces and subhumans of street life, embrocated with sex, drugs, danger, and poverty.

The interpenetrating spaces of print media, television, and cyberspace collapse the public image of street folk into one type: the *nóias*. This monolithic stereotype of all inner-city poor as irrational persons is particularly efficacious for the government charged with policing and regimenting street people through reforms in the name of public health (Goode 2002). Furthermore, media hyping of drug use and violence, which neglects the nexus between prohibition and drug-related violence, is great politics for media-savvy politicians. As *O Panóptico* (July 27, 2009) reports, one of the principal architects of the "social cleansing," the vice mayor of the Centro region, "has found a new form to propagandize his ideas: Twitter posts . . . with the promise to attend directly to the population through the channel."[12] In one tweet, the vice mayor states that there are "many street dwellers on the stoops of São João and Boa Vista streets . . . [but] old Centro is almost good." *O Panóptico* responds: "Centro is almost good, if all the street dwellers would die all at once it would be excellent."

Earlier this year, the conservative mayor of São Paulo, Gilberto Kassab, asserted, "In a short time we will have one of the most beautiful and modern regions of the world," referring to requalification of the Luz district, which, as noted by other officials in the same clip, will follow the "great dynamic of the market" ("Projeto Nova Luz: prefeiturakassab," YouTube, May 22, 2009). One can see the progress, such as the stream titled "Demolition of a building *nóia-center*" (Nova Luz—São Paulo: Demolição de prédio nóis-center, YouTube, October 24, 2008). Indeed, even by mid-2008 the mayor claimed victory, stating that Cracolandia "não existe mais" (Folha de São Paulo, February 14, 2008; no longer exists): mission accomplished.

But where did all the *nóias* go? What are they doing now? Most people doubt the mayor's optimism, agreeing with an earlier TV news story, "Cracolandia Will Never End" (Fantastico, May 2008). This belief is supported by recent posts to YouTube, such as the six-part "Cracolandia: O Drama dos Viciados" (The Drama of the Addicts) (August 10, 2009) and Al Jazeera's "Drug Addicts a Challenge for Sao Paulo" (September 28, 2009), which points out that "sweeping the addicts out . . . has pushed them out into other areas." The Al Jazeera team, following the common "duck-blind" approach to videotaping (after the photographer was attacked by one of the drug addicts), reports that social workers say that drug abuse is a criminal problem, and the police say it is a social problem. Furthermore, rehabilitation programs for addicts say that over 80 percent reject those services. The reason might seem obvious: such programs offer no long-term solution to the underlying conditions of poverty and misery, homelessness and joblessness, which dominate their lives. As of 2010, the drug traffic and street drug use in Nova Cracolandia is still going strong and has seeped into neighboring areas.

The highly public campaign against *nóias*, whether framed as an immediate crisis of public health and social control or policing, glosses over the deeper history and more complex patterns of sociality in Centro. These news reports reflect largely non-working-class consumer interests, like the US fixations in the media on reality TV, law and order, tragedy, and terrorism. One need not excavate too deeply into digital archives to see what the public wants: crime, danger, and inner-city terror personified by the *nóia*. The inner-city lives of Centro's diverse "urban outcasts," outside of Luz and the street life of *nóias*, are conspicuously absent. Instead, the threat of the *nóias* is the justification for a wholesale house-cleaning of the downtown area. Also typically absent are the voices of the street folk themselves, from whom we hear not a single tweet.

Digital archives, including Internet images and text, can be used in a highly selective manner and, like other forms of cultural memory including the cityscape itself, "every act of memory carries with it a dimension of betrayal, forgetting, and absence" (Huyssen 2003, 4). At the same time that digital media expand or even explode the space of representation, creating a new historicity of urban spaces and lives, they are often used in a way that flattens and excludes diverse histories and social lives, like the virtual models of urban planners. Obviously, digital media are highly diverse and the brief examples used here are merely intended to illustrate the common use of media by social and political elite in their representations of inner-city poor. They perpetuate views of the homeless as free-floating, lacking social networks, and living in transient communities, if they are considered communities at all. But, at the same time, the use of digital media, particularly the Internet and amateur video, has important potential to incorporate diverse voices, including those of the urban poor.

The more engaged cyber-voyeur can, of course, uncover public controversies, for example, as commentators on social justice and NGOs advocating the rights of the homeless weigh in on urban operations and poverty. However, these are overwhelmed by the vastly dominant images and streams of the *nóia*, the icon of inner-city irregulars in the digital culture industry as marginal bodies and shadow lives. These cyber-caricatures are duplicitous with state propaganda in reinforcing an essentialized image of street folk as not only homeless but simply "less," subnormal, and thus unhumanized, solidifying public sentiment that the best solution is eradication and rehabilitation. Thus, digital media, here largely referring to images and commentary on the Internet, and state agendas often converge in the propagandizing of "preposterous violence," referring to the exaggerated representations of violence in the media and, notably, "the way in which internal 'democracy' calls for the suppression of those deemed criminal, delinquent, and disaffected" (Twitchell 1989; Whitehead 2004, 61).

Despite routinized digital imagery, however, homelessness is not a fixed category but collapses a variety of ways of life and persons without fixed residence or permanent or "regular" employment. The emergent novelty or self-organization on the street in Centro stands in stark contrast to what outsiders witness on YouTube or the cyber-propaganda of the conservative, neoliberal programs of municipal government. Somewhere between the picturesque scenes of the city center, also prominent in digitalscapes, and dystrophic scenes of *nóia-landia* are the real lives of people across Centro, which as communities of practice, subjectivities, and social agents are highly varied and complex and deeply situated in the historical landscapes of the city center.

CONCLUSION

In *Precarious Lives*, Butler (2004, 36) explores how cultural frames for thinking the human set limits on the kinds of losses we can avow as loss. Specifically, certain lives are not considered lives at all and are dehumanized at the level of public discourse: "[V]iolence against those who are already not quite living, living in a state of suspension between life and death, leaves a mark that is no mark" (ibid., 36). Digital subjectivities, it would seem, radically change the relationship between discourse and humanization, opening and expanding the space of representation. And, the assumption, as Butler goes on to say, is that "those who gain representation, especially self-representation, have a better chance of being humanized, and those who have no chance to represent themselves run a greater risk of being treated as less than human, regarded as less than human, or indeed, not regarded at all" (2004, 141).

However, the digital subjectivities, served up for popular consumption, conspire with the neoliberal agendas of city planners, who wish to recapture the city, protect it from invasive and pathological "others," and "grow" new cities based on reason, tradition, and harmony. They conspire to create "virtual bedtime stories," following Stacey (1999, 33): Once upon a time there was a magical land, in this case the landscapes of grandeur and cultural consumption envisioned by urban planners; evil came to this fairytale land, invaded by subnormals, rogues, and zombies: the *nóias*; rebellious, disrespectful, and irrational, the "bandits" spurned authority, tradition, and convention of the "good people." I needn't belabor the point that "the plot line, imagery, and production values owe more to . . . [audio-visual] archives, and to power and knowledge shifts in the academy, economy, and polity, than they do to ethnographic, demographic, or analytical acumen" (ibid., 33). But it is critical to emphasize the willful ignorance of real historical subjectivities, including deep histories, social networks, and legacies of structural and symbolic violence, which make it easier to deny the urban outcasts, drug users, prostitutes, homosexuals, and pavement dwellers any rights to this small piece of city real estate, amounting to about one square kilometer. Yet there they linger.

In closing, it is worth emphasizing that working or even talking with people on the street, not to mention representation of their subjectivities and humanity, poses significant challenges to standard ethnographic approaches, as Frúgoli and Sklair (2008) noted in their study of the Luz district and is widely noted by the ethnographers of "urban outcasts" (Bourgois 2003; Bourgois and Schonberg 2009; Frúgoli 2000; Wacquant 2007, 2008).[13] Among these, the social realities of Centro highlight the role of anthropologists not only as observant participants and commentators in both real and virtual worlds but also as witness to the lives and histories that suffer the threat of being erased—or at least flattened—in public discourse and cultural memory.

NOTES

1. The notion of computers as a prosthesis obviously further complicates this subject/object dichotomy.

2. Although beyond the scope of the present discussion, two themes explored by Benjamin are of particular note here: first, Benjamin's "Arcades Project" provides a classic study of the interpenetrating spaces of normative cultural consumerism and "marginal" activities and social traffic, such as prostitution, in Paris's hyper-designed city center, themes previously explored by Charles Baudelaire; and, second, his discussions and debates regarding the powerful and transformative effects of mass media.

3. In 2008, PricewaterhouseCoopers ranked São Paulo as the tenth richest city in the world and is projected to be the sixth in 2025, behind Tokyo, New York, Los Angeles, London, and Chicago, all with growth rates less than 2.2 percent (GDP rankings for megacities published at https://www.ukmediacentre.pwc.com/Media-Library/GDP-rankings-between-2008-2025-61b.aspx, accessed May 29, 2010).

4. Centro refers to the core area of downtown São Paulo, largely within the district of República. It is situated in the submunicipality of Sé, which is composed of several districts or bairros (neighborhoods) with a residential population of roughly 375,000. Population density is among the highest in the broad metropolitan area (approximately 14,250 per km^2) and dominated by high-rise apartment buildings).

5. Populations vary significantly between the core urban area and greater São Paulo, but population trends are clearly precipitous: 32,000 (in 1872), 65,000 (1890), 240,000 (1900), 580,000 (1920), 1,500,000 (1940), 2,333,346 (1950), 4,005,361 (1960), 7,866,659 (1970), 12,183,634 (1980), 15,183,612 (1990), and 19–22 million (2007).

6. See Collins (2008) and Espinheira (1984) on the revitalization of Salvador's Pelourinho city center.

7. The Old Republic was overthrown by a military coup in 1930, after which the New State period (1937–1945) ensued.

8. Rosa and colleagues (2008) discuss chat groups relating to adult cinemas in Centro.

9. Brenner and Theodore (2002) provide a brief but incisive summary of common neoliberal strategies of urban reformation, which include "privatization" of urban public spaces, placing access and control in the hands of politico-economic elite and characterized by fundamental transformations of the built environment and urban form, for example, "elimination and/or intensified surveillance of urban public spaces and destruction of traditional working-class neighborhoods in order to make way for speculative redevelopment" (2002, 371).

10. Spatial change has reoriented drug trade and street use from Luz, on the northern and eastern side of the praça, to República, Campos Elísios, Santa Cecília, Vila Buarque, Higienópolis, and Bela Vista on the northwestern, western, and praça's southwestern edges.

11. As recently noted by Sebastião Nicomedis of the Movimento Nacional dos Moradores de Rua, "City government realizes operations to collect objects of street people, pressuring them to leave these areas. One need only go any time of day to see what the government is doing; but, at night, when no discretion is needed, things are worse still: sending water trucks to the locations, spraying down everyone who is sleeping there" (Correio da Cidadania, http://www.correiocidadania.com.br, accessed December 11, 2009; A prefeitura realiza operações para recolher objetos dos moradores de rua, pressionando-os a deixar o local onde estão . . . É só ir lá a qualquer hora do dia que é possível ver o que a prefeitura está fazendo; mas, de noite, quando não é necessária nenhuma discrição, a coisa é pior ainda: mandam caminhões-pipa lavarem o local, molhando todos os que estão dormindo).

12. The NGO Forum Centro Vivo states that "those responsible for the social cleansing of [Centro] São Paulo have a name and profession. They are the vice mayor of Sé and secretary of metropolitan districts Andréa Matarazzo, the Secretary of Habitation Orlando de Almeida, and the ex-mayor José Serra (*ReporterBrasil*, May 31, 2006; Os responsáveis [states the NGO Forum Centro Vivo] pela limpeza social de São

Paulo têm nome e profissão. São eles: o Subprefeito da Sé e Secretário das Subprefeituras, Andréa Matarazzo; o Secretário de Habitação, Orlando de Almeida; e o ex-prefeito José Serra). As *O Panóptico* (July 27, 2009) notes, Matarazzo uses Twitter to "directly attend to the population," from which they selected and comment on a few recent posts to reveal his "politically correct tone" and "way of thinking" (um pouco em baixa nos bastidores do poder paulistano, encontrou uma boa forma de propagandear suas idéias: postar no twitter. Com a promessa de atender a população diretamente através do canal, as frases postadas revelam, num tom politicamente correto, sua forma de pensar):

> **AM:** "No centro, muitos moradores de rua nas marquises da Av São joão (no início num bingo abandonado) e na Boa vista. Centro velho esta quase bom." (http://twitter.com/AndreaMatarazzo/status/2849059760; In Centro, many street people on stoops of Av. São João [starting at an abandoned bingo] and in Boa Vista. Old Centro is almost good.)

> *O Panóptico:* "Poxa, o centro está quase bom. Se todos os moradores de rua morressem de uma vez só, ficaria ótimo." (Wow, the center is almost good. If all the street people died at once, it would be great.)

> **AM:** "Não tem perigo. O que é sim, é muito triste. Claro que não desço do carro. Embora os dependentes da novaluz não oferecem perigo." (http://twitter. com/AndreaMatarazzo/status/2848935697; There is no danger. What it is, is very sad. Of course, I didn't get out of the car. Although the addicts of Nova Luz don't pose a danger.)

> *O Panóptico:* "Trata-se de uma técnica de observação da fauna selvagem? Uma técnica de camuflagem? Ou é apenas a sensação de segurança trazida por uma tonelada de aço com arranque rápido? Se 'não tem perigo' qual seria o motivo de 'conhecer a realidade' de dentro do carro? Quem seriam os perigosos? Os moradores do bairro?" (Does he treat it as a form of observation of wild animals? A technique of camouflage? Or, is it only a sense of security provided by a tone of steel with a quick escape? If "there is no danger," what is the reason to "know the reality" from inside a car? Who would be the dangerous people? The residents of the neighborhood?)

13. During the course of nearly twenty years, I have had lengthy conversations with well over a hundred individuals living and working on the streets of downtown, particularly during the period from August 2007 to May 2009, and in the case of about a dozen persons I conducted multiple, long informal interviews during this time. I do not report on these interactions specifically here, because of the difficulty of obtaining "informed consent" when working with socially marginalized groups. Furthermore, as noted in the photo essay titled "Land of the Living Dead" (http://blogs.reuters.com/ photo/2010/05/21/land-of-the-living-dead/, accessed January 6, 2010), the reality of crime in some downtown areas "can turn the simple action of anyone photographing or filming into a fatal mistake." Even note taking or audio taping can be a sensitive and potentially dangerous action.

REFERENCES

Barbosa da Silva, Jose Fabio. 1959. "Aspetos sociológicos de homossexualismo em São Paulo." *Sociologia* 21: 350–60.

Benjamin, Walter. 2002. *The Arcades Project*. Cambridge, MA: Harvard University Press.

Biehl, João, Byron Good, and Arthur Kleinman. 2007. *Subjectivity: Ethnographic Investigations*. Berkeley: University of California Press.

Bourgois, Philippe. 2003. *In Search of Respect: Selling Crack in El Barrio*. Cambridge: Cambridge University Press.

Bourgois, Philippe, and Jeff Schonberg. 2009. *Righteous Dopefiend*. Berkeley: University of California Press.

Brenner, Neil, and Nick Theodore. 2002. "Cities and the Geographies of 'Actually Existing Neoliberalism.'" *Antipode* 34 (3): 349–79. http://dx.doi.org/10.1111/1467-8330.00246.

Butler, Judith. 1993. *Bodies that Matter: On the Discursive Limits of Sex*. New York: Routledge.

Butler, Judith. 2004. *Precarious Lives: The Power of Mourning and Violence*. London: Verso.

Caldeira, Teresa. 2000. *City of Walls: Crime, Segregation, and Citizenship in São Paulo*. Berkeley: University of California Press.

Carvalho, J.N.B., and M.C.S. Schicchi. 2007. "A Área da Luz em São Paulo: Reabilitação de edifícios históricos versus recuperação urbana." *Os Urbanitas* 4(5). http://www.aguaforte.com/osurbanitas5/Carvalho&Schicchi2007.html)

Collins, John. 2008. "'But What If I Should Need to Defecate in Your Neighborhood, Madame?' Empire, Redemption, and the 'Tradition of the Oppressed' in a Brazilian World Heritage Site." *Cultural Anthropology* 23 (2): 279–328. http://dx.doi.org/10.1111/j.1548-1360.2008.00010.x.

DaMatta, Roberto. 1991. *Carnivals, Rogues, and Heroes: An Interpretation of the Brazilian Dilemma*. Notre Dame, IN: University of Notre Dame Press.

De Certeau, Michel. 2002. *The Practice of Everyday Life*. Berkeley: University of California Press.

Deleuze, Gilles, and Felix Guattari. 1983. *Anti-Oedipus*. Minneapolis: University of Minnesota Press.

Espinheira, Gey. 1984. *Divergência e Prostituição*. Salvador: Tempo Brasileiro.

Fausto, Boris. 2001 [1984]. *Crime e Cotidiano: A Criminalidade em São Paulo, 1880–1924*. São Paulo: EdUSP.

Frúgoli, Heitor, Jr. 2000. *Centralidade em São Paulo: Trajetórias, conflitos, e negociações na metrópole*. São Paulo: EdUSP.

Frúgoli, Heitor, Jr., and Jessica Sklair. 2008. "The Luz District in São Paulo: Anthropological Perspectives on the Phenomenon of Gentrification." Paper presented at the 9th Conference of the Brazilian Studies Association, New Orleans, March.

Gilroy, Paul. 1987. *There Ain't No Black in the Union Jack*. London: Hutchinson.

Goode, Judith. 2002. "How Urban Ethnography Counters Myths about the Poor." In *Urban Life: Readings in the Anthropology of the City*, ed. G. Gmelch and W. P. Zenner, 279–95. Prospect Heights, IL: Waveland.

Green, James. 1999. *Beyond Carnival: Male Homosexuality in Twentieth Century Brazil*. Chicago: University of Chicago Press.

Guimarães, Antonio. 2002. Classes, Raças e Democracia. São Paulo: Editora 34.

Harrison, Faye. 1998. "Introduction: Expanding the Discourse on Race." *American Anthropologist* 100 (3): 609–31. http://dx.doi.org/10.1525/aa.1998.100.3.609.

Hermann, Lucia. 1944. "Estudo de desenvolvimento de São Paulo através da análise de um radial—a estrada do café, 1935." *Revista de Arquivo Municipal* 99: 7–45.

Holston, James. 2009. *Insurgent Citizenship: Disjunctions of Democracy and Modernity in Brazil*. Princeton, NJ: Princeton University Press.

Huyssen, Andreas. 2003. *Present Pasts: Urban Palimpsests and the Politics of Memory*. Stanford, CA: Stanford University Press.

Jameson, Fredric. 2006. *Archaeologies of the Future: The Desire Called Utopia and Other Science Fictions*. London: Verso.

Johnson, Steven. 2001. *Emergence: The Connected Lives of Ants, Brains, Cities, and Software*. New York: Scribner.

Low, Setha. 2001. *On the Plaza: The Politics of Public Space and Culture*. Austin: University of Texas Press.

Low, Setha, Dana Taplin, and Suzanne Scheld. 2005. *Rethinking Urban Parks: Public Space and Cultural Diversity*. Austin: University of Texas Press.

Marcuse, Herbert. 1962. *Eros and Civilization*. New York: Vintage Books.

Mitchell, Don, and Lynn Staeheli. 2006. "Clean and Safe? Redevelopment, Public Space, and Homelessness in Downtown San Diego." In *The Politics of Public Space*, ed. Setha Low and Neil Smith, 143–175. New York: Routledge.

Müller, N. L. 1958. "A Área Central da Cidade." In *A Cidade de São Paulo: Estudos de Geografia urbana*: vol. 3, *Aspetos da Metrópole Paulista*, ed. A. de Azevedo, 121–182. São Paulo: Companhia Editora Nacional.

Needell, Jeffrey. 1987. *A Tropical Belle Epoche: Elite Culture and Society in Turn-of-the-Century Rio de Janeiro*. Cambridge: Cambridge University Press.

Perlman, Janice. 2007. "Marginality from Myth to Reality: The Favelas of Rio 1968–2005." http://info.worldbank.org/etools/docs/library/117812/Chapter4.pdf.

Perlongher, Nestor. 1987. *O negócio do michê: Prostituição viril em São Paulo*. São Paulo: Editora Brasiliense.

Rosa, A. J., A. Valerini, C. A. Fabio, and D. C. Nascimento França. 2008. "Cinemas Pornôs da Cidade de São Paulo." *PontoUrbe* 2(3). http://www.n-a-u.org/pontourbe03/cinespornodesaopaulo.html.

Sherif, Robin. 2001. *Dreaming Equality: Color, Race, and Racism in Urban Brazil*. New Brunswick, NJ: Rutgers University Press.

Stacey, Judith. 1999. "Virtual Social Science and the Politics of Family Values." In *Critical Anthropology Now: Unexpected Contexts, Shifting Constituencies, Changing Agendas*, ed. George Marcus, 29–54. Santa Fe, NM: SAR Press.

Twitchell, James. 1989. *Preposterous Violence: Fables of Aggression in Modern Culture*. Oxford: Oxford University Press.

Wacquant, Loic. 2007. *Urban Outcasts: A Comparative Sociology of Advanced Marginality*. New York: Polity.

Wacquant, Loic. 2008. "The Militarization of Urban Marginality: Lessons from the Brazilian Metropole." *International Political Sociology* 2 (1): 56–74. http://dx.doi.org/10.1111/j.1749-5687.2008.00037.x.

Weinstein, Barbara. 1996. *For Social Peace in Brazil: Industrialists and the Remaking of the Working Class in São Paulo*. Chapel Hill: University of North Carolina Press.

Whitehead, Neil. 2004. "On the Poetics of Violence." In *Violence*, ed. N. L. Whitehead, 55–77. Santa Fe, NM: SAR Press.

12

Are We There Yet?

The End of Anthropology Is Beyond the Human

Neil L. Whitehead

For anthropology the recognition of multiple modernities, both now and in the past, and the existence of other globalized worlds beyond that of the Western sensorium and the expansion of that sensorium enabled by new digital worlds (Jones 2006) suggest that many of the central categories of Western intellectual experience, such as the cultural and the natural, the modern and the traditional, and the global and the local are all deeply entwined in any discussion of society, history, environment, and the beings through which such abstractions are constituted. This is true throughout the humanistic and social science disciplines, not just anthropology. In this context the notion of "posthuman" presents itself as a historical and intellectual judgment as to what is, a revelation as to what we already know and experience. This chapter, in seeking to find an end, a purpose, to anthropology beyond the idea of simply the "human," looks to what might be the objects of future anthropological enquiry and why anthropology should be directed toward these new purposes.

The alternative to rethinking anthropology's methodologies and objects along these lines would be a collapse into intellectual conservatism and political

DOI: 10.5876/9781607321705.c12

quietism in the face of burgeoning new cultural worlds that, as chapters in this volume show, have become otherwise functionally un-interpretable and un-researchable. This does not mean that such cultural worlds are unimportant, although such an assumption no doubt would perfectly suit many current regimes of intellectual and political power. Academia does not exist in a cultural vacuum, so our sense of what is a priority and whose experiences are relevant to intellectual understanding are part of wider cultural discussions. In this way an uncritical ethnography practiced as part of a normative anthropological agenda can easily slip into an unthinking co-option by military, industry, and government interests (Price 2008), suggesting that ethnography's epistemological ancestry makes this a persistent danger for those, like most anthropologists, who would rather use ethnographic engagements to foster emancipatory and advocacy goals (Whitehead 2009a).

However, a critique of ethnographic epistemology alone is not sufficient, because it simply returns us to the question of what anthropology and ethnography are for. It is here that the meaning of the debate about the posthuman becomes all-important because we face a crisis of ontology, not just of epistemology. As all the chapters in this volume show, it is the multiple ontologies generated in online worlds and present in occluded offline worlds that have been overlooked or actively ignored because we lack adequate methodologies to engage immaterial, digital subjects ethnographically or the ethical issues raised by participant observation among violent, drug-taking, insurgent, and criminal subjects seem insurmountable (Whitehead 2009b). The limits of standard ethnographic methodology challenge us to develop new forms of engagement, as the authors in this volume demonstrate. However, beyond methodological questions we still need to consider what the goals of anthropological knowledge are or should be. Assuming that "ethnography" stands outside of social relationships is clearly an untenable position, and although the profession has been questioning the relation between researcher and subject in many effective ways over the last two decades, recent events suggest that much remains to be done. In particular, the avid interest of government security agencies in recruiting anthropologists as a means to "weaponize" cultural knowledge has resulted in important analyses and critique of this kind of co-option (Kelly et al. 2010; González 2009; Price 2008). But if the kind of cultural knowledge that ethnography produces can be "weaponized" in this way, further thought needs to be given about how this can occur, given the largely progressive and emancipatory aims of most anthropological practice.

In these ways anthropology faces fundamental challenges to its unexamined epistemological and ontological assumptions. Without rethinking both the goals of anthropological knowledge and the forms of ontology ethnography needs to engage to achieve such knowledge, anthropology risks becoming a mere catalog of the exotic and diverse. At the same time ethnography risks becoming a generalized methodology, stripped of the complexities arising from long-term subjective engagement and reduced to little more than the protocols that institutional review boards require to govern human-subject interview techniques.

The chapters here amply illustrate important forms of collective association and practice that highlight such issues, and the authors' responses to these challenges of ontological and epistemological reformulation do much to show us new ends and means to a future anthropology. It is also critical to consider how such case studies suggest the need for a wider critique that can reveal the systematic implications of these approaches for a reformulated anthropology. To that end, the rest of this chapter will consider how the essays collected here stake out new anthropological fields and take us beyond the human.

TRADITION, MODERNITY, AND THE COLLAPSE OF CULTURE

The question of what anthropology should have as its knowledge goals is not unique to this volume. Arguably, the last two decades of the "reflexive turn"— the notion that problems of inequitable and colonizing epistemologies are overcome when the observers participate with the subjects of their observation—has adequately de-centered any lingering naive modernism about the possibility for achieving total "knowledge" of others. However, this shift has not led to any indication of what our post-colonial knowledge goals should be and how we can pursue them in a way that does not continually reproduce the cultural superiority of observers over observed, whatever the manner of engagement with those other lives (Mbembe 2001).

To some extent the force of such questions was blunted by attempts to salvage the anthropological tradition as it has been constituted so far (Ortner 2006; Rabinow et al. 2008) and even with the new opportunities of the digital online world kept front and center (Boellstorff 2008). In an afterword (notably not in the introduction), Rees writes of the discussion he mediated between Rabinow Marcus and Faubion:

> [They] explore some of the ways in which anthropology has been
> developing since the 1980s and seek to articulate . . . the conceptual
> challenges these developments imply for the practice of anthropological
> inquiry today. Today, what is anthropology? What could it be? Where does
> it come from and in which way might it develop? What's the role of culture,
> the place of society where we anthropologists no longer exclusively—or
> predominantly—address culture and/or society? What new objects have
> been emerging? What new concepts? What's the role of fieldwork under
> these renewed circumstances? What constitutes ethnographic data and
> what could serve as a measure for descriptive thickness? (Rabinow et al.
> 2008, 115–6)

That such questions, but not their answers, conclude the work suggests that this is not another moment for "recapturing" anthropology (Fox 1991) or, as that work terms it, "redesigning" anthropology. In any case, some form of design "makeover" hardly seems to meet the need to examine the deep structure and history of the discipline at a critical intellectual juncture. In short, the outcomes of failing to address such epistemological and ontological problems are already with us and have proliferated, leading to serious ethical and political issues in professional practice with, at times, even lethal consequences (Tierney 2002; Whitehead 2009a).

This failure to address our problems has led others to question anthropology's purpose and to identify a tendency for anthropology to devolve into a species of area studies as comparative religion, literary studies, political science, geography, and sociology all discover "field work" and a untroubled program of synthesizing ethnography to undergird it. All of this occurs at a moment when the anthropological sciences—archaeology and biology—are also seeking to find practices that problematize their own forms of knowledge gathering and subjective engagements to reinvent new ends suitable to those purposes (El Haj 2002; Schmidt and Patterson 1996; Atlan and de Waal 2007; Schmidt 2009).

For exactly the same reasons, the Brazilian anthropologist Viveiros de Castro asks in his recent volume *Métaphysiques cannibales*, "Conceptually, what should anthropology be to the peoples it studies?" (2009, 1, my translation). Through this question, Viveiros de Castro is trying to go beyond all those studies generally grouped under the label of "reflexive anthropology" by showing the inadequacy of the traditional opposition between a naively objectivist anthropology that systematically reveals others through writing about them and a postmodernism that insists on a unique particularism among others that forever eludes translation or interpretation, and thus the theoretical construction of "culture." Although Viveiros de Castro is quite right about the epistemological limits of a reflexive anthropology, the notion of culture is still unquestioned and the issue of ontology replaced as one of viewpoint. But although such "perspectivism" (discussed below) is a powerful insight into translation among different epistemological regimes, it leaves the question of ontology untouched because, for Viveiros de Castro, to have a "perspective" it is necessary also to have an interior form of "humanity" (2009, 1).[1] How viewpoints and ontologies are interrelated and how ways of being produce ways of seeing nonetheless require more thought. The chapters in this volume begin some of that work by showing how digital lives are not experienced and cannot be known through observational practices alone. Rather, participation—that is, the development of one's own digital subjectivity—is a prerequisite for any observational activity (Whitehead 2009b), and this fundamental principle guides how ethnography may be reformulated. For this reason we can pluralize "perspectives" endlessly, but then such "perspectives" only function philosophically as "culture" once did.

In North American anthropology, Arjun Appadurai's iconic *Modernity at Large* (1996) continues to give anthropology a powerful vision of culture as a mobile, plural, and ever-changing phenomenon, unlike earlier more static and essentialist models. By suggesting that a global modernity was effectively linking even the most isolated populations, Appadurai's work seemed to offer a way out of the impasse of trying to invent new strategies for "writing culture" that had all foundered when faced with the impossibility of identifying what "culture" meant in such literary exercises (Clifford 1988; Clifford and Marcus 1986; Marcus 1998; Marcus and Fischer 1999). It also perfectly matched the post-Soviet moment by suggesting a social philosophy of democratic and entrepreneurial freedom through the globalization of "glasnost," or openness and transparency, which was celebrated as the source of Soviet internal collapse and a key difference between the Soviet system and Western democracy. Since the notion of culture itself has remained problematic, the notion of global modernity supplanted culture as a guiding theoretical category. Consequently, Clifford (1997) was now writing "mobility" rather than "culture," and, as Sahlins (2000) announced it, the topic for anthropology in the twenty-first century became ethnographies of global modernity's "indigenization," that is, of "culture[s] in their practice," to paraphrase the title of Sahlins's book. But the isomorphism of modernity and culture for such authors ignores the way in which the ideas of "culture" and "modernity" are historically contingent and culturally particular. Thus, there may be multiple and alternative modernities that do not necessarily match the chronology of American and European history or express the liberal democratic values that the advent of this latest version of "modernity" is supposed to entail.

Many anthropologists and historians of non-Western cultures have been more open to the idea that invasive modernity has been experienced in other times and places, specifically as a result of domination by one of the early regional empires in, for example, Mexico, Egypt, Rome, the Indus Valley, or China (Ferguson and Whitehead 2000; Gaonkar 2001; Abu-Lughod 1991). In any given historical and cultural context, "modernity" cannot be understood apart from those ideas that also give meaning and content to the idea of "tradition." In this sense, "modernity" is both ancient and plural, an aspect of the continuous construction of "tradition," closely interrelated and historically contingent, the mutual condition of their possibility. The expansion of industrialized capitalism in the last 200 years was a contingent historical phenomenon, bringing along with it particular notions of tradition and modernity formed largely in colonial encounter.

Nineteenth-century anthropology had an important role to play in generating these categories through the contemplation and classification of "primitive" peoples that were encountered, and it is those notions of tradition and modernity that have been globalized in our version of a "modern" world. This process is not permissive, because even if local meaning and form is given to the modern, what the process should be is a matter of continuous debate and sometimes embittered conflict for those on the point of imminent envelopment by national states and international corporations (Comaroff 2001; Ferguson 2006; Scott 2009; Whitehead 2002). In short, there has not been a "convergence" of modernities, as suggested by both Marx and Durkheim, to produce a global social and cultural uniformity but rather an explosion of alternative modernities.

In this frame, the need to become modern is less a precursor to the inevitable advent of a set of uniform social and cultural conditions as invented in Euro-America over the last 200 years than it is a signal of a political and economic condition of marginalization from current global systems. This frame of reference also allows a different kind of understanding of not only cultural tradition and its allure but also those cultural fundamentalisms that seem poised to challenge Western modernity as morally bankrupt, spiritually dissolute, and socially competitive.

Thinking about the global nature of modernity is thus a way of focusing on the cultural process through which certain regimes of power—states and corporations—are established over and against local folklore and traditions in the social and cultural sphere. In turn, this process often represents an assertion of the individuality of "human" rights and obligations in relation to the state and the denial of other forms of collectivity—family, clan, mosque, or church. This is not an end to culture, or to anthropology, but it is a theoretical impasse for an anthropology wedded to notions of culture that cannot allow for this expanded frame of reference in writing about the local and global, the traditional and the modern. Supposedly, nothing could be more "modern" than the digital, but virtual, mobile worlds are arguably ancient (Zielinski 2008) and perfectly compatible with "tradition" as demonstrated by the chapters in this volume by Alemán, on the use of digital media by indigenous peoples, and Wisniewski, on globalized social consciousness among Amazonian peoples.

CULTURE, NATURE, AND THE POSTHUMAN

In the same way that notions of "culture" collapse when faced with the dynamics of how people deploy their traditions and modernities, so too is the binary of culture/nature or natural/human destabilized by how people practice relationships with non-humans and things and to the extent that culture is seen as a unique property of the "human" (Santos-Granero 2009; Whitehead 2012). In the same way that debates about modernity supplanted theorizing about culture, the use of mediating concepts such as "perspectivism" and "landscape" have been put forward as ways in which the categories of "human" and "natural" can be sustained despite the long-overdue acknowledgment of the agency of animals and objects, as well as the digital and unhuman subjects that are at the core of this book. Just as notions of the theater state (Geertz 1981), the magical state (Coronil 1997; Taussig 1997), and the state as exception (Agamben 2005) showed the state to be a quasi-object (after Latour 1993), eluding typology and definition through social science, so too the ideas behind the notions of "perspectivism" and "landscape" show "nature" and "human" to be quasi-subjects.

However, as Latour (1993) suggests, such mediation still leaves the poles of the binary intact and thus, by itself, fails to address ontological questions, even while providing clarification of epistemological issues. Anthropologies and histories of landscapes, commodity chains, and the labor that creates them have been extensively researched over the last three decades, particularly in South America beginning in 1970s with Alfred Crosby's groundbreaking work *The Columbian Exchange* (1973; Mintz 1986; Stewart and Strathern 2003; Tsing 2004; Feld and Basso 1997; Hirsch and O'Hanlon 1995; Topik, Frank, and Marichal 2006; Striffler, Moberg, and Joseph 2003). Nonetheless, the centrality of the "human" as an analytical category still persists, like a nagging hangover from Enlightenment categories. As a result, the human continues to be constituted through reason and its cultural expression as language, whereas embodiment is mapped through biological, neurological, and zoological understandings of psychology, physiology, and genetics.

Cary Wolfe (2009) in *What Is Posthumanism?* has carefully unpicked both affectual and ethical theoretical positions that have stemmed from the various attempts to bring animals and other non-humans into this theoretical landscape (e.g., Haraway 1990, 2007). However, the intent here seems to be to provide "humanism-humanities" with a more adequate theoretical foundation and the means for détente with science. Thus, for Wolfe the proper way to craft an ethical pluralism that gives place to the animal other is to arrive at this animal other by way of ethical theory and reason. As Wolfe (2009, xv) puts it, through an intensification of humanism, when theory is done "well enough," we will eventually discover that other animals are not Other in the sense of belonging to some wholly foreign "outside" but rather constitute a radical difference and alterity that structures "the human" in its very core. But such a hope for the triumph of theory and reason not only excludes the animal as ontological Other but also reproduces the human as merely an ethical entity rather than as a fully spiritual being. To paraphrase Bruno Latour (1993), God is still crossed out, which is another way of saying that Cartesian models are highly reductive of both the human and the animal.

Although most theorists see the problem in terms of animalizing the human or humanizing the animal, the absence of other biotic taxa (insects, fish, microbes) in such a project is matched by an exclusion of all those people considered subhuman/unhuman—junkies, abusers, thugs and gangstas, insurgents, terrorists, the insane or disabled, and the damaged or deformed, as well as those considered non-human, such as avatars, networked identities, and the whole realm of digital actors described in this volume. For these reasons, Wolfe's formulation fails to escape the logic of capitalism and colonialism since the universalization of "human" rights and the extension of those rights to "animals" beg too many questions about animality and humanity, as well as the emancipatory potential of the human rights discourse itself. The logic of domination is inherent in "human rights" discourse; thus, in our attempts to write animals in, just as with the category of "children," the perceived lack of opportunity or ability to "speak for oneself" invites the rescuing discourse of inherent rights to supplant this silence. The "rescue missions" under way in Iraq and Afghanistan should, therefore, give us pause in uncritically accepting such a discourse at face value. Likewise, among the wild beasts, the "naturals," the occurrence of thrill killing, rape, and mono-gendered and trans-species sexuality, as well as myriad other forms of "biological exuberance" (as Bagemil [1999] has called it), cannot fit into these reasonable theories that Wolfe aims to construct and that seem to result in another glorious triumph for reason and science. But in some arenas of anthropology, the human has already been surpassed in a more proactive attempt to replace the logos of anthropology with experience-based concepts rather than those of biologized identity. In just this way, the notion of trans-species formations is being used by anthropologists and historians of South America to track how, through the exercise of imperial biopower, the manipulation of all life continually creates and redefines the speciation and destiny of both naturals and humans (Few and Tortorici 2011). However, although we still preserve the notions of speciation, or its the exemplar the human, in ordering such narratives we have yet to escape from a discourse that also enables power and domination over a threatening and foreign "nature." To that end we might direct our attention to non-Western thinking about nature and its "perspectival quality" (Århem 1996; Viveiros de Castro 2000).

This perspectival character to epistemological and cosmological systems results in viewing the world as inhabited by different sorts of subjects or persons. Such persons apprehend experience from distinct ontological positions, which we bifurcate into just two classes—human and non-human. As many anthropologists have already concluded, the classic distinction between nature and culture cannot be assumed to describe domains internal to non-Western cosmologies. This has led to the suggestion that "multi-naturalism," as opposed to Western "multi-culturalism," is a key and revealing difference here. To paraphrase Viveiros de Castro's (2000) analysis, multi-culturalism, the plenitude of culture, is founded for Western thought on an assumption of the unity of nature but the plurality of cultures. The natural proceeds from a supposedly objective universality of body and substance; the cultural is generated by the subjective particularity of affect (spirituality) and meaning. To express this multi-naturalism through a Western lens, non-Western conceptions suppose a spiritual unity and a corporeal diversity in which culture or the subject is the form of the universal, whereas nature or the object is the form of the particular. So humans do see humans as humans, animals as animals, and spirits as spirits; however, animals and spirits may also see humans as animal-prey to the same extent that animals (as prey) see humans as spirits or as animal-predators. In this way, the houses or villages of parrots, piranhas, peccaries, or jaguars—their places—give rise to their own particular forms of culture. Fur, feathers, scales, fins, claws, teeth, and beaks are indeed seen and worn as body decorations and as cultural instruments for loving and killing by both animals and humans, as we term them. So, too, in a direct inversion of sociobiology, the naturals see their social systems as human institutions of chiefs, shamans, rituals, and marriages. Moreover, indigenous perspectivism is not just a latent ahistorical symbolic category but a living theory of cultural practice, most dramatically in hunting and war. And we encounter here perhaps the most fundamental way of loving, being, and killing animals as others and humans as ourselves.[2]

CONCLUSION

Sustained engagement with other ontologies and epistemologies through ethnographic participation in hunting (or fishing), as well as petkeeping and household husbandry, thus suggests new methodologies for centering the naturals in history and anthropology. This requires close attention to the meaning-laden contexts of action and behavior that provide an extended hermeneutic for the interpretation of ultimately ineffable others, whatever their forms of speciation (Grandin 2009). By the same token, the variously unhuman digital, marginal, criminal, and tribal persons that are the central subject of this volume achieve a more complete theoretical status through inclusion within such a hermeneutic.

Anthropology, in the field of the human, has long realized that totalizing "holistic" explanation is impossible. No one can say why another does as they do, because we cannot even do that for ourselves. Therefore, it is the purposes of knowledge rather than hope for its completeness that needs to drive our explanatory projects of humans, naturals, and the plenitude of trans-species, online/offline formations to which all of life gives rise.

We are not adapted; we are just here. But like the "well-bred" show dogs that cannot survive without veterinary intervention, the Enlightenment project of the "human" was not a process of discovery but one of exclusion of the savage, the animal, the inferior, and the superstitious from the fully human. In time, colonial civilization developed these subhumans into the fully rational self-maximizing entrepreneurs, and the early Christian Gnostic claim—that

God had made an imperfect world and then abandoned it in disgust—was put aside. Only with the mass slaughter of the First and Second World Wars did the notion that we are all crippled, damaged, somehow "hollow men" again take hold. The carnage we inflict on ourselves and others reveals that "modern" life is unlivable. Our militarized subjectivities, the "war machines" that we have become (Deleuze and Guattari 1987), now give rise to subjectivities that are also profoundly enchained to prosthetic systems of communication supported by digital devices, without which we can no longer function as fully "modern humans." But it is not the entanglement in prosthetics that is the problem so much as the inequalities of access to the relevant technologies. In the spirit world of amodern peoples the shaman exhibits control over the techniques of ecstasy, prophecy, and sacrifice, but in this case the technologies are intellectual and organic and thus accessible in social ways unlike an iPod or Reaper Drone.[3] Indeed, by reason of their ontological congruence with people, even animals can be seen to use these shamanic technologies while obviously being no less excluded from high-end digital technology.[4] Nonetheless, they are disciplined by human speciation and state-sponsored ecological management, and their wildness is "nomadic" (after Deleuze and Guattari 1987) and so inimical to the state no less than the savage cannibal on a desert isle or in a forest fastness. War, counterinsurgency, special policing, riot control, homeland security, and its economic profits through energy and resource extraction drive the perpetual colonialism of wild animals and wild people by erasing their codependent landscapes and their subjugation to those regimes of capitalist modernity delineated by Marx and Foucault. For these reasons, an understanding of magic and spirituality is necessarily part of the project of going beyond the rational Enlightenment human as well as its counterpart, the unthinking animal. Popular resistance to the strictures of modernity is then directly reflected in the global resurgence of sorcery—precisely, "the modernity of witchcraft," to borrow Peter Geschiere's (1997) phrase—no less than the animal-rights and human-disabilities movements in the "developed" West.

If we have never been and never will be modern, we never were traditional. Therefore, it is not what makes us different from or the same as other animals (unhumans) that is significant but rather what experiences we include or exclude as relevant to our attempts to live, that is, to achieve a satisfaction for the desires we experience—something that we envy in animals but have new possibilities through the digital experience. The neologism "zoosomnial blurring" (*New York Times*, op-ed, September 12, 2010), the notion that animals probably do not distinguish much between dreaming and being awake, nicely captures the envy of those trained to practice a Cartesian consciousness for those who have managed without such a bifurcation of mind and world. This envy, however, is always restrained by a fear of the consequences of unthinking belief or the "unexamined" life.[5]

Reflexively examined or not, the suffering of the battery chicken is no less theoretically relevant to the future anthropological project than the agonies of the military torture room, and in any case, no practical difference between these situations can ethically allow us to exclude either experience from an anthropology that goes beyond the human. Ethnography is also a relational practice that establishes the limits of human variety under the guise of the ethnic and linguistic. But this sorting of subjects, as Latour (1993) showed us, is apt to produce its own marginalizations precisely at the boundary of the human, thereby producing animals as unhumans, the disabled and virtual as para-humans, and the asocial as subhumans/savages. Thus, the issue becomes whether ethnographic methodology can perpetually recuperate the human among those marginalized and expanding groups of quasi-humans (the virtual, digital, criminal, insane, and insurgent), or should it relinquish its role in policing those borders to reconceptualize the existing results and future strategies of the discipline? The answers must be "yes," and the essays in this volume show both why and how that can occur. But we are not there yet.

NOTES

1. As Pierre Charbonnier notes in his review (L'Anti-Narcisse de Viveiros de Castro, *La Vie des idées*, 4/15/2010), "Dans la mesure où toute entité, humaine ou non humaine, est réputée être dotée d'une intériorité analogue à celle de l'homme, elle est aussi dotée d'un point de vue sur ses partenaires écologiques et sociaux. Et la particu larité de ce point de vue est donnée par le « vêtement » matériel qui envelope cette intériorité: un corps de jaguar, de singe, d'homme, etc."

2. However, "multi-culturalism" has not meant that the idea of a genetic-biological core of the idea of the "human" has likewise been critiqued, as Maurice Bloch's (2011) essay on the "phenomena of people" shows. He writes that we should see "people as natural organisms rather than as the abstractions of unclear ontological status," but despite acknowledgment of the instability of human ontology, problems with the idea of "natural" are not considered.

3. Bruce Kapferer (1997), following the works of Deleuze and Guattari (1987), characterizes both "war machines" and state governance as practices of power. Kapferer also explicitly and productively references such practices as forms of sorcery, seen as quintessentially operating outside the normal relations of modern capitalism, disrupting established hierarchies of value, and perpetually transforming material realities (1997, 274–285).

4. Jaguars consume the hallucinogen *yajé*, as shamans do; see footage from a BBC documentary here: http://www.youtube.com/watch?v=OqGDv0KCJl8.

5. The Socratic warning is that "[t]he unexamined life is not worth living for a human being" (ho de anexetastos bios ou biôtos anthrôpôi). But Mark Twain riposted that "[t]he unexamined life may not be worth living, but the life too closely examined may not be lived at all."

REFERENCES

Abu-Lughod, Janet L. 1991. *Before European Hegemony: The World System A.D. 1250–1350.* New York: Oxford University Press.

Agamben, Giorgio. 2005. *State of Exception.* Chicago: University Press of Chicago.

Appadurai, Arjun. 1996. *Modernity at Large: Cultural Dimensions of Globalization.* Minneapolis: University of Minnesota Press.

Århem, Kaj. 1996. "The Cosmic Food-Web: Human-Nature Relatedness in Northwest Amazonia." In *Nature and Society: Anthropological Perspectives*, ed. Gisli Pálsson and Philippe Descola, 185–204. London: Routledge.

Atlan, Henri, and Frans B.M. de Waal. 2007. *Les frontières de l'humain.* Paris: Pommier.

Bagemil, Bruce. 1999. *Biological Exuberance: Animal Homosexuality and Natural Diversity.* New York: St. Martins Press.

Bloch, Maurice. 2011. "The Blob." *Anthropology of this Century.* http://aotcpress.com/articles/blob/.

Boellstorff, Tom. 2008. *Coming of Age in Second Life: An Anthropologist Explores the Virtually Human.* Princeton, NJ: Princeton University Press.

Clifford, James. 1988. *The Predicament of Culture: Twentieth-Century Ethnography, Literature, and Art.* Cambridge, MA: Harvard University Press.

Clifford, James. 1997. *Routes: Travel and Translation in the Late Twentieth Century.* Cambridge, MA: Harvard University Press.

Clifford, James, and George E. Marcus, eds. 1986. *Writing Culture: The Poetics and Politics of Ethnography.* Santa Fe, NM: SAR Press.

Comaroff, John L., ed. 2001. *Millennial Capitalism and the Culture of Neoliberalism.* Durham, NC: Duke University Press.

Coronil, Fernando. 1997. *The Magical State: Nature, Money, and Modernity in Venezuela.* Chicago: University of Chicago Press.

Crosby, Alfred W. 1973. *The Columbian Exchange: Biological and Cultural Consequences of 1492.* Westport, CT: Greenwood.

Deleuze, Gilles, and Félix Guattari. 1987. *A Thousand Plateaus: Capitalism and Schizophrenia.* Minneapolis: University of Minnesota Press.

El-Haj, Nadia Abu. 2002. *Facts on the Ground: Archaeological Practice and Territorial Self-Fashioning in Israeli Society.* Chicago: University of Chicago Press.

Feld, Steven, and Keith H. Basso, eds. 1997. *Senses of Place.* Santa Fe, NM: SAR Press.

Ferguson, James. 2006. *Global Shadows: Africa in the Neoliberal World Order.* Durham, NC: Duke University Press.

Ferguson, R. Brian, and Neil L. Whitehead, eds. 2000. *War in the Tribal Zone: Expanding States and Indigenous Warfare.* Santa Fe, NM: SAR Press; London: James Currey.

Few, Martha, and Zeb Tortorici. 2011. *Centering Animals in Latin America.* Durham, NC: Duke University Press.

Fox, Richard, ed. 1991. *Recapturing Anthropology: Working in the Present.* Santa Fe, NM: SAR Press.

Gaonkar, Dilip Parameshwar. 2001. *Alternative Modernities.* Durham, NC: Duke University Press.

Geertz, Clifford. 1981. *Negara: The Theatre State in Nineteenth-Century Bali.* Princeton, NJ: Princeton University Press.

Geschiere, Peter. 1997. *The Modernity of Witchcraft: Politics and the Occult in Postcolonial Africa.* Charlottesville: University of Virginia Press.

González, Roberto J. 2009. *American Counterinsurgency: Human Science and the Human Terrain*. Chicago: Prickly Paradigm Press.

Grandin, Temple. 2009. *Animals Make Us Human: Creating the Best Life for Animals*. Boston: Houghton Mifflin Harcourt.

Haraway, Donna Jeanne. 1990. *Simians, Cyborgs, and Women: The Reinvention of Nature*. London: Routledge.

Haraway, Donna Jeanne. 2007. *When Species Meet*. Minneapolis: University of Minnesota Press.

Hirsch, Eric, and Michael O'Hanlon. 1995. *The Anthropology of Landscape: Perspectives on Place and Space*. Oxford: Oxford University Press.

Jones, Caroline A. 2006. *Sensorium: Embodied Experience, Technology, and Contemporary Art*. Cambridge, MA: MIT Press.

Kapferer, Bruce. 1997. *The Feast of the Sorcerer: Practices of Consciousness and Power*. Chicago: University of Chicago Press.

Kelly, John D., Beatrice Jauregui, Sean T. Mitchell, and Jeremy Walton, eds. 2010. *Anthropology and Global Counterinsurgency*. Chicago: University of Chicago Press.

Latour, Bruno. 1993. *We Have Never Been Modern*. Cambridge, MA: Harvard University Press.

Marcus, George E. 1998. *Ethnography through Thick and Thin*. Princeton, NJ: Princeton University Press.

Marcus, George E., and Michael M.J. Fischer. 1999. *Anthropology as Cultural Critique: An Experimental Moment in the Human Sciences*. Chicago: University of Chicago Press.

Mbembe, Achille. 2001. *On the Postcolony*. Berkeley: University of California Press.

Mintz, Sidney W. 1986. *Sweetness and Power: The Place of Sugar in Modern History*. New York: Penguin.

Ortner, Sherry B. 2006. *Anthropology and Social Theory: Culture, Power, and the Acting Subject*. Durham, NC: Duke University Press.

Price, David H. 2008. *Anthropological Intelligence: The Deployment and Neglect of American Anthropology in the Second World War*. Durham, NC: Duke University Press.

Rabinow, Paul, George E. Marcus, James Faubion, and Tobias Rees. 2008. *Designs for an Anthropology of the Contemporary*. Durham, NC: Duke University Press.

Sahlins, Marshall D. 2000. *Culture in Practice: Selected Essays*. New York: Zone Books.

Santos-Granero, Fernando, ed. 2009. *The Occult Life of Things: Native Amazonian Theories of Materiality and Personhood*. Tucson: University of Arizona Press.

Schmidt, Peter, ed. 2009. *Postcolonial Archaeologies*. Santa Fe, NM: SAR Press.

Schmidt, Peter R., and Thomas C. Patterson. 1996. *Making Alternative Histories: The Practice of Archaeology and History in Non-Western Settings*. Santa Fe, NM: SAR Press.

Scott, James C. 2009. *The Art of Not Being Governed: An Anarchist History of Upland Southeast Asia*. New Haven, CT: Yale University Press.

Stewart, Pamela J., and Andrew Strathern. 2003. *Landscape, Memory and History: Anthropological Perspectives*. London: Pluto Press.

Striffler, Steve, Mark Moberg, Gilbert M. Joseph, eds. 2003. *Banana Wars: Power, Production, and History in the Americas*. Durham, NC: Duke University Press.

Taussig, Michael T. 1997. *The Magic of the State*. New York: Routledge.

Tierney, Patrick. 2002. *Darkness in El Dorado: How Scientists and Journalists Devastated the Amazon*. New York: W. W. Norton.

Topik, Steven, Zephyr Frank, and Carlos Marichal, eds. 2006. *From Silver to Cocaine: Latin American Commodity Chains and the Building of the World Economy, 1500–2000*. Durham, NC: Duke University Press.

Tsing, A. L. 2004. *Friction: An Ethnography of Global Connection*. Princeton, NJ: Princeton University Press.

Viveiros de Castro, Eduardo. 2000. "Cosmological Deixis and Amerindian Perspectivism." *JRAI (new series)* 4: 469–88.

Viveiros de Castro, Eduardo. 2009. *Métaphysiques cannibales*. Paris: PUF.

Whitehead, Neil L. 2002. *Dark Shamans: Kanaima and the Poetics of Ritual Death*. Durham, NC: Duke University Press.

Whitehead, Neil L. 2009a. "Ethnography, Torture and the Human Terrain/Terror Systems." *Fast Capitalism* 5: 2. http://www.uta.edu/huma/agger/fastcapitalism/5_2/Whitehead5_2.html.

Whitehead, Neil L. 2009b. "Post-Human Anthropology." *Identities (Yverdon)* 16 (1): 1–32. http://dx.doi.org/10.1080/10702890802605596.

Whitehead, Neil L. 2012. "Loving, Being, Killing Animals." In *Centering Animals*, ed. Martha Few and Zeb Tortorici. Durham, NC: Duke University Press. Forthcoming.

Wolfe, Cary. 2009. *What Is Posthumanism?* Minneapolis: University of Minnesota Press.

Zielinski, Siegfried. 2008. *Deep Time of the Media: Toward an Archaeology of Hearing and Seeing by Technical Means*. Cambridge, MA: MIT Press.

Afterword

Anne Allison

In this provocative collection, two questions are continually provoked: what has happened to the human condition in an era of heightened digitality and deterritorialization, and what is happening to the anthropological condition in an era when place-based ethnography has become so out-of-date? Indeed, in these times of "digital subjectivities" and "unhuman subjects," are we facing a condition of being "human no more" that announces the "end of anthropology"? In what I take to be a resounding "no" to both questions, the authors overwhelmingly endorse anthropology as an enterprise that not only can but must stretch its notion of place—and the human subject—to the terrain of digitality. They also accord the digital subject a humanness and sociality that has long been the purview of anthropology. Even when this subject is referred to as "posthuman," as Jennifer Cool does, the intention is not to signal an evisceration or eclipse of humanity altogether but to register a shift in the ways humans inhabit space, negotiate identity, and assemble "life," including that with other living or virtual beings in the increasingly digitalized world of the twenty-first century. As Cool says, citing Katherine Hayles,

DOI: 10.5876/9781607321705.c13

the posthuman does not really mean the end of humanity. It signals instead the end of a certain conception of the human, a conception that may have applied, at best, to that fraction of humanity who had the wealth, power, and leisure to conceptualize themselves as autonomous beings exercising their will through individual agency and choice. What is lethal is not the posthuman as such but the grafting of the posthuman onto a liberal humanist view of the self. (Hayles 1999, 286)

But what Hayles disdains as a "liberal humanist view of the self" has long been the disdain of anthropology, a discipline built—at least after its evolutionist beginnings—on a much more expansive and elastic notion of the human, a humanness that assumes a variety of forms in the efforts waged to produce and reproduce life in circumstances as diverse as hunting and gathering, laboring as a slave on sugar plantations, or living in a Brazilian favela. And amid terrain of varying kinds, what is identified as "human" may be rigidly personcentric or may barely distinguish between human and, say, a tree or rock, or someone already dead or not yet born. As Lévi-Strauss once said about the logic of binaristic opposition underlying (his notion of) culture, this logic may be culturally universal but it takes locally specific forms, such as with the cannibalistic group that boiled their friends but roasted their enemies. This practice reveals a sociality—and identity—brokered through dead and reanimated body parts, which may or may not be at radical odds to anything in a video game or on an anonymous website.

This is not to say that the world has not radically changed or been dramatically altered by the digital makeover that has spread so deeply into life (all of it and all over) that robots now handle surgery and revolutions are plotted on cell phones. Place is certainly transformed, and anthropology, to keep up, must go where people are to grasp "the imponderabilia of everyday life" (Malinowski 2002 [1922], 24). Now many people live a wired existence through their machines, where they hook up and revirtualize their identities online. Therefore, anthropologists should not hold on to a static and stale notion of the village study. "I was there" means going somewhere else today sometimes without leaving one's office. From the comfort of an office, a researcher can teleport to a virtual or remote world using an avatar that makes sense to the subjects being studied. But shifting the orbit of place remains somewhat a methodological issue. More critical, if related, is the matter I see as much more constitutive of anthropology's scholarly "condition" both today and always, which is figuring out not only how people live—on the ground (or wired) and in the flesh (or online)—but also how they interact with one another, the interpersonal and trans-subjective pursuit of collectivity, connection, and commonwealth (Hardt and Negri 2009). How precisely do anthropologists tap into and measure these things in an era when, as so many of the authors investigate in their chapters here, belonging and identity are being reworked and all too often frustrated or dispersed?

This issue is deftly handled by Radhika Gajjala and Sue Ellen McComas in her study of South Asian diasporic subjects on Second Life. Calling this a transitional place, she tracks how it connects users to both a comforting community online but also faraway worlds with which they can now engage, as if actually there. Community is no longer imagined in the Benedict Andersonian sense today as much as rendered through what Gajjala calls "digital diasporic networks." But Michael Wesch encounters something quite different in the Internet antics of Anonymous. Registering not as "someone" but as "no one," users to the site purposely wreak havoc, performing wild hacks and releasing awesome viruses as acts of vigilantism or just for hilarity, at least for those in on the joke. As Wesch trenchantly notes, the feeling of being socially ignored, overlooked, or simply invisible has rapidly risen under conditions of late modernity, and this social state of anonymity has also contributed to the cult of celebrity in media culture. This structure of feeling—both the hystericism of celebrity worship and the sinking dread of anonymity—is what the Anonymous activists mock. But is this parody or acquiescence? Or a battle cry of—or beyond—human alienation, still expressing the desire to be part of a collective even though one's identity is masked within the group?

As Arjun Appadurai has recently argued in *Fear of Small Numbers* (2006), it is the anxiety and fear of disbelonging—to a nation, community, or simply humanity—that fuel the upsurge in ethnic violence of a savage "vivisectionist" sort around the world today. In the face of neoliberalist restructuring, ongoing warfare, environmental destruction, and the widening of inequity around the globe, people still cling to the desire to fit in, live safe, and be a member of a community even when their ability to do so is shockingly at risk. Now is the time that we must heed Donna Haraway's clarion call, issued some two decades ago, to see in the cyborg an "ironic political myth." This hybrid of organism and machine, at once "a matter of fiction and lived experience," that situated within "a struggle over life and death" offers us a way of imagining/struggling beyond (Haraway 1991, 149). The cyborg gives us a rubric and apparatus for contemplating and challenging the inadequacies, social biases, and disparities (ideological and of real power) so attached to the naturalistic world and human bodies within it. As Haraway argued, the posthuman can be a good thing. As anthropologists, we should understand it better and perhaps nurture it along.

REFERENCES

Appadurai, Arjun. 2006. *Fear of Small Numbers: An Essay on the Geography of Anger.* Durham, NC: Duke University Press.

Haraway, Donna. 1991. "A Cyborg Manifesto: Science, Technology, and Socialist-Feminism in the Late Twentieth Century." In *Simians, Cyborgs and Women: The Reinvention of Nature*, 149–181. New York: Routledge.

Hardt, Michael, and Antonio Negri. 2009. *Commonwealth*. Cambridge, MA: Belknap Press of Harvard University Press.

Hayles, N. Katherine. 1999. *How We Became Posthuman: Virtual Bodies in Cybernetics, Literature, and Informatics*. Chicago: University of Chicago Press.

Malinowski, Bronislaw. 2002 [1922]. *Argonauts of the Western Pacific*. London: Routledge.

Contributors

STEPHANIE W. ALEMÁN
Assistant Professor
Department of Philosophy
University of Wisconsin–Stevens
 Point
Stevens Point, Wisconsin

ANNE ALLISON
Robert O. Keohane Professor of
Cultural Anthropology
Duke University
Durham, North Carolina

MATTHEW BERNIUS
Cornell University
Ithaca, New York

JENNIFER COOL
Postdoctoral Teaching Fellow
Department of Anthropology
University of Southern California
 Los Angeles, California

RADHIKA GAJJALA
Director
American Culture Studies Program
Bowling Green State University
 Bowling Green, Ohio

GRAY GRAFFAM
Lecturer
Media Studies
University of Toronto
Toronto, Canada

Founding Member of the Games
  Institute
University of Waterloo
Waterloo, Canada

MICHAEL HECKENBERGER
Associate Professor
Department of Anthropology
University of Florida
Gainesville, Florida

JAMES HOESTEREY
Assistant Professor
Department of Religion
Emory University
Atlanta, Georgia

SUE ELLEN McCOMAS
Assistant Professor
Speech Communications
Bowling Green State University,
  Firelands
Firelands, Ohio

JENNY RYAN
University of California, San Diego
  San Diego, California

ZEYNEP TUFEKCI
Assistant Professor
School of Information and Library
  Science
University of Maryland, Baltimore
  County
Baltimore, Maryland

MICHAEL WESCH
Associate Professor
Sociology, Anthropology, and Social
  Work
Kansas State University
Manhattan, Kansas

NEIL L. WHITEHEAD
Professor
Department of Anthropology
University of Wisconsin, Madison
Madison, Wisconsin

KENT WISNIEWSKI
Instructor of Anthropology
Department of Behavioral Sciences
Santa Rosa Junior College
Santa Rosa, California

Index

Page numbers in italics indicate illustrations.